Inhalt

1	**Form and layout**	4
2	**General office communication**	14
3	**Enquiries**	26
4	**Offers and quotations**	40
5	**Orders**	51
6	**Dealing with orders**	67
7	**Payment and reminders**	81
8	**Complaints**	99
9	**Credit enquiries**	114
10	**Looking for a job**	126
Deutsch-englisches Glossar		142
Alphabetisches Wörterverzeichnis		154
Transcript		169
Incoterms		174

Form and layout

Model letter: a sales letter

Parts of a business letter: company stationery, reference number, inside (or recipient's) address, attention line, date, subject line, salutation, body of the letter, complimentary close, punctuation, signatures, enclosures, copies

There are several forms of written communication in and between companies: letter, fax, email and memo.

- The **letter** is mostly used for inter-company communication. In the USA and in Britain, there are conventions which companies apply more or less strictly for outgoing mail and which give companies more scope for interpretation. They are not as strict as the German DIN-standards.

- For a **fax** the same rules apply as for a business letter, only the means of communication is different. A fax, however, is often also used for the speedy transmission of urgent messages or information; in this case a much less standardised form of layout and more informal language will be used.

- **Email** messages by their very nature have a standard format. Only the message counts. So there are no rules. Depending on your relationship with your business partners the family name or the first name can be used in the salutation. For the complimentary close people choose the more informal *Yours, Best wishes, (Kind) Regards* or even the short form *Rgds*.

- The **memo** is mostly used for intra-company communication. Again there no conventions and there certainly is no standardised format. Memos are meant just to convey information and messages in hand-written or typed form.

Layout of business letters

Here is a sales letter from a credit card company.

STC Card Services

Scotcard House   2 – 10 Burns Square
Edinburgh EH2 5BA

Ms Fiona J Clark
17 Morris Court
Cupar
Fife
KY4 8JS

17 December 20..

DS 78463

Low-cost credit card – Start to save now

Dear Ms Clark

With Christmas bills coming in and the January sales offering tempting bargains, it's important to act quickly if you want to cut your credit card bill – before you pay a penny more than you need to.

So, if the card you use now has a higher interest rate than we're offering today – and it's quite likely that it does – it makes sound financial sense to apply for a STC Scotcard right away.

Then, as soon as you receive your new credit card, you can pay off your more expensive cards – simply by asking us to move the balance to your STC Scotcard account. We'll do the transfer work. And you'll start to save – thanks to our special reduced interest rate offer.

Once you have completed the attached application form, simply return it in the reply-paid envelope provided. As soon as your application has been approved, we'll send you your STC Scotcard – together with a simple form to help you transfer other card balances.

I wish you a very Happy New Year and hope to soon be welcoming you to all the advantages and savings of STC Scotcard.

Yours sincerely

Karen Leyland

Karen Leyland
Manager, Customer Services

125/Dec20../025369
00271981ScotBank plc
63-67 The Royal Mile
Edinburgh EH1 3 BS
Registered in Scotland, England
and Wales: Number 1098352

Study this business letter and find the following:

1. address of the recipient
2. address of the sender
3. date
4. subject line
5. the function of the writer

B Parts of a business letter

1 Company stationery

Sender's address/letterhead

Business letters have a printed letterhead which often gives information about the company. Together with the sender's address you normally also find the sender's telephone number, the fax number, the email address and the website.

Type of company

The type of business organisation is usually indicated after the name of the company. Here are some of the more common forms:

PLC or plc (Public Limited Company)	=	Aktiengesellschaft (AG)
LTD or Ltd (Limited = Private Limited Company)	=	Gesellschaft mit beschränkter Haftung (GmbH)
Co (company)	=	Firma (Fa)
Son(s)	=	Sohn/Söhne
Bros (Brothers)	=	Gebrüder
Inc (Incorporated) (used in the USA)	=	eingetragene Gesellschaft (AG oder GmbH)
Pty (proprietary company) (used in Australia and South Africa)	=	*etwa* GmbH
Corp (Corporation) (used in the USA)	=	Gesellschaft mit beschränkter Haftung (GmbH)

Additional information

The following information can often be found on company stationery:

- the company's registered office
- the registration number
- in GB the VAT number (value added tax); in the US the sales tax number

Note: In the USA and GB there is usually no indication of the names of the chief officers or the company's bank account.

2 Reference number

Sometimes reference is made to earlier correspondence. In this case either the sender's or the recipient's reference numbers may be used. Some companies use file numbers, eg *774/2001* or initials for the writer and the secretary, eg *DE/PF*. This is shown by the short form of *Your Ref* or *Our Ref*. Sometimes both are used. The reference is found below the recipient's address.

3 Inside (or recipient's address)

The inside address is written as in the model letter. Postal indications such as *AIR MAIL*, *Registered* or *Printed Matter* are mentioned above the inside address. Do not forget to state the name of the country.

Title

If you know the name of the person you are writing to, you write *Mr* for a male or *Ms* for a female person. For reasons of political correctness the form *Mrs* is not commonly used any more. This is followed by the person's initials or his/her first name and the initial for the middle name, eg

Mr J E Smith	or	Ms F J Simmons
Mr John E Smith	or	Ms Frances J Simmons
Mr. J.E. Smith	or	Ms F.J. Simmons

In the USA there is a tendency to use punctuation after *Mr.* or *Ms.*

Messrs is used for partnerships when the company name consists of the partners' names (eg *J Humble & Co, Greggs & Sons* or *Howard & Co Ltd*). If you do not know the name of the person you are writing to, you can speed up the processing of the letter if you know her/his position in the company (*The Sales Manager*) or the department (*The Purchasing Department*).

Arrangement of addresses

The following arrangement should be used for addresses:

Messrs F Hynes & Co	Messrs F Hynes & Co		
Merton House	Merton House		
34–38 Craigton Road	34–38 Craig Road		
Bolton	Bolton	or:	Bolton
Lancashire	BL4 8TF		Lancashire BL4 8TF
BL4 8TF	UNITED KINGDOM		
UNITED KINGDOM			

In England and Wales, the name of the county (here: Lancashire) is not necessary, but many people and firms still use it as part of the address. In Scotland there are regions. There are some abbreviations for counties:

Buckinghamshire	Bucks	Middlesex	Middx
Hampshire	Hants	Northamptonshire	Northants
Lancashire	Lancs	Nottinghamshire	Notts

A typical address from the USA:

VoicePower Inc.	VoicePower Inc
Box 14526	Box 14526
St. Louis, MO 63178	St. Louis, MO 63178
U.S.A.	Missouri/USA

The American postal code consists of the abbreviation for the state name and the ZIP-Code (Zone Improvement Plan) which is a five-digit number. The state name is sometimes repeated in full. Some abbreviations for US states (second column) and postal abbreviations (third column):

California	Cal/Calif	CA
Michigan	Mich.	MI
Missouri	Mo.	MO
New Jersey	N.J.	NJ
New York	N.Y.	NY
Pennsylvania	Penn/Pa	PA
Texas	Tex/Tx	TX
Virginia	Va	VA

4 Attention line

This special reference *(For the) Attention of ...* , or *Attn ...* is found just below the address and is used when the letter is addressed to a company and intended for a particular person only.

> InternetWare Ltd
> 1–3 Barrow Drive
> Liverpool
> L22 5PL
>
> For the attention of the
> Production Manager
>
> or   Attn Mr J M Donald
>
> or   For the attention of Richard Delaney, Export Sales

Phrases like *Private and confidential*, *Confidential*, *Strictly confidential* are in the same place.

5 Date

The date is mostly written below the recipient's address on the left. The following forms can be used:

24 October 20..	or	October 24, 20..
24th October 20..		October 24th, 20..
24 Oct. 20..		Oct. 24, 20..

In informal documents (email, fax, memo) the date may be written as follows:

> 24/10/20..
> 24-10-20..
> 24.10.20..

The Americans put the month first, then the day and finally the year (eg 10/24/20..).

6 Subject line

In business letters there is usually a headline to indicate what the letter is about, the subject line or reference line. There is normally no introduction or short form like *Ref* or *Re*. Only the topic of the letter is mentioned. In letters where the block form is used the subject line can be put above or below the salutation and starts at the left margin. It may be underlined or in bold.

In the semi-block form, it may also be placed below the salutation, ie before the body of the letter. In this case it is underlined and put in the centre of the page.

7 Salutation

Here again there is a difference in usage between Britain and the USA.
Dear Sir or Madam is used to address a person in a company in the UK or a Commonwealth country if the name of the addressee is not known. The following forms are also used: *Dear Sirs; Dear Sir/Madam.*
Ladies and Gentlemen (or sometimes *Gentlemen*) is now commonly used in the USA to open a letter to a person in a company if the name or sex is not known. Note: this is usually followed by a colon.
If the name is known it should be used, eg *Dear Mr Penney* or *Dear Ms Jones.*

8 Body of the letter

The first paragraph always begins with a capital letter, although there may have been a comma or colon at the end of the salutation. The first line of each paragraph may be indented (ie it does not start at the margin but after the first tab stop) or written in semi-block form with each line beginning at the left margin or even in full block form with all the lines beginning at the left margin and ending at the right margin. (Note: When the full block form is used, the date, the reference line, the subject line and the signature section all start at the left margin.) When using the semi-block or full block forms, it is helpful to leave a line space between paragraphs.

9 Complimentary close

The appropriate ending for letters starting with the formal salutations mentioned above are *Yours faithfully* in the UK or *Yours (very) truly*, *(Very) Truly yours*, *Sincerely yours*, *Sincerely* or *Yours sincerely* in the USA.
When you use the name of the addressee you use *Yours sincerely* in the UK or *Sincerely yours* or *Yours sincerely* in the USA.

It is important to remember the following:

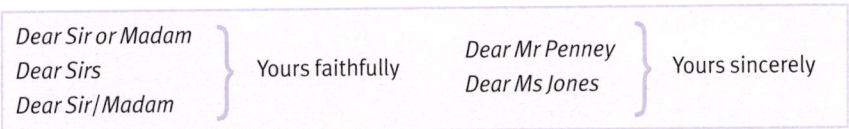

If two business persons know each other well, they may use less formal forms: the letter may begin with the first name (especially when it is not passed on to or read by other people in the company), eg *Dear Roger* or *Dear Janet* and the letter may close with the following: *Sincerely*, *With kind regards*, *With best wishes*, *Yours*.

10 Punctuation

British usage

If the salutation has no comma (ie *Dear Mr Keracher*), then the complimentary close ends without a comma. This also means that the date should be written without a comma. This is the preferred form.

If punctuation is used in the salutation (ie *Dear Ms Keracher,*), then the complimentary close must also end with a comma. In this case the date can be written with a comma.

American usage

A comma is used after the salutation. The impersonal salutation *Ladies and Gentlemen* or *Gentlemen* may be followed by a colon or a comma.
In the USA it is much more common than in Britain to use a full stop after abbreviations, eg *Mr., Ms.* or *No.*.

The complimentary close always ends with a comma.

11 Signatures

The handwritten signature should always contain your initials or your first name.
The name is usually printed below the signature. For female persons it is important to indicate their preferred title (*Ms* or *Mrs*) in brackets. Mostly the position or job title and department are also mentioned. This helps the addressee in the follow-up correspondence. Employees signing for (or for and on behalf of) another person or their company use the abbreviation *pp* or *per pro.* (*per procurationem*). This does not have the same meaning as the German *ppa*.

12 Enclosures

Occasionally enclosures (eg catalogue, price-list) are added. This is indicated in the lower left-hand corner by the word *Enclosure(s)* or by one of the abbreviations *Enc(s)* or *Encl(s)*. Sometimes the items enclosed are listed individually. (Note: The punctuation rules apply here too, ie if no punctuation has been used with the date, the salutation and complimentary close, no punctuation will be used with *Enc*. If punctuation has been used with the salutation and the complimentary close, however, punctuation must be used here, too.)

13 Copies

When copies are sent to people other than the person addressed, *cc* (*carbon copy* or *copies*) often followed by the names of the respective persons or department is written at the end of the letter.

D Useful words

(Mit) Luftpost	(By) Air Mail, AIRMAIL
Einschreiben	Registered (Mail)
Durch Eilboten	(By) Express, Special Delivery [US]
Persönlich	Personal
Drucksache	Printed Matter
Postfach	P.O. Box
Eilt	Urgent
Bitte nachsenden	Please forward / To be forwarded
Zurück, falls unzustellbar	Return if undelivered
Empfänger unbekannt verzogen	Moved, address unknown
Muster-, Formbrief	model/specimen/form letter
Briefentwurf, Konzept	first draft, rough copy
Briefrückseite	reverse (of letter)
adressierter Freiumschlag	self-addressed/stamp-addressed envelope (SAE)
Ablage	filing
Akten(ablage), Aktenvorgänge, Registratur	files, records
Brief-, Posteingang	incoming letters, inward mail [US]
Brief-, Postausgang	outgoing letters, outward mail [US]
Postgebühren	postal rates/charges
Porto	postage
Inlands-, Auslandsporto	inland/overseas postage
Internationaler Postantwortschein	international postal reply coupon
mit gleicher Post	with/by same mail/post
mit getrennter Post, mit getrenntem Umschlag	under separate cover
postwendend, umgehend	by return of mail/post, by return (mail)
leeres/ausgefülltes Formular	blank/filled-out form
Briefvordruck	printed letter form
Notizblock	memo pad
Durchschlag	carbon copy
Schreib-, Briefpapier; Schreibwaren	stationery

2 General office communication

Model letters: making a hotel reservation, confirming a hotel reservation, making an appointment, invitations and thank-you letters

Useful phrases: hotel reservations, appointments, invitations and thank-you letters

As part of daily office work many messages (letters and emails) are written to communicate with customers and staff on matters other than the buying and selling of products or services. These may involve the booking of accommodation or conference facilities in hotels, the arrangement of appointments, invitations to special events, thank-you letters, letters informing about changes of address, new appointments, changes of responsibility and many more.

In the introductory paragraph clearly state what the letter is about (briefly give the reason for making contact; in the reply, thank your partner for making contact). Then explain your requirements in detail or, in a reply, give the required details or explain the arrangements you have made. Always close with a polite phrase.

Make sure you use paragraphs (and, if need be, indentation) to arrange your message/information clearly.

General office communication   UNIT 2

3 Making an appointment

This fax is to arrange a meeting with a business partner.

FAXmessage

Visit of Sales Director

In connection with the Hannover Computer Fair, our Sales Director, Mr Peter Marsh, will be visiting customers in Germany. He would like to call on you in the last week of March to discuss the possibility of joint projects.

Please let us know whether that week would be suitable and which particular date you prefer. Of course, we would appreciate any help you are able to give regarding accommodation.

An early reply would be helpful as we need to arrange a timetable for the visits.

We look forward to hearing from you at your earliest convenience.

Yours sincerely

Janet Rowland (Ms)
(PA/Secretary)

This is a reply to the fax from Computech Ltd above.

Dear Ms Rowland

Visit of your sales director

Thank you for your fax announcing the visit of your Sales Director, Mr Peter Marsh. We shall be pleased to welcome him in our office on any day during the last week in March, although Monday to Wednesday would be preferable. Herr Freier, our Technical Director, has some appointments on Thursday and Friday, but these could be changed if necessary.
We will, of course, be pleased to make the necessary hotel booking, as soon as you can give us the definite date of Mr Marsh's visit. Please let us know further details once the itinerary has been finalised.
We look forward to hearing from you again soon.

Yours sincerely

Pamela Winter
Abteilungssekretariat

This email is in reply to the letter on page 17.

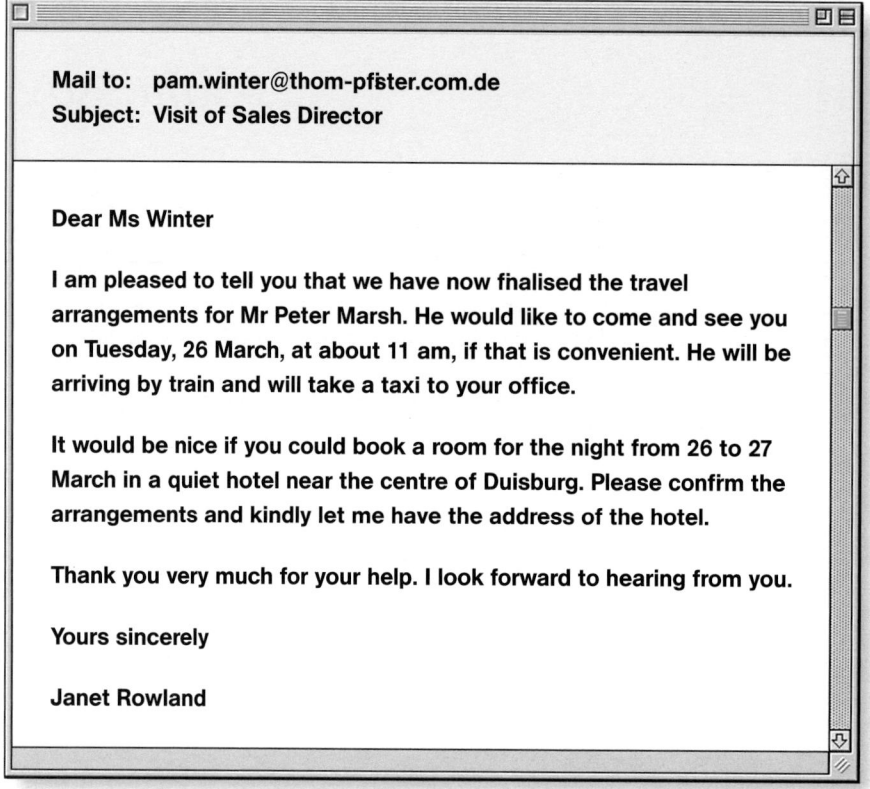

Pamela Winter informs her British colleague by mail about the arrangements made. Complete the text using the following (there are more items in the box than you need):

| booked | facilities | faithfully | hope | journey | Mr | Ms | sincerely | single | Thank you | visiting | welcoming |

Dear ... [1] Rowland

... [2] for your letter of 25 February. I ... [3] a ... [4] room with en-suite ... [5] for Mr Marsh for 26 March in the Adelphi-Hotel, Königstr 15, 47045 Duisburg, Tel. 0203/334521. We ... [6] Mr Marsh will have a good ... [7] and look forward to ... [8] him at our office.

Yours ... [9]

4 Invitations and thank-you letters

This letter is an invitation to a customer to a trade fair.

Dear Mr and Mrs Jones

Cadeaux-Messe in Leipzig

The Cadeaux Fair in Leipzig in March was a great success. We trust that you were pleased with the business that you did at the fair and that our goods have been well received in your market. The feedback we have had from the trade has been very encouraging.

Today we have the pleasure of inviting you to visit the Autumn Cadeaux Fair in Leipzig and enclose two complimentary tickets. The fair is due to take place from 15 to 18 September. The Cadeaux Autumn Fair is certain to be a much bigger event with many more exhibitors from an even larger number of countries. It is an ideal occasion in the run-up to the Christmas season to add to your range of gifts suitable for the festive season.

We ourselves have made a great effort to develop our product lines even further. When you look at the enclosed autumn catalogue, we are sure you will agree that there have been some highly attractive additions to our various ranges.

But you will want to see for yourselves. We look forward to welcoming you at our stand at the Cadeaux Fair in Leipzig.

Yours sincerely

Mr and Mrs Jones decide they want to go to Leipzig. Their assistant finds a note on her desk. Complete the details.

Cadeaux ... in ... from ... September. Please ... hotel accommodation and also ... from London to Berlin and ... from Berlin to Leipzig. Any ... is suitable, but 18 Sept ... Thank you.   Paul

This letter is to thank for hospitality received and to give some feedback on a newly developed software program.

Dear Karen

Just a quick note to say how much I enjoyed seeing you again at the fair in Utrecht. And I would like to thank you very much indeed for the warm welcome at the fair stand and the hospitality. The restaurant was well chosen with a nice atmosphere and a very interesting menu. The food was excellent. Altogether, a most enjoyable evening. Thank you very much again and I hope you will give me the opportunity to take you out for a meal next time we meet.

After my return home, I tried out your new software. It works perfectly and I could imagine that we may want to consider buying it for the management of trucking operations. I'll certainly talk to Frank about it. The one little snag there might be is that as yet there is only an English-language version. Perhaps you could do something about that. I like the program and hope it will find plenty of buyers here in Germany, too.

Well, thank you again. And I'll be in touch.

Yours

Stefanie

B Useful phrases

1 Hotel reservations

Für unsere Konferenz / unser Seminar benötigen wir ...	For our conference/seminar we require ...
Für die Dauer der ...-Messe benötigen wir Hotelunterkunft / Zimmer mit Dusche / WC ...	For the duration of the ... Fair we require accommodation/rooms with en-suite facilities ...
Schicken Sie uns bitte Ihren Hotelprospekt.	Please send us a brochure of your hotel.
Für unsere ... Leiterin und ihren Mann möchten wir ein Zweibettzimmer reservieren.	We wish to book a twin room for our ... manager and her husband.
Der Preis für Übernachtung und Frühstück beträgt / beläuft sich auf ...	The price for bed and breakfast is ...
Der Preis versteht sich einschließlich Mehrwertsteuer.	The price is inclusive of VAT (value added tax).
Wir wünschen Ihnen einen angenehmen Aufenthalt in ...	We hope that you will have a pleasant stay in ...
Leider müssen wir Ihnen mitteilen, dass ...	We are sorry to inform you that ...
... müssen wir die Zimmerreservierung leider stornieren.	... we must unfortunately cancel the room booking.
Bei Stornierungen müssen wir leider eine Stornogebühr in Höhe von ... berechnen/erheben.	Cancellations are subject to a cancellation charge/fee of ...
Wir bitten um Bestätigung unserer Reservierung / Für eine kurze Bestätigung wären wir dankbar.	Please confirm our reservation. / Please let us have your confirmation by return.
Sollten Sie keine Zimmer (mehr) frei haben, ...	Should you have no vacancies, ...

2 Appointments

Herr/Frau ... reist nach ...	Mr/Ms ... will be travelling to ...
Wir freuen uns, Sie darüber zu informieren ...	We are pleased to inform you ...
... und würde sich freuen, Sie zu besuchen / Ihnen einen Besuch abzustatten.	... and would be pleased to pay you a visit / to call on you.
... um Ihnen unser neues ...-Gerät vorzuführen.	... in order to demonstrate our new ... machine.
... um mit Ihnen die weitere Geschäftsentwicklung zu besprechen.	... to discuss the future business development.
Wir hoffen, dass Ihnen dieser Termin gelegen ist.	We hope that this date will suit you / will be convenient.

Sollte dieser Termin / diese Woche unpassend sein, …	If the date/week is not convenient/ suitable / is inconvenient …
… nicht in Ihre Zeitpläne / Ihren Terminplan passt …	… does not fit in with your plans/ schedule …
… wäre … ohne weiteres in der Lage umzudisponieren.	… would be quite willing to make alternative arrangements.
Bestätigen Sie bitte …	Please/Kindly confirm …
Ich wäre Ihnen sehr dankbar, wenn Sie … buchen könnten.	I would be obliged / very grateful to you if you could book …
Teilen Sie mir bitte mit, ob …	Please let me know whether …
… wird wegen einer anderen Verpflichtung / eines anderen Termins nicht im Haus/Betrieb/ Büro sein.	… will not be in the office because of another commitment.
Deswegen möchten wir bitten/vorschlagen, …	Therefore we would like to suggest …

3 Invitations and thank-you letters

Bei dieser Gelegenheit möchten wir …	We take this opportunity to …
Wir würden uns sehr freuen, Sie … willkommen zu heißen.	We would be pleased to welcome you …
… geben sich die Ehre, Sie zu … einzuladen.	… have the honour of inviting you … / request the pleasure of your company at …
Wir würden uns sehr freuen …	We would be delighted …
Vielen Dank für Ihre freundliche Einladung …	Thank you for your kind invitation …
…, die wir gern annehmen.	… which we have pleasure in accepting.
Leider sind wir wegen einer anderen Verpflichtung verhindert.	Unfortunately, we are unable to attend due to a previous engagement.
… können wir leider nicht annehmen.	… we must decline / are unable to accept …
… möchte Ihnen auch im Namen von … herzlich danken.	… would also like to thank you on behalf of …
Bitte leiten Sie meinen aufrichtigen Dank auch an … weiter …	Please pass on my sincere thanks to …
Ihre Freundlichkeit möchten wir gern erwidern …	We would be pleased to be able to reciprocate / return your kindness …
Wir haben einen äußerst angenehmen Abend verbracht.	We enjoyed the evening very much.
… möchten Ihnen ganz herzlich danken.	… would like to thank you most warmly.

C Practising language

1 Choose from the following to complete the text.

> agreement | be attending | bath and toilet | book | brochure | confirmation | costs | en-suite | make a booking | present | prospectus | rates | require | use

Dear Sir or Madam

We ... [1] accommodation from 13 to 18 October for our Export Sales Manager, Mr Hartmut Jung, who will ... [2] the Logistics Fair at the Birmingham Exhibition Centre in October. We would therefore like to ... [3] a single room with ... [4] facilities. Please let us have your ... [5] and also send details of your ... [6] and a hotel ... [7].

Yours faithfully

2 Complete sentences 1–9 below. Use the parts a–k. There are two more items than you need.

Dear Mr Saunders

1 Two of our executives will be attending ...
2 They would like to use this occasion to visit ...
3 Arrangements have already been made to meet ...
4 Therefore the visit to your company could be fixed ...
5 As no detailed plans have yet been made for the visits, ...
6 As soon as we have drawn up an itinerary, ...
7 We would be pleased if you could suggest ...
8 Then we could arrange ...
9 We hope that such a visit is convenient ...

Yours sincerely

a ... a suitable hotel near your office.
b ... accommodation from here.
c ... and look forward to hearing from you.
d ... and thank you for mailing us.
e ... for the days immediately before or after that.
f ... phone you to arrange the details of the visit.
g ... some buyers on 4 August.
h ... some of our important customers in Germany.
i ... the Düsseldorf Igedo from 2 to 5 August.
j ... we will mail you.
k ... we would ask you to let us know your preferred dates.

3 The parts of this letter have been mixed up. Put them in the correct order. There are three sentences altogether.

Dear Herr Kramps

On my return home I should like to thank you …
become acquainted with the way
and especially for your kind hospitality.
for the useful meeting
I would be pleased
It was certainly most interesting
to visit your company and
very much indeed
we had at your office last Wednesday
Whenever you are in this country
your business is run.
… to return your kindness.

Yours sincerely

4 Correct the mistakes in these sentences.

1 We will hold the appointment in our conference room at 10 o'clock.
2 Next week, I will become more information about the details of the visit.
3 The time of the meeting does not fit me.
4 Unfortunately, I have another date on Wednesday.
5 At our house, we make many high-tech products.
6 From our company there were only seven people who visited the conference.
7 I hope, you had a good travel.
8 If I'm not at home you can always call me on my handy.
9 I would like to invite you to a meal, if you are free tonight.

Listening comprehension

5 Write a memo.

Listen to this telephone message on the answering machine and write a short memo in German to inform the persons involved in the meeting.

6 Listen to the dialogue on the CD and then do the exercise.

Listen to this extract from a telephone conversation. As the hotel receptionist make notes for the conference manager and write down the important points.

Letter writing

1 Write an email or a letter in reply.

As the reservations officer, confirm the reservation made in exercise C1, page 22. Indicate that the daily rates for B&B accommodation are £55.00 per night including VAT, also that evening meals are available at a moderate price. Enclose a brochure and a list of the standard room rates. End with a polite phrase.

Addresses
Sender: Birmingham City Hotel, 50 Canal Close, Birmingham, B3 6ZP,
Tel +44 121 456 9821
reservations@bhamcity-hotel.co.uk

Recipient: EVA Interlogist GmbH, Hüttenstr. 57, 44315 Dortmund, 0231/48 64 481
vera.lang@eva-interlogist.de

2 Ask for information.

Write an email to a guesthouse in Northern Ireland. You want to spend a week's holiday in the area with your friend. Enquire about prices for bed and breakfast. Ask for a brochure. Choose the guesthouse that you like best.

MANOR GUEST HOUSE **	
Miss A Graham, 23 Olderfleet Rd, Harbour Highway, Larne, BT40 1AS, Tel (028) 2827 3305. Fax 2826 0505. B&B from £27.50. Vouchers accepted. 2 mins walk from ferry terminal and train station.	8 en-suite rooms. All rooms have CTV, hairdryer, clock/radio alarm, trouser press, tea/coffee making facilities, double glazing and controlled central heating. Early breakfasts catered for. AA selected ♦♦♦♦.

SEAVIEW GUEST HOUSE **	
Marion Muir, 156 Curran Rd, Larne, BT40 1BX Tel & Fax (028) 2827 2438. B&B from £26. Vouchers accepted. 2 mins from harbour towards town centre.	8 rooms, 5 en-suite, well established guest house. All rooms have colour TV, hospitality tray. Guest lounge with Sky TV. Convenient to Glens of Antrim, Carnfunnock Country Park and the famous Coast Road to the Giant's Causeway. Personal attention and warm welcome assured.

3 Write an email.

You are the assistant to the product manager Dore Göbel. Write a mail to inform your visitor Ms Clark that for urgent reasons your boss will not be able to see her as agreed on Monday at 9.00 am. Your boss will be free to see Ms Clark at 2.00 pm on the same day. Say that your boss is sorry. Ask for Ms Clark's confirmation of the change of time.

Addresses
Sender: doris.goebel@Hanser-Schmiedekunst.com.de
Recipient: liz.clark@av-craft.co.uk

4 Rewrite this email as a formal letter.

> Dear Ms Hanley
> We are delighted that you are coming to see us in Essen at the Equitana this year. If you have nothing to do in the evening, why don't we go out for a meal. Then we can talk about our business. Tell me whether you like the idea. Let me know soon.
> Yours
> Karl Drömer

E Useful words

1 Hotel reservations

buchen, reservieren	to make a booking/reservation
Buchung/Reservierung stornieren	to cancel a booking/reservation
ein Zimmer reservieren/buchen	to book accommodation
Einzelzimmer	single room
Zweibettzimmer	twin room
Doppelzimmer	double room
Übernachtung mit Frühstück	bed and breakfast (B&B)
Vollpension	full board
Halbpension	half board
Zimmer mit Bad/Dusche und WC	room with en-suite facilities
belegt	no vacancies
Zimmer frei	vacancies
Unterkunft; Unterbringungsmöglichkeit	accommodation
Konferenzpaket	conference facilities
Tagungsraum	conference room
schriftliche Bestätigung	confirmation in writing
Stornogebühr	cancellation fee/charge
Hotelprospekt	hotel brochure
Parkmöglichkeit	parking facilities
jdn in einem Hotel / in einer Pension unterbringen	to accommodate sb in a hotel / B&B
Zimmerpreis	room rate

2 Appointments

Geschäftsreise	business trip
auf Geschäftsreise	away on business
geschäftlich/dienstlich unterwegs sein	to travel on business
im Haus/Büro/Betrieb	in the office
da/anwesend sein; im Betrieb sein	to be in
am/für den ... vorgesehen/geplant sein	to be scheduled for
umdisponieren	to make alternative arrangements
Termin vereinbaren/machen	to make an appointment
Treffen/Termin verlegen	to postpone a meeting / an appointment
anderweitig verhindert sein	to have another commitment
nicht verfügbar sein	to be not available
Treffen, Konferenz, Sitzung	meeting
Terminplan, (Termin)Kalender	(appointments) diary
in der Woche vom ...; in der ... Kalenderwoche	in the week commencing ...

3 Invitations and thank-you letters

jds Freundlichkeit erwidern	to return sb's kindness
Gastfreundschaft erweisen	to extend hospitality
Einladung zum Essen	invitation to a meal
jdn besuchen / jdm einen Besuch abstatten	to visit sb
jdn aufsuchen/besuchen	to call on sb
u.A.w.g. (um Antwort wird gebeten)	RSVP (répondez s'il vous plaît)
im Namen von, für	on behalf of
aufrichtigen Dank	sincere thanks
Feierlichkeiten	celebrations
jdn beglückwünschen zum/zur	to congratulate sb on

3 Enquiries

Model letters: a general enquiry, a specific enquiry

Useful phrases: opening lines; asking for catalogues, sales literature, price-lists etc; asking for details of quality; asking for samples, patterns, demonstrations; prices, terms, methods of payment, discounts; goods on approval, sale or return, trial order; further conditions; closing lines

An enquiry is usually the first contact between buyer and seller. It is a request for information about a product or service (**general enquiry**) and very often also a request for a quotation (**specific enquiry**).

While a phone call, a postcard or a reply coupon may be appropriate forms to ask for information, a specific enquiry involves much more detail about the product or service the customer is interested in. Specific enquiries are therefore commonly made by phone, email, fax or letter. In either case the potential supplier needs to know the customer's address and the kind of information required.

In the specific enquiry the source of information should be stated – business partner, fair contact, advertising, trade directory (Yellow Pages, CD-ROM), trade association, Chamber of Commerce, website etc. For the seller it may be useful to be given some information about the buyer's business. Depending on the product or service the customer will require sales literature, want to examine samples and/or patterns, and even ask for a representative or an agent to visit him/her to discuss details. The possibility of discounts, the terms of payment and delivery may be raised even at this early stage.

A Model letters

1 A general enquiry

In this email the customer responds to a magazine advertisement and wants to find out more about computer games.

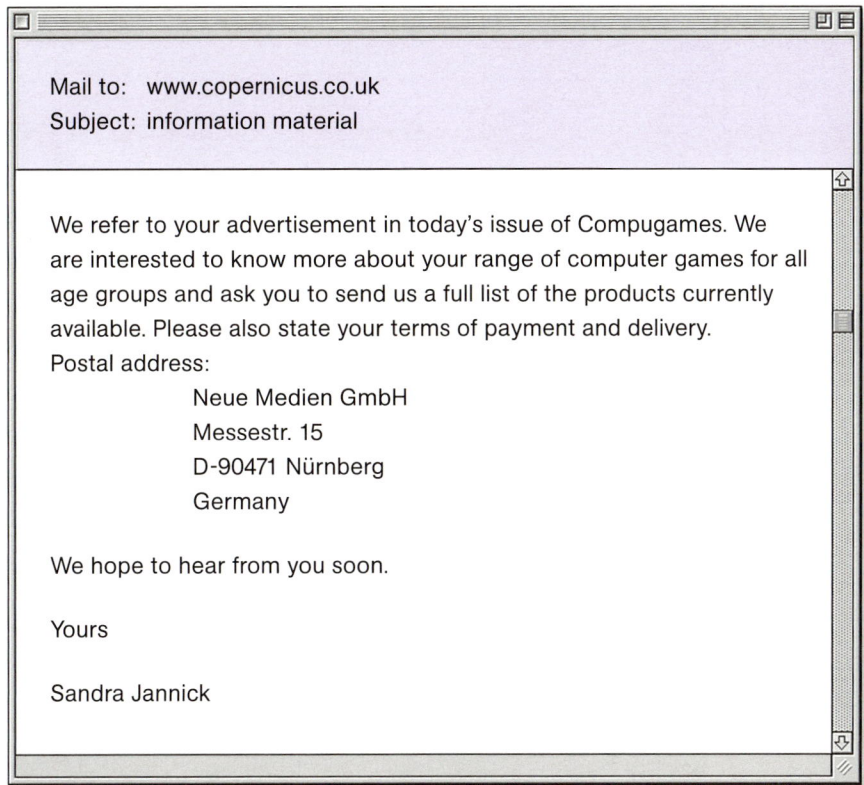

Mail to: www.copernicus.co.uk
Subject: information material

We refer to your advertisement in today's issue of Compugames. We are interested to know more about your range of computer games for all age groups and ask you to send us a full list of the products currently available. Please also state your terms of payment and delivery.
Postal address:
        Neue Medien GmbH
        Messestr. 15
        D-90471 Nürnberg
        Germany

We hope to hear from you soon.

Yours

Sandra Jannick

Use the following to rewrite the email as a full letter.

… and are interested …
Dear Sirs
Our postal address is as follows:
Request for information material
Therefore we kindly ask …
We look forward to hearing from you shortly.
Yours faithfully

2 A specific enquiry

In this letter a customer requires detailed information about the products advertised and asks for specimens for testing purposes.

Geschenkhaus
GmbH & Co KG

Braunschweiger Str. 34
10104 Berlin
Fon 030 353 505 1
Fax 030 353 505 248
E-Mail:
satt.well@geschenkhaus.com.de

Royal Denby Ltd
38 Stafford Road
Stoke
ST3 4QA

England

28 February 20..

Dear Sir or Madam

Request for information

We saw your series of advertisements in the recent issues of the trade journal *Porzellan und Glas*. The variety of designs and shapes of your ranges of china and earthenware is very impressive. The colouring is very attractive, too.

As a well-established specialist retailer for glass and china with outlets in all the major towns in the region, we feel that your products could be successfully marketed here.

Please send us the relevant literature for your ranges of china, earthenware and glassware. We would also appreciate it if you could let us have some specimen pieces for testing purposes. Kindly state details concerning your discounts and your terms of payment and delivery.

We look forward to hearing from you soon.

Yours faithfully

Annette Reppel

Annette Reppel
Chief Buyer

Kommanditges.,
Sitz u. Registergericht
AG Nürnberg HRA 2967

Persönlich haftende
Gesellschafterin
Sattler & Wellert GmbH
AG Nürnberg HRA 2165

Geschäftsführer:
R. Sattler, G. Wellert

Bankverbindung:
Commerzbank Nürnberg
Kto.-Nr. 43567405
BLZ 760 400 61

Decide which of the following comes closest to the terms used in the letter on page 28 (left column).

1 range	a assortment	b lot	c pallet
2 attractive	a interesting	b lovable	c nice
3 major	a big	b large	c minor
4 marketed	a delivered	b sold	c supplied
5 literature	a brochures	b news	c texts
6 appreciate it	a be pleased	b like it	c thank you
7 terms	a conditions	b dates	c times

Letter plan for a general enquiry

- ☐ State your interest in a particular product or product line.
- ☐ Ask for information (printed material).
- ☐ Close with a polite phrase.

Letter plan for a specific enquiry

- ☐ State the source of the seller's address.
- ☐ Briefly describe your company.
- ☐ State the reason for your enquiry and product (range).
- ☐ Ask for information about the product/service (sales literature; samples/patterns; visit by a representative).
- ☐ Ask for a quotation (prices, discounts, terms of payment and delivery).
- ☐ Mention the possibility of providing references (may be omitted).
- ☐ Close with a polite phrase.

UNIT 3 Enquiries

B Useful phrases

1 Opening lines

Ihren Namen haben wir von … erhalten.	We were given your name by …
Sie wurden / Ihre Firma wurde uns von … empfohlen.	You were / Your company was recommended to us by …
Unsere Geschäftspartner/Geschäftsfreunde äußern sich sehr positiv über …	Our associates / business partners speak highly of …
(Unsere Geschäftsfreunde) … teilte(n) uns mit, dass Sie … liefern können.	We were advised by … / Our business partners … advised us that you can / are able / are in a position to supply …
In der letzten/neuesten (laufenden) Ausgabe von … haben wir Ihre Anzeige / Ihr Inserat gesehen.	We saw your advertisement in the latest/current issue of …
Wir haben Ihre Webseite/Homepage im Internet gesehen.	We saw your website/homepage on the internet.
Wir beziehen uns auf Ihre Anzeige in der … Ausgabe vom …	We are replying to your advertisement in the … issue of …
Während … Messe/Ausstellung in … haben Sie eine große Auswahl an … gezeigt.	At the recent … exhibition/fair in … you displayed a broad range of …
Von der Auswahl von … , die Sie an Ihrem Messestand gezeigt haben, waren wir beeindruckt.	We were impressed by the selection of … displayed on your stand.
Wir sind Facheinzelhändler mit zahlreichen Ladenlokalen / einem ausgedehnten Netz von Verkaufsstellen / einem ausgedehnten Vertriebsnetz.	We are a specialist retailer with many outlets / an extensive network of outlets / an extensive sales network.
Als eine große Vertriebsgesellschaft für … spezialisieren wir uns auf …	As a major distributor of … we specialize in …
Wir sind ein Großhändler / eine Großhandelsgenossenschaft mit Sitz in …	We are a wholesaler / wholesale society based in …

2 Asking for catalogues, sales literature, price-lists etc.

… würden wir gern mehr über Ihre Produkte wissen.	… we would like to know more about your products.
Für Produkte dieser Art besteht gegenwärtig eine starke/hohe Nachfrage.	There is currently a strong demand for goods of this kind.
Wir haben von Ihrer neuesten Maschine / Ihrem neuesten Gerät für … gehört.	We have heard about your latest machine/appliance for …

... und würden gern weitere Einzelheiten erfahren.	... and would like to know further details.
(Über)Senden Sie uns bitte ... / Lassen Sie uns bitte ... zukommen. / Wir bitten um Zusendung von ...	Please send us ... / Kindly let us have ...
... Ihren aktuellen Katalog / Ihre Sommer-/ Winterbroschüre und Ihre Preisliste für... / ... das verfügbare Informationsmaterial.	... your current catalogue / summer/winter brochure and price-list for ... / ... any information you can supply.

3 Asking for details of quality

Wir hätten gern Informationen zu den technischen Daten Ihrer ...	We would be pleased to receive specifications for your ...
Bitte teilen Sie uns genaue Einzelheiten über die Qualität ihrer Produkte mit.	Please let us have precise information about the quality of your products.
Wir sind nur an Produkten von höchster Qualität interessiert.	Only products of the best quality will be acceptable to us.
Bitte teilen Sie uns mit / Wir würden gern wissen, ob die Qualität Ihrer Produkte schwankt / Schwankungen unterliegt.	Kindly let us know / We would be grateful to know whether the quality of your goods is subject to variation.
... ob Sie Waren dieser Qualität über einen längeren Zeitraum liefern können.	... whether you are in a position to supply the same quality goods over an extended period of time.
Wir sind an Ihren Waren nur dann interessiert, wenn Sie hinreichende Garantien geben können.	Your products are acceptable only when covered by an adequate warranty.

4 Asking for samples, patterns, demonstrations

Bitte fügen Sie Ihrer Antwort eine Musterkarte bei.	Please enclose a pattern card when replying.
Wir würden uns über die Zusendung einiger Muster freuen ...	We would also appreciate it if you could send some samples of the material ...
Schicken Sie uns (daher) bitte je 2 Stück von ...	Please send us two each of the following ...
Bevor wir Ihre Produkte verkaufen, möchten wir sie gern auf ihre Sicherheit testen.	Before selling your ... we would like to test them for safety.
Bitte senden Sie uns einige kostenlose Muster/Musterstücke Ihres Sortiments.	Kindly send us without charge some samples/specimens from the range of goods you manufacture/distribute.
... , damit wir das Gewebe / die Beschaffenheit und die Qualität untersuchen können.	... , so that we can examine the texture and the quality.

Wir möchten noch die Frage der Wartung erörtern ...	We would like to discuss the problem of maintenance ...
... , bevor wir entscheiden, welches Modell wir einbauen/installieren.	... before deciding which model to install.
... wenn Sie den Besuch eines Ihrer Vertreter veranlassen könnten.	... if you could arrange for one of your representatives to call on us.

5 Prices, terms, methods of payment, discounts

Wegen des starken Wettbewerbs hier bitten wir Sie um die Angabe Ihrer günstigsten Konditionen/Preise.	In view of the strong competition here we advise you to quote your most favourable terms/prices.
Bitte geben Sie Ihre Preise netto/brutto/CIF/FOB an.	Please quote your prices net/gross/CIF/FOB.
... welche Rabatte Sie gewähren (können).	... which discounts you are prepared to grant.
Wir bitten (auch) um Angabe Ihrer Lieferbedingungen.	Please (also) state your delivery terms and conditions.
Darüber hinaus möchten wir Sie um Einzelheiten bezüglich Ihrer Zahlungsbedingungen bitten.	We would also appreciate (receiving) information about your terms of payment.
Unsere Lieferanten räumen uns ein Zahlungsziel von drei Monaten ein / rechnen monatlich ab.	Our suppliers allow us three months credit / to settle by monthly statement.
Falls erforderlich können wir die üblichen Empfehlungen vorlegen.	We can offer/furnish the usual trade references if required.

6 Goods on approval, sale or return, trial order

Wir können einen Auftrag nur wie üblich mit Rückgaberecht erteilen.	We would only consider placing an order provided it was on the usual basis of sale or return.
Wenn Sie diese Ware zur Ansicht liefern können, würden wir gern ... Stück auf Lager nehmen, um zu sehen, wie sie sich verkaufen.	If you would supply these goods on approval, we would be pleased to hold ... items to see how they sell.
Bitte teilen Sie die Mindestmenge für eine Probelieferung mit.	Please let us know the minimum quantity for a trial shipment.

7 Further conditions

Zum Schluss möchten wir betonen, dass wir auf Auslieferung bis zum ... bestehen müssen.	Finally, we would like to point out that delivery before ... is essential.
Vorausgesetzt Sie können die Auslieferung innerhalb von vier Wochen nach Auftragseingang verbindlich zusagen, ...	Provided you can guarantee deliveries within four weeks from receipt of order, ...
Wenn die Ware unseren Vorstellungen / Bedürfnissen entspricht, ...	If the goods come up to our expectations / meet our requirements, ...
Sollte die Erledigung unseres Erstauftrags zu unserer Zufriedenheit ausfallen, ...	Should the the execution of our initial order prove satisfactory, ...
Wenn die verlangten Preise wettbewerbsfähig sind und die Qualität den Anforderungen entspricht, ...	If the prices quoted are competitive and the quality is up to standard, ...
Wenn die Ware von unseren Kunden gut aufgenommen wird, können Sie mit einem flotten Umsatz rechnen.	If the goods meet with / find our customers' approval you can expect a brisk turnover.
Wenn Sie uns die gewünschten Zugeständnisse machen, können wir Ihnen einen größeren/umfangreicheren Auftrag zusagen/erteilen.	If the concessions we have asked for can be met, we would certainly place a substantial order.
Wir hoffen, dass Sie uns dies zusichern können.	... , and we hope you can offer us this guarantee.
... können Sie mit regelmäßigen Aufträgen in beträchtlicher Höhe rechnen.	... you can count on / expect regular and considerable orders from us.
... werden wir regelmäßige Aufträge erteilen.	... we will order on a regular basis / place regular orders with you.

8 Closing lines

Für Ihre Bemühungen danken wir.	Thank you for your attention.
Wir hoffen bald von Ihnen zu hören.	We hope to hear from you in the near future.
Ihrer umgehenden Antwort sehen wir gern entgegen. / Über Ihre baldige Antwort würden wir uns freuen.	We would be grateful for an early reply. / A prompt reply would be much appreciated.

C Practising language

1 Complete the sentences below with suitable phrases from the box. There are two more items than you need.

> appreciated | broaden | deliver | delivery periods | demand for | distributor | hearing | leading manufacturer | price-list | quantity | recommended to | sales literature | shop | specialist retail trade

Your company was ... [1] us as a ... [2] of toys made from wood.
We are a ... [3] of toys to the ... [4]. As the ... [5] toys made from wood is steadily increasing, we are interested to ... [6] our range and, therefore, are looking for new suppliers.
We would like to ask you to let us have your ... [7] and current ... [8]. Please also quote your trade and ... [9] discounts. In view of the seasonal nature of our business detailed information on your ... [10] would be much ... [11].

We look forward to ... [12] from you soon.

2 Rearrange these sentences in the proper order.

Dear Sirs,

a During the ECR in Vienna we visited your stand and gained information about your product range.
b Our highly skilled staff is also available to take care of the after-sales service.
c Should you be interested in working together with us, we would be pleased to hear from you.
d We are a marketing and service company in medical technology and are looking for partners with products in the field of the production of diagnosis equipment and related software.
e We look forward to hearing from you in the near future.
f We would appreciate your sending us detailed information about the full range of your products as well as your terms and conditions.
g With our extensive sales network we are in a position to market your products everywhere in the German-speaking countries.

Yours faithfully,

3 Rewrite these sentences in better English.

1 When I read the paper I saw your ad.
2 I need information about your products.
3 What are your prices?
4 Tell me about your conditions.
5 What rebates do you give?
6 If we like your conditions, we will buy a lot.
7 Write soon.

4 Study the useful phrases and match adjectives and nouns in the lists below.

Adjective		Noun
1 adequate	a	catalogue
2 brisk	b	competition
3 competitive	c	customer
4 comprehensive	d	furniture
5 current	e	importer
6 high-quality	f	information
7 illustrated	g	order
8 keen	h	price
9 leading	i	price-list
10 long-standing	j	range
11 precise	k	turnover
12 substantial	l	warranty

5 Complete this text.

Dear Sirs

Your company was recommended to us by a business partner. We are a wholesaler dealing in office equip… and a… interested in y… overhead projectors. Kindly s… us detail… information ab… the techni… data o… your mach… . Please l… us al… have y… current p…-list quot… your m… competitive exp… prices. Inform… about y… terms … payment … delivery w… be m… appreciated. Fur…, we w… like t… know w… quantity dis… you a… able t… grant f… substantial ord… . If … machines me… our expect… , we wi… first pl… a trial ord… to te… the qual… of y… products a… your serv… .
We … forward t… hearing f… you.

Y… faithfully

6 Replace the words in *italics* with more suitable ones.

1. We saw your advertisement in the February *edition* of "Furniture Monthly".
2. The *items* you *demonstrated* at your stand at the Hannover Fair were very impressive.
3. At the Logistics *exhibition* in Birmingham we *spoke about* shelf systems.
4. Your *assortment* of vacuum cleaners is very attractive.
5. Please send us your *prospectuses*.
6. We also *want* information about your prices.
7. Kindly *tell* us about your terms.
8. We would be grateful to *get* information about your *supply periods*.
9. Please let us know your *conditions* of payment.
10. If your prices are *low*, we will *make* a large order.
11. We will place a *test* order to *examine* the local market.
12. Your *offer* of ladies outerwear *pleases us*.

7 Form complete sentences to write a letter of enquiry.

1. at recent Igedo fashion show/attractive designs/display of accessories/impress with/in Düsseldorf/see/and
2. based in Munich/chain of ladies fashion houses/well-established
3. handbags and gloves/interested in/particularly/range of suede and leather goods
4. current price-list/comprehensive catalogue/most competitive prices/please/quote/send
5. come up to/count on/expectations/if/products/regular and considerable orders
6. as usual/expect to be granted/in Germany/off net prices/25 % trade discount
7. hear from you/hope/near future

8 Write a summary in German of the enquiry below.

> Dear Sir or Madam
>
> We have heard from our business partners Carruthers in Perth, Scotland that you are one of the leading manufacturers of repro furniture in Germany.
> One of our major customers specializes in refurbishing country hotels throughout Britain and is looking for a reliable supplier of repro furniture to equip hotel lounges, bars and rooms. Therefore we are particularly interested in your ranges of leather and imitation leather armchairs, settees, occasional furniture etc.
> Kindly send us your literature, catalogues and price-lists for your full range quoting your keenest export prices, the discounts available and your terms of sale and delivery. Please also indicate your delivery periods. If your products prove to be suitable for our purposes you can expect big orders on a regular basis.
> Should you wish to enquire about our company, we would be happy to provide first-class references from customers and banks.
> We look forward to hearing from you at your convenience.
>
> Yours faithfully

Listening comprehension

9 Listen to the message on the answering machine twice. Copy the memo and complete the details.

10 Listen to this telephone dialogue twice and then, as the caller Petra Schnitzler, write a summary in German for your boss.

Letter writing

1 Write a letter of enquiry to a manufacturer of fashion goods.

You are interested in shoewear, leather goods and garments or a similar product group of your choice. Use as many of the following terms and phrases as possible.

> appreciate receiving additional information about …
> at the recent … fair in …
> your prices are competitive
> detailed catalogue and current price-list
> at reasonable prices
> latest range of …
> look forward to an early reply
> might find a ready market
> place a trial order
> reductions for large orders
> terms and conditions
> test the local market
> very much like the design and patterns

2 Write a general enquiry using the following information.

> Für Kundendienst (Abt. Tiermedizin – *veterinary medicine division*)
> Suche nach tragbaren Röntgengeräten *(portable x-ray machines)*;
> Bitte um Zusendung von geeignetem Informationsmaterial.

3 Write an email using the following notes.

> Auf der Messe „Ideal Home Exhibition" in London im Juni haben Sie den Stand der Firma Britelight besucht. Die Lampenschirme haben Ihnen besonders gefallen. Sie haben allerdings nur eine Visitenkarte *(business card)* mitgenommen.
>
> Bitten Sie nun um die Zusendung eines ausführlichen Katalogs und der gültigen Preisliste. Fragen Sie auch nach Lieferfristen und Rabatten bei größeren Aufträgen.
>
> Teilen Sie Ihre Anschrift mit.

4 Write a letter of enquiry.

Für die Einkaufsleitung Ihres Unternehmens entwerfen Sie einen Brief an Textile Machines plc, 28 Smithfield Way, Horsley Business Park, Horsley, LS15 7TS. Beziehen Sie sich auf das Gespräch am Firmenstand von Textile Machines während der Hannover Messe. Nach Durchsicht der Kurzinformationen über computergesteuerte Webmaschinen (*computer-controlled weaving machines*) sind Sie nun an dem vollständigen Katalog und den weiteren technischen Einzelheiten interessiert. Fragen Sie nach den Liefer- und Zahlungsbedingungen. Stellen Sie die Bestellung mehrerer Maschinen in Aussicht.

5 Write a letter from notes.

Sie haben die Anzeige der Firma Sports & Leisure Fashions, 17 Manningham Lane, Bradford, BD4 9LT in der letzten Ausgabe der Fachzeitschrift „Sports Today" gesehen. Ihre Firma vertreibt Freizeitbekleidung (*leisurewear*). Insbesondere der Fachhandel gehört zu den Kunden. Da die Nachfrage stetig steigt, wollen Sie Ihr Sortiment erheblich erweitern und insbesondere um hochwertige Sportbekleidung (*high-quality sportswear*) ergänzen.

> **Aufgabe**
> Schreiben Sie eine Anfrage an Sports & Leisure Fashions und berücksichtigen Sie dabei folgende Punkte:
> - Verweis auf die Anzeige
> - Vorstellung Ihrer Firma
> - Nachfrage nach Bekleidung für Golf, Tennis und Squash
> - Bitte um illustrierten Katalog und gültige Preisliste
> - Frage nach Rabatten insbes. für umfangreiche Aufträge
> - Liefer- und Zahlungsbedingungen
> - Zusendung von Mustern

6 Write a letter from notes.

Durch Geschäftspartner sind Sie auf die Firma Gordons Silver Ltd, 36 Forth Road, Musselburgh, EH14 7OX aufmerksam gemacht worden. Sie sind ein führender Importeur von qualitativ hochwertigen Silberwaren (*high-quality silverware*). Britische Silberwaren erfreuen sich wachsender Beliebtheit. Die Produkte werden vorwiegend an den Facheinzelhandel vertrieben. Sie sind zunächst an Besteck mit Silberauflage (*silver-plated cutlery*) und Geschenkartikeln (*giftware*) aus Silber interessiert.

> **Aufgabe**
> Schreiben Sie eine Anfrage an Gordons Silver Ltd und berücksichtigen Sie dabei folgende Punkte:
> - Informationsquelle
> - Vorstellung Ihrer Firma / Beschreibung der Marktsituation
> - Bitte um vollständigen bebilderten Katalog und aktuelle Preisliste
> - Frage nach Rabatten, Lieferfristen, Liefer- und Zahlungsbedingungen
> - Frage nach Möglichkeit des Kaufs auf Probe
> - Angabe von Referenzen möglich

E Useful words

Prospektmaterial, Prospekte	(sales) literature, sales material
(bebilderter) Katalog	(illustrated) catalogue/catalog [US]
Prospekt, Broschüre	brochure
Heft, Faltblatt	booklet
Informationsblatt, Prospekt	leaflet
Werbeprospekt (Schule/Universität); Börsenzulassungsprospekt	prospectus
gültige/aktuelle Preisliste	current price-list
Ausstellungsraum	showroom
Ausstellung	exhibition
(Fach-)Austellung, (Fach-)Messe	(trade) fair
Ausstellungsstück	exhibit
Messebesucher	visitor (to the fair)
Aussteller/in	exhibitor
Probe(stück), Muster	sample
Muster (Stoff etc.)	pattern
Beschaffenheit, Struktur	texture
Muster(stück) (in Originalgröße)	specimen
Gestaltung, Ausführung, Muster	design
(allgemeine) Geschäftsbedingungen, Bedingungen	terms and conditions
Vergünstigungen/Nachlässe einräumen/gewähren	to offer/grant concessions
Skonto, Barzahlungsrabatt	cash discount
Wiederverkäuferrabatt, Handelsrabatt	trade discount
Mengenrabatt	quantity discount
zur Ansicht, zur Probe	on approval
mit Rückgaberecht, in Kommission	on sale or return
Probesendung, Probelieferung	trial shipment
Beschaffung, Einkauf	purchasing, buying
Beschaffung (Staat)	procurement
wettbewerbsfähiger/günstiger Preis	competitive/keen price
unverzügliche Lieferung	prompt delivery
Empfehlungsschreiben, Referenz; Verweis, Hinweis	reference
Referenz vorlegen	to furnish/submit/supply a reference
Handelsvertreter/in	representative
Agent/in, Vermittler/in, Vertreter/in	agent
Auftraggeber/in, Unternehmer/in	principal
Sortiment, Produktpalette	range (of products)
langjähriger Kunde	long-standing customer
gut eingeführt	well-established
Angebot machen/unterbreiten	to submit an offer
ein günstiges Angebot vorlegen/machen	to offer/make a favourable quotation
nach Auftragseingang, nach Eingang der Bestellung	after receipt of order
jdm. etw. zukommen lassen	to provide so. with sth.
den Anforderungen entsprechen	to be up to standard

Offers and quotations

Model letters: a general offer, a specific offer

Useful phrases: opening lines; 'selling' the product; availability of the product; catalogues, price-lists, demonstrations; prices, discounts, terms of payment and delivery; instructions and closing sentences

A reply to a **general enquiry** (general offer) usually does not require a letter. Everything the customer may need to know about the product or service will normally be available in printed form, especially as the products in question do not often require much explanation.

In your reply to a **specific enquiry** (specific offer) let your prospective customer know immediately whether you have the product or can provide the service s/he is enquiring about. In order to encourage him/her to do business with you, mention one or two selling points including any warranties you offer. Suggest an alternative if you cannot supply the article in question or even refer the prospective customer to another supplier.

Enclose current catalogues and price-lists to inform the customer of the full range of goods available. If samples are sent, this should be mentioned. In some cases it may be helpful or even necessary to demonstrate the product. Make suitable suggestions for your representative to call on the customer or invite him to visit a stockist's or agent's showroom.

Let the customer know for how long the offer is valid. Prices may be quoted firmly, although this is not legally binding, or subject to confirmation. Net prices do not include any other costs or charges. It is common practice to grant special discounts to sellers or industrial users (trade discounts), for orders of a certain amount (quantity discount) or for payment within a short period of time (cash discount). The terms of delivery should also be mentioned in sufficient detail. Sometimes it may be useful to be specific about possible delivery dates.

Do not forget to thank the customer for his enquiry and to encourage enquiries for further details. Make sure all items mentioned in your letter (catalogues, price-lists, samples etc.) are either enclosed or dispatched under separate cover immediately. Assure the customer of the prompt and careful execution of any order.

A Model letters

1 A general offer

This letter is a reply to the general enquiry from Neue Medien about computer games (see page 27).

Copernicus Ltd   15 Castle Drive   Durham DH1 4UH

Neue Medien GmbH
Messestr. 15
D-90471 Nürnberg
Germany

Attn Ms Jannick
25 April 20..

Dear Ms Jannick

Enquiry about computer games

Thank you for your enquiry of 20 April about our computer games. As requested we are sending you our comprehensive catalogue and current price-list.

In this fast-moving market new products are being developed at a very rapid rate, as you will no doubt realise. We therefore update our list every month to add new titles and delete out-of-stock material. To avoid disappointment we would advise that, when ordering, you check with us whether the titles you require are still available. It is our policy to fulfil orders within 24 hours.

There is no charge for packaging and transport for overseas orders in excess of £250. For payment within a fortnight of receipt of invoice we grant the usual 2% cash discount.

We trust that you will find our comprehensive list of titles of interest for your clientele and look forward to receiving your order.

Yours sincerely

B. Stevens

Brian Stevens
Sales Manager

Encls

Write a list of the important points raised in this letter. Mention at least 5 points.

Letter plan for a general offer

- Refer to the enquiry.
- Mention any items enclosed/sent under separate cover.
- Provide any other information considered useful to attract a sale.
- Close with a polite phrase.

2 A specific offer

This letter is a reply to the special enquiry Annette Reppel from Geschenkhaus GmbH sent to Royal Denby Ltd (see page 28).

Dear Ms Reppel

Information about our product range

Thank you for your letter of 28 February and your interest in our ranges of china, earthenware and glassware.

The new catalogues for these ranges have just come off the press. In addition to the sets and individual pieces of china which we highlighted in our advertising campaign you will find a variety of traditional and modern designs for dinner and coffee sets. The delicate patterns, the quality of the material and the finishing will certainly appeal to the discerning customer.

Over the past 12 months we have considerably extended our selection of high-quality crystal and ornamental glassware. The new ranges have proved very popular, and we trust that you will like them too.
We can give a 10-year supply guarantee on all our standard ranges of china and glassware.
Of course, we are happy to send you a few specimens for testing purposes: a selection of items is being shipped to you today.
Our terms of payment and delivery for trade customers are explained in detail in the catalogues. But should you have any queries, please do not hesitate to contact us.
For most items and sets we can promise shipment within a fortnight of receipt of your order. Should production take longer we will, of course, notify you immediately.
We trust that you will like our products and look forward to receiving your order in due course.

Yours sincerely

Which of these statements are incorrect? Change the statements if necessary.

1 The letter is in reply to an offer.
2 The new catalogues have only just come in.
3 The advertising campaign appealed to many customers.
4 It has taken 12 months to design the range.
5 The 10-year supply guarantee only applies to the china and glassware ranges.
6 The specimen pieces are sent free of charge.
7 The terms for trade customers and other customers are the same.
8 It takes a fortnight to deal with orders.

Letter plan for a specific offer

- [ ] Refer to the enquiry.
- [ ] Provide information about the product / range of products.
- [ ] Outline any specific features of the product (selling point).
- [ ] Inform the potential buyer about the availability of the product.
- [ ] Mention any items enclosed (sales literature, samples etc.).
- [ ] Give information about prices, discounts, terms of delivery and payment.
- [ ] Promise good and fast service (optional).
- [ ] Close with a polite sentence.

B Useful phrases

1 Opening lines

Vielen Dank für Ihre Anfrage vom … / Für Ihre Anfrage (Bezugsnr. …) vom … danken wir.	Many thanks / Thank you for your enquiry (Ref. No. …) of … / We would like to thank you for your enquiry of …
Ich nehme / Wir nehmen Bezug / Wir beziehen uns auf Ihre Anfrage vom …	In reply / With reference to your enquiry of …
Gern unterbreiten/machen wir Ihnen folgendes Angebot. / Wir freuen uns Ihnen folgendes Angebot unterbreiten zu können.	We have the pleasure of submitting / We are pleased to submit the following quotation.
… bieten wir Ihnen wie folgt an …	… offering you the following …
… fügen wir unseren Kostenvoranschlag für die Lieferung von … bei.	… enclosing our estimate for the supply of …

2 'Selling' the product

Wir haben eine umfangreiche/umfassende Auswahl an …, die … sicherlich gefallen wird.	We have a wide selection of … that will appeal to …
Wir dürfen Sie zur Wahl dieser Artikelgruppe / dieses Artikels/Modells/Typs/Erzeugnisses beglückwünschen.	We think you have made an excellent choice in selecting this line/model/ type/product.
Wir dürfen Ihnen versichern, dass die … eine hervorragende Maschine ist.	We can assure you that the … is an outstanding machine.

3 Availability of the product

Wir haben eine große Auswahl an Farben und Größen vorrätig.	We have a wide range of colours and sizes in stock.
Wir führen das komplette Sortiment aller bedeutenden Marken.	We stock the full range of all major brands.
Diese Menge können wir ab Lager liefern.	We can supply this quantity from stock.
Alle im Katalog angeführten Produkte sind ab Lager lieferbar.	All the products listed in this catalogue are available from stock.
Das von Ihnen verlangte Modell ist nicht vorrätig / nicht mehr verfügbar / wird nicht mehr hergestellt.	The model you ask for is out of stock / no longer available / out of production.
Jedoch können wir Ihnen folgenden Ersatz anbieten: …	But we are pleased to be able to offer you the following substitute: …
Wir können Ihnen jedoch eine Alternative in einer ebenso guten Qualität anbieten.	But we can offer you an alternative product of an equally high standard.

Zur Herstellung dieser Menge benötigen wir ... Wochen/Monate.	We require ... weeks/months to manufacture this quantity.
Die Auslieferung wird sich daher um ... Wochen/Tage verzögern.	Delivery will therefore be delayed by ... weeks/days.
Wegen der überaus großen Nachfrage nach diesem Artikel sind wir nicht in der Lage, ...	Because of the heavy demand for this product we are unable to ...

4 Catalogues, price-lists, demonstrations

Beiliegend übersenden wir Ihnen unseren neuen Herbstkatalog sowie die derzeit gültige Preisliste.	Please find enclosed / Enclosed are our recent autumn catalogue and the current price-list.
... und übersenden Ihnen gern die erbetenen Unterlagen /die Unterlagen, um die Sie gebeten haben.	... and are pleased to send you the literature you asked for / as requested.
Hiermit übersenden wir ihnen Informationsmaterial für unser Angebot/Sortiment von ...	Our literature for our range of ... is enclosed.
... und weisen darauf hin, dass die angegebenen Preise sich wegen der unbeständigen Marktlage verändern können.	... and should like to point out that due to unstable market conditions the prices stated are subject to change.
In dem beigefügten illustrierten Katalog finden Sie alle notwendigen Einzelheiten.	The enclosed illustrated catalogue will give you all the details you require.
Wir möchten Ihnen vorschlagen, sich in den Ausstellungsräumen unseres Vertreters in Ihrem Bezirk umzusehen (vgl. nachstehende Anschrift).	May we suggest that you visit the showrooms of our agent in your area whose address is given below.

5 Prices, discounts, terms of payment and delivery

Der Nettopreis für diesen Artikel beläuft sich auf ...	The net price for this article is ...
Bei den Preisen handelt es sich um Nettopreise.	The prices quoted are net.
Hinzu kommen noch die Kosten für Verpackung und Transport.	... to which must be added the costs of packaging and transport.
Unsere Preise gelten ab Werk/Lager.	Our prices are ex works/mill/warehouse.
... , so dass sich der Bruttopreis einschließlich der Versandkosten / Gesamtpreis auf ... pro 100 Stück beläuft.	... making a gross price, inclusive of delivery charges, / an all-inclusive price of ... per 100 items.
Dieser Preis versteht sich einschließlich Fracht und Verpackung.	Freight and packing are included in this price.
Unsere Preise gelten FOB Southampton / FAS Felixstowe / CIF Bremen.	Our prices are quoted FOB Southampton / FAS Felixstowe / CIF Bremen.

Wir können Ihnen einen Rabatt in Höhe von 10 % für Mengen von mehr als 1000 Stück anbieten.	We can offer you a discount of 10% for quantities in excess of 1000 items.
Auf die genannten Preise gewähren wir einen Wiederverkaufsrabatt/Fachhandelsrabatt von 25 % des Nettopreises.	The prices quoted are subject to a 25% trade discount off the net price.
Für Begleichung innerhalb von 14 Tagen nach Rechnungserhalt / Für Barzahlung gewähren wir 2 % Skonto.	For payment within a fortnight of receipt of invoice / For cash payment we allow/grant a 2% cash discount.
Da wir bisher noch keine Geschäftsbeziehungen miteinander hatten, würden wir gern per Nachnahme abrechnen.	As we have not done business before, we would prefer payment to be made cash-on-delivery (COD).
Unsere üblichen Bedingungen sind netto Kasse.	Our usual terms are net cash.
Die Zahlung soll durch 30-Tage-Wechsel / 3-Monats-Wechsel, Dokumente gegen Akzept erfolgen.	Payment is to be made by 30-day bill of exchange (B/E) / 3-month bill of exchange, documents against acceptance (D/A).
Als Zahlungsmodus möchten wir unwiderrufliches und bestätigtes Akkreditiv vorschlagen.	We would prefer payment by irrevocable and confirmed letter of credit (L/C).

6 Instructions and closing sentences

Wir danken Ihnen nochmals für Ihr Interesse an unseren Produkten / für Ihr Schreiben und sind gern bereit, bei Bedarf noch weitere Fragen zu beantworten.	Once again we would like to thank you for your interest in our products / for writing to us and would welcome any further queries you would like us to answer.
… und dürfen Ihnen versichern, dass Ihr Auftrag umgehend erledigt wird.	… and can assure you that your order will be dealt with promptly.
Wenn Ihnen dieses Angebot zusagt, würden wir uns freuen, bald einen Auftrag zu erhalten.	If this offer is acceptable to you, please let us have your order by return.
Wir erwarten eine rege Nachfrage nach diesem attraktiven Artikel und schlagen deshalb vor, frühzeitig zu bestellen.	As we expect a rush of orders for this attractive product we advise you to order early.
Die Aufträge werden in der Reihenfolge ihres Eingangs erledigt, da unsere Vorräte begrenzt sind.	Orders will be dealt with in the order we receive them as our supplies are limited.
Dieses Angebot gilt für einen Monat. / Wir halten uns einen Monat an dieses Angebot gebunden.	This offer is binding/firm for one month.
Wir würden uns freuen, wenn Sie von diesem günstigen Angebot Gebrauch machen würden.	We hope you will make use of this advantageous offer.
Ein Probeauftrag wird Sie von der Qualität unserer Produkte und Leistungen unseres Hauses überzeugen.	A trial order will convince you of the excellence of our products and the quality of our service.

C Practising language

1 Choose the correct term.

Dear Mr Patel

We have *got/had/received* [1] your *demand/enquiry/request* [2] and are *glad/happy/pleased* [3] to send you our *last/latest/newest* [4] catalogue and *actual/current/running* [5] price-list.

The 'Delta' *assortment/group/line* [6] of cutlery is very *admired/liked/popular* [7] with younger *buyers/clients/customers* [8], whereas the classic 'Gamma' *design/pattern/sample* [9] appeals more to other age groups.

All our *commodities/goods/wares* [10] can be *packed/sent/supplied* [11] from stock. The usual 2 per cent *discount/rebate/reduction* [12] is *acceptable/available/possible* [13] for cash payment.

We look forward to *receipt/receive/receiving* [14] your *command/instruction/order* [15] which will be dealt with *fast/promptly/quickly* [16].

Yours *cordially/faithfully/sincerely* [17]

2 Use the following to complete the sentences below. There are more items than you need.

> cash discount | cash payment | customised | ex stock | firm |
> in strict rotation | net | out of stock | quantity discount |
> subject to confirmation | terms of delivery | trade discount

1. An offer is ... , if the prices change very quickly.
2. A buyer who orders large quantities may be granted a ...
3. If the offer is valid for 30 days, it is called ...
4. If supplies are limited, orders will often be handled ...
5. If the goods are available immediately, they are sold ...
6. ... goods are made to the customer's specifications.
7. A buyer who pays cash may be entitled to a ...
8. The buyer must pay for packaging and transport, if the prices are quoted ...
9. Often a ... is granted to customers who resell the goods.
10. The goods are ... , if the supplier cannot deliver them immediately.

3 Changing the beginning of your sentences. Replace the *we*-structures with those in brackets.

1. We thank you for your enquiry of 10 July. (Thank ...)
2. We can assure you that the 'Zeta' power drill is an outstanding machine. (Be ...)
3. We have enclosed our latest catalogue and current price-list. (Our ...)
4. We can supply all our products from stock. (All ...)
5. We have enclosed our autumn catalogue. (Enclosed ...)
6. We would suggest that you visit one of our showrooms. (May ...)
7. We will deal with new orders in the order we receive them. (New ...)
8. We expect a rush of orders, and therefore we advise you to order early. (As ...)

4 Write full sentences to inform your customer.

1 Say thank you for a phone call showing interest in your products. Specify a product.
2 Say that you are sending the information the customer asked for.
3 Say that you are sending textile material so that it can be examined.
4 Say that you have stopped making this product as it didn't sell well. Specify a product.
5 State that you can send another item that is even better and can be bought at a lower price. Specify a product.
6 Say that this product is sold out and that it takes at least two weeks to get new goods. You are very sorry. Specify a product.
7 Tell the customer that there are many people wanting this product; a quick decision is needed. Specify a product.
8 Inform the customer that you want to sell the summer goods at very low prices to make room for the autumn goods. Everything has to go.

5 Express these terms and prices in idiomatic English.

1 Die Preise sind ab Werk.
2 Es handelt sich um Bruttopreise, d.h. einschließlich Fracht und Verpackung.
3 Es gibt 2% Skonto für Bezahlung innerhalb von 10 Tagen nach Rechnungsdatum.
4 Bei Kauf von mehr als 20.000 Stück gibt es einen Mengenrabatt von 15%.
5 Da es ein neuer Kunde ist, verlangen Sie Bezahlung bei Lieferung.
6 Sie arbeiten nur mit geringen Margen, um die Preise günstig zu halten. Preisnachlässe sind deshalb nicht möglich.
7 Die Zahlung soll durch unwiderrufliches und bestätigtes Akkreditiv erfolgen.
8 Sie können Lieferung innerhalb von 10 Tagen zusagen.

Listening comprehension

6 Listen to the dialogue and then complete this memo.

```
MemoMemoMemoMemo

Date:     12/7/20..
Called:
Discussed:
Action:
Address:
```

Spell the name and address of your company or a company you know to a partner.

D Letter writing

1 Write a general offer from notes.

Reply to a request for product information and samples of fabrics for curtain materials. Use the terms and phrases listed below.

> broad range of modern and traditional designs | colour code | colour combinations stated in attached list | delivery within five working days | look forward to | material and design reference number | minimum order volume per item | most items available from stock | pattern books and assortment of samples of fabrics | pleased to receive enquiry | prices indicated in pattern books | quantity discount of 15% for orders exceeding €10,000 | return pattern books within 10 days | trust you will like | under separate cover | usual cash discount | when ordering please state

2 Write a reply to a request for sales literature.

Refer to the printed material enclosed. Point to the wide range of goods offered at very competitive prices. Express expectation that customer will like the products. Point out one or two novelties. Goods immediately available. Terms and conditions in catalogue. Quantity discounts upon request. Express hope for order.

3 Write a reply to an enquiry.

> Messrs
> Carton & Co.
> 293 Colemore Road
> London SW27 4NP
>
> Dear Sir or Madam
>
> Enquiry for metal polish for cars
>
> We read with interest the article about your newly developed car polish 'Carshine' in the current issue of Motorist Monthly. We invite quotations for your range of metal polish and in particular of 'Carshine'. If your products prove satisfactory and your prices are competitive we should be prepared to give you the bulk of our business.
>
> It will be necessary, however, for us to put your polish through a rigorous test, to which we have no doubt you will agree. Naturally, we are prepared to pay the market price for a trial supply of 5 500g tins for testing purposes. But in view of the fact that a satisfactory result would lead to our placing a contract for 20 tons or more annually, we feel that some discount should be allowed. We must therefore ask you to state the best terms you can offer.
>
> An early reply would be appreciated and we look forward to hearing from you.
>
> Yours faithfully

> **Aufgabe**
> Schreiben Sie ein Angebot und berücksichtigen Sie folgende Punkte:
> - Dank für die Anfrage und Verweis auf das beigefügte Informationsmaterial zum gesamten Sortiment für die Fahrzeugreinigung
> - Testversuche an Tankstellen (*petrol station*) und in Betrieben mit großen Fahrzeugflotten (*car fleet*) sehr zufriedenstellend verlaufen
> - Verbrauch geringer als bei Vergleichsprodukten
> - Einführungssonderpreis (*special introductory price*) auf 3 Monate beschränkt
> - 5 Dosen zu Testzwecken kostenlos
> - Versand noch heute
> - Bei Abnahme größerer Mengen Rabatt von 25% auf den Listenpreis
> - Sie hoffen, dass der Kunde mit der Ware zufrieden sein wird

4 Write a letter from notes.

Als Mitarbeiter/in der Verkaufsabteilung Ihres Unternehmens Brandmann & Söhne GmbH in 80231 München, Dachauer Str. 291 beantworten Sie die Anfrage eines Neukunden (Home Design Ltd, Craigfield Business Park, Unit 15, Kirkby, L15 6PN) nach Designer-Möbeln für den gehobenen Geschmack.

> **Aufgabe**
> Verfassen Sie ein Angebot unter Berücksichtigung der folgenden Punkte:
> - Dank für Anfrage und Interesse an Produkten
> - Formschöne und qualitativ hochwertige Produkte (Material, Verarbeitung – *workmanship*)
> - Einzelheiten in beigefügtem Katalog
> - Preisliste gültig bis 30.10. d.J.
> - Lieferzeiten ca. 4 Wochen, da Produktion nur nach Bestellung
> - Mengenrabatt möglich bei Auftragswert von mindestens €310.000
> - Verpackung und Versand zum Selbstkostenpreis
> - Zahlung 14 Tage nach Rechnungsdatum

5 Write a letter from notes.

Die Maschinenfabrik Hartmann und Braun GmbH, Dachauer Str. 241, 80924 München, hat von der Northwest Trading Ltd., 21 Walmsley Drive, Liverpool L7 8TF Großbritannien, eine Anfrage zur Anfertigung und Lieferung von 4 Transportbandanlagen (*conveyor belt systems*) für zwei Lagerhallen (*warehouse*) erhalten.

> **Aufgabe**
> Bereiten Sie ein Angebotsschreiben unter Berücksichtigung folgender Punkte vor:
> - Preis der Transportbandanlagen: €57.500 pro Stück FOB norddeutscher Seehafen
> - Lieferung ca. 3 Monate nach Auftragserteilung
> - Zahlung durch unwiderrufliches, bestätigtes Akkreditiv (SEC-Bank in München)
> - Auftragsausführung nach Akkreditiveröffnung
> - Aufstellung und Inbetriebnahme (*assembly and putting into operation*) durch Servicepersonal der Hartmann und Braun GmbH zum Pauschalpreis von €20.000
> - Gültigkeit des Angebots: 3 Monate
> - Verweis auf allgemeine Lieferbedingungen in der Anlage

E Useful words

Verkaufsargument	selling point
Produkt herausstellen/fördern/bewerben	to promote a product
Sonderfertigung, Einzelstück, nach Kundenangaben hergestellter Artikel	customised/tailor-made article
Probeauftrag	trial order
Erstauftrag, Neuauftrag	initial order
Ersatz-, Nachfolgebestellung	repeat order, follow-up order
feste Bestellung, Festauftrag	firm order
unverbindlich, ohne Kaufverpflichtung, (Angebot) freibleibend	without any obligation, subject to confirmation
Gegenangebot	counter offer
Großeinkauf	bulk purchase
die Läger räumen	to clear/reduce stocks
das Lager wieder auffüllen	to replenish stocks, to restock
Lagerräumung	stock clearance
Ware auf Lager nehmen	to lay/take goods in stock
vorrätige Ware	goods in stock
nicht mehr vorrätige Ware	goods out of stock
voll ausgelastet sein, die Kapazität voll ausschöpfen	to be working to capacity
jds Bedürfnisse befriedigen, jds Bedarf decken	to meet sb's requirements
Auftrag bearbeiten/abwickeln	to handle/process an order
Kaufinteressent, potenzieller Kunde	prospective buyer
Gesamtkosten	overall/total cost
Restbetrag, Restsumme, Saldo, Restmenge	balance
Begleichung (Rechnung)	settlement
wirksam werden, in Kraft treten	to become effective
Liefertermin nennen	to quote a delivery date
Liefertermin/Lieferfrist einhalten	to meet a delivery date
(Aus-)Lieferung, Anlieferung, Belieferung	delivery
Sendung, Lieferung	consignment/shipment
Partie, Gebinde	lot
Angebot, Vorrat, (Lager-)Bestand, Lieferung	supply
Nachfrage, Bedarf, Anforderung	demand

5 Orders

Model letters: a trial order, a repeat/follow-up order, a counteroffer, a reply to a counteroffer

Useful phrases: opening lines; prices; buyer's confirmation of agreed discounts; buyer's confirmation of the terms of payment; seller's rejection of requested terms of payment; buyer's confirmation of terms of delivery; buyer's forwarding and packing instructions; closing lines

An offer usually provides the basis for an **order**. The customer has all the necessary information at his disposal: information about the goods (quality, size, measurement, weight, colour, material etc.), the quantities in which they are sold, availability, prices and discounts, delivery periods, cost of packaging and delivery, terms of delivery and payment, and warranties if applicable.

In the order, the buyer states clearly which goods are to be purchased by giving a goods description mentioning the product name and any additional extras (letters and/or numbers) and also indicating the catalogue number, item number, model number etc. This is usually preceded by an indication of the quantity (number of items, cases, containers, bottles) or volume of weight required. The agreed price(s), discounts and terms of delivery and payment are repeated to confirm the agreement reached between buyer and seller.

In legal terms, the order is binding on both parties and constitutes a contract. For the seller it involves the obligation to supply the goods as described in the order, provided the order is placed on the basis of a firm offer. For the buyer, the order entails the obligation to accept the goods supplied in conformity with the order and to pay for such goods.

In order to avoid any misunderstanding and because of the legal implications, an order is commonly placed in writing. This can be done by way of a letter or an order form provided by the seller or a special form. In either case this will result in an order number being allocated to the transaction which is quoted in all future communication.

There are different types of order:
- **Initial order:** first business transaction between the buyer and seller.
- **Trial order:** an order to test whether an article is suitable for the buyer's purpose.
- **Follow-up/repeat order:** an order placed when the goods originally bought proved to be suitable or have sold very well.
- **Regular/standing order:** order placed at regular intervals.
- **Order on call:** order for a part delivery under the terms of a large-scale order, often used in just-in-time (jit) delivery arrangements.

If the order is placed at a price which is lower than the price originally quoted by the seller a **counteroffer** may result (the supplier may even decide not accept the order at the terms stated by the buyer). In this case agreement between both parties must be reached about the terms (prices and discounts), before the order can be executed.

UNIT 5 Orders

A Model letters

1 A trial order

This letter is a reply to the offer from Copernicus Ltd for the supply of computer games (page 41).

Neue Medien GmbH

Messestr. 15
D-90471 Nürnberg
E-Mail: sandra.jannick@neue-medien.co
Tel.: 09 11/73 85 51
Fax: 09 11/73 85 511

Copernicus Ltd
15 Castle Drive
Durham
DH1 4UH
England

16 May 20..

Dear Mr Stevens

Order for computer games

Thank you for your letter of 25 April and your catalogue. We found your range of titles very attractive and would like to place a trial order to test the local market, although we are confident that your products will sell well.

Please find attached our order for a variety of computer games. It is understood that in view of the size of this order there will be no charge for packaging and transport. Payment will be made by bank transfer upon receipt of your invoice.

We look forward to receiving the computer games in due course.

Yours sincerely

S. Jannick

Sandra Jannick
Purchasing officer

Encl. Order form

Decide which of the following comes closest to the terms used in the letter above.

		a	b	c
1	range of titles	collection of titles	line of titles	selection of titles
2	test	examine	experiment	try out
3	be confident	believe	confirm	doubt
4	a variety of	many different	a large number of	some
5	it is understood	we are certain	we are aware	we are confident
6	no charge	no fee	no costs	no payment
7	upon receipt	when we get	when you send	we hear from you
8	invoice	list of charges	packing list	statement of price to be paid

2 A repeat/follow-up order

This letter and the order form on page 54 are a follow-up order after a consignment of specimens proved to be very satisfactory. (See also offer on page 42).

Geschenkhaus
GmbH & Co KG

Braunschweiger Str. 34
10104 Berlin
Fon 030 353 505 1
Fax 030 353 505 248
E-Mail:
satt.well@geschenkhaus.com.de

Royal Denby Ltd
38 Stafford Road
Stoke
ST3 4QA

England

14 April 20..

Dear Mr Treacher

Order for chinaware

Thank you for your consignment of specimens which you sent so promptly. We have, in the meantime, examined the goods and are very pleased with the designs and the finish. Therefore we have no doubt that your goods will find a ready market here.

Please find attached a trial order for a selection of items from your various ranges. We are confident that further business will develop as soon as our customers have come to appreciate the quality of your goods. When this happens we hope you will see your way to improving the terms and discounts as stated in your catalogues. For the time being we are quite willing to accept these terms.

Please make sure that the goods are shipped to our warehouse at the following address:

    Geschenkhaus GmbH & Co KG
    Erlanger Str. 281
    12053 Berlin

We look forward to hearing from you.

Yours sincerely

Annette Reppel

Annette Reppel
Chief Buyer

Kommanditges.,
Sitz u. Registergericht
AG Nürnberg HRA 2967

Persönlich haftende
Gesellschafterin
Sattler & Wellert GmbH
AG Nürnberg HRA 2165

Geschäftsführer:
R. Sattler, G. Wellert

Bankverbindung:
Commerzbank Nürnberg
Kto.-Nr. 43567405
BLZ 760 400 61

Royal Denby Ltd   38 Stafford Road   Stoke ST3 4QA

ORDER FORM

Article no.	Description	Quantity	Unit price	Total price
15738 A	Golden Eagle Dinner set	15	€ 75.00	€ 1125.00
15739 A	Buzzard Dinner Set	15	€ 77.50	€ 1162.50
15740 A	Kestrel Dinner Set	15	€ 85.00	€ 1275.00
15743 A	Hawk Dinner Set	15	€ 65.00	€ 975.00
16312 B	Dover Breakfast Set	25	€ 30.00	€ 750.00
16314 B	Brighton Breakfast Set	25	€ 27.50	€ 687.50
16317 B	Bristol Breakfast Set	25	€ 32.00	€ 800.00
16318 B	Cardiff Breakfast Set	25	€ 25.00	€ 625.00
16320 B	Carlisle Breakfast Set	25	€ 35.00	€ 875.00
20011 C	Sherry glasses Edinburgh	20	€ 27.50	€ 550.00
20013 C	Whisky tumblers Edinburgh	20	€ 40.00	€ 800.00
20015 C	Hock glasses Edinburgh	20	€ 35.00	€ 700.00
20036 C	Whisky Decanter Edinburgh	5	€ 25.00	€ 125.00

Delivery: within 30 days, franco domicile
Payment: 30 days net, 2 per cent cash discount for payment within 10 days of receipt of invoice

Answer these questions.

1. Have the specimens turned out to the buyer's expectations?
2. What are the sales prospects?
3. What kind of order does the buyer place?
4. What does the buyer say about the expected market reaction?
5. When does the buyer expect the terms and conditions to be improved?
6. When does the buyer expect to receive the goods?

Letter plan for an order

- Refer to the offer.
- State the catalogue, brochure or price-list on which the order is based.
- Specify in detail the item(s) required, quoting item/catalogue number, quality, colour, size, dimensions etc.
- State the price per unit.
- Repeat the discounts agreed.
- Mention the terms of delivery.
- Mention the terms of payment.
- (State date of delivery.)
- Add specific instructions, if necessary, and/or special arrangements.
- Close with a polite phrase.

3 A counteroffer

This letter is written to persuade the supplier to offer better terms.

25-29 Great Western Road
Leeds LS3 6BX

Adventis Damenmoden GmbH
Odenwaldstr. 25
63743 Aschaffenburg
Germany

Dear Ms Jensen

Order for Ladies' Winterwear

Thank you for both your offer of 3rd March and the samples of the materials you use for your range of ladies winter coats.
In the meantime we have been able to test the materials and are very pleased with the result. While appreciating the good quality of the fabrics and also the excellent workmanship of your ladies' outerwear that we saw at the IGEDO Fashion Fair, we find the prices of these goods rather high for the market in which we operate. We also have to point out that good quality ladies' outerwear is now available from several European manufacturers in the Far East. All of these are available at prices from 15% to 25% below yours.
We should like to place our order with you, but must ask you to reconsider your offer.
As our order would be worth around £15,000, you may think it worthwhile to make a concession. We look forward to hearing from you again shortly.

Yours sincerely

Liz Bryant
(Purchasing Manager)

Answer the questions.

1. Why do Gaffeys ask for lower prices?
2. How do Gaffeys try to persuade Adventis to reduce their prices?
3. Decide which of the following options you would choose for your reply and give reasons for your decision.
   a Ms Jensen could try to get the order by lowering the price by 10 to 15 per cent.
   b Ms Jensen could offer a quantity discount.
   c Ms Jensen could say 'no' to the request for a reduction in price.

Letter plan for a counteroffer

- ☐ Refer to the order.
- ☐ State reason for requesting new terms.
- ☐ State new terms required.
- ☐ Close with a polite phrase.

4 A reply to a counteroffer

In this reply the supplier, Adventis Damenmoden GmbH, states reasons for the pricing policy. There is hope for a reduction in the future if certain conditions have been met.

Dear Ms Bryant

Order for Ladies Winterwear

Thank you for your letter of 24th April and your comments on our products. You may remember that we discussed prices and terms at the IGEDO trade fair last autumn. We realise that good quality ladies' wear is being offered by some of our competitors with production facilities in the Far East. But, as tests over a long period of time have shown, the quality of workmanship leaves something to be desired. And we would advise you to examine the products very carefully.

You will understand that this is not the market segment in which we wish to operate. We have always concentrated our efforts on supplying the top end of the market and meeting the demands of fashion-conscious and discerning customers. The feedback we have had in the past strongly supports this business strategy. Therefore we think, it would not be very helpful in the long term to try to compete with lower-priced products from the Far East, which we would find very difficult anyway, because our cost structure is different from that of our competitors with non-European production facilities.

The order volume that you indicate seems very attractive and may allow for some economies of scale. We would certainly be prepared to revise our discounts, if you can demonstrate that the order volume now under discussion can be maintained over a longer period of time.

We hope you will understand our position in this matter and look forward to your comments. Your order will have our best attention.

Yours sincerely

---

1. What do Adventis say about the competition?
2. Describe the type of customer Adventis are looking for.
3. Why is competing with products from the Far East a problem?
4. Why is the order volume attractive?
5. What do you think about the compromise?

Letter plan for a reply to a counter-offer

- Refer to the order.
- State reason for non-acceptance of requested terms.
- Make an alternative offer if possible.
- Close with a polite phrase.

Useful phrases

1 Opening lines

Wir danken Ihnen für Ihr Angebot vom … / Für Ihr Angebot vom … danken wir.	Thank you for your offer of …
Auf der Grundlage Ihres Katalogs Nr. … möchten wir wie folgt bestellen: …	On the basis of your catalogue No. … we would like to order the following …
Beiliegend übersenden wir Ihnen unseren Auftrag (Nr. B 561) über … / Wir erteilen Ihnen hiermit nachstehenden (Probe-)Auftrag.	Enclosed you will find our order (No. B 561) for … / We are pleased to place the following (trial) order with you.
Unter Bezugnahme auf Ihr Inserat in … möchten wir … bestellen.	We refer to your advertisement in … and would like to order …
Die in Ihrem Katalog angebotenen Produkte sind offenkundig von guter Qualität. Wir bitten Sie um die Zusendung folgender Artikel, damit wir sie prüfen können.	The products offered in your catalogue appear to be of the best quality. Please send us the following items for examination.
Vielen Dank für die schnelle Zusendung von Mustern. Nach eingehender Prüfung konnten wir feststellen, dass das Material für unsere Zwecke sehr wohl geeignet ist. Unsere Bestellung haben wir beigefügt.	Thank you for being so prompt in sending us the samples as requested. After rigorous tests we have found that the material is quite suitable for our purposes. Please find our order attached.
In Bestätigung unserer Bestellung, die wir heute Morgen telefonisch durchgegeben haben, senden wir Ihnen hiermit unser Auftragsformular 1278CE.	In confirmation of the order we placed with you by phone this morning we enclose our order form No. 1278CE.
Die Qualität Ihrer Erzeugnisse hat uns beeindruckt. Wir erteilen Ihnen daher diesen ersten Auftrag, obwohl ihre Preise etwas über denen der Konkurrenz liegen.	The quality of your products has impressed us. Therefore we are placing this initial order although your prices are somewhat higher than those of your competitors.

2 Prices

Unsere Bestellung erteilen wir auf der Basis Ihrer Preisliste Nr. …	Our order is placed on the basis of your price-list No. …
Wir gehen davon aus, dass Verpackung und Transport in Ihren Preisen enthalten sind.	We take it that your prices are inclusive of charges for packing and transport.
Es gilt als vereinbart, dass bei der Preisberechnung für diesen Auftrag die üblichen Rabatte berücksichtigt werden.	It is understood that you allow the usual discounts when calculating the price for this order.

3 Buyer's confirmation of agreed discounts

Für die Einräumung eines Wiederverkäuferrabatts in Höhe von 25% und eines Mengenrabatts von 10% danken wir.	We thank you for the 25% trade discount and the 10% quantity discount you allowed us.
Von Ihren Skonti für sofortigen Rechnungsausgleich werden wir sicher Gebrauch machen.	We will certainly take advantage of the cash discounts you offered for prompt settlement.
Für den Einführungsrabatt von 15% danken wir.	Thank you for granting us a 15% introductory offer discount.
Wir sind enttäuscht über den geringen Handelsrabatt von 10%. Hiermit erteilen wir Ihnen einen Probeauftrag und gehen davon aus, dass Sie uns bald günstigere Bedingungen einräumen können.	We were disappointed at the low trade discount of 10%. We will place a trial order and trust that this reduction can be reviewed at some time in the near future.

4 Buyer's confirmation of the terms of payment

Für diese Lieferung gilt Barzahlung.	As agreed we will pay cash on delivery.
Die Zahlung erfolgt vereinbarungsgemäß durch Banküberweisung / per (Verrechnungs-)Scheck.	Payment will be made by bank transfer / (crossed) cheque as agreed.
Ein Zahlungsziel von 30 Tagen gilt als vereinbart.	It is understood that payment will be made 30 days after receipt of the goods.
Da Sie bei neuen Kunden Zahlung bei Auftragserteilung verlangen, haben wir einen Scheck über ... beigefügt. Wir gehen davon aus, dass diese Bedingung bei zukünftigen Aufträgen geändert wird.	As you require cash with order for first-time customers we enclose a cheque for .... We take it that these terms will be revised for future orders.
Wir bitten um Lieferung per Nachnahme.	Please supply the goods COD (cash on delivery).
... und wir sind übereingekommen, dass die Begleichung vierteljährlich nach Eingang der Abrechnung erfolgen soll.	... and we agreed that payment would be made against quarterly statement.
Wie vereinbart ziehen Sie auf uns mit 30 Tagen Sicht Dokumente gegen Akzept/Annahme. Die Dokumente werden unserer Bank in ... übersandt.	As agreed you will draw on our account at 30 days documents against acceptance with the documents being sent to our bank at ...
Wir bestätigen Ihnen hiermit, dass die Zahlung durch unwiderrufliches Akkreditiv erfolgt. Wir haben bereits einen entsprechenden Antrag an unsere Bank gerichtet.	We would like to confirm that payment is to be made by irrevocable letter of credit for which we have already applied at our bank.

5 Seller's rejection of requested terms of payment

Es wäre unrentabel für uns, unsere Produkte zu den von Ihnen geforderten Rabatten anzubieten, da wir mit niedrigen Spannen bei schnellen Umsätzen arbeiten.	It would be uneconomical for us to offer our products at the discounts you suggest as we work on a fast turnover and low profit margins.
Der übliche Fachhandelsrabatt beträgt bei uns 15 % und liegt damit 5 % niedriger als der von Ihnen genannte Rabatt.	The usual trade discount is 15 % in this country, which is 5 % lower than the figure mentioned in your letter.
Die Zahlung erfolgt ausschließlich durch Akkreditiv.	We only accept payment by letter of credit.
Bei Erstaufträgen gewähren wir grundsätzlich kein Zahlungsziel von drei Monaten, auch solchen Kunden nicht, die Referenzen beibringen können. Wenn wir jedoch eine feste Geschäftsbeziehung aufgebaut haben, können wir diese Frage erneut prüfen.	We never offer quarterly terms on initial orders, even to customers who can provide references. However, we might consider this sort of credit once we have established a trading relationship.

6 Buyer's confirmation of terms of delivery

Die bestellte Ware wird dringend benötigt.	We require the ordered goods immediately. / We are in urgent need of the goods ordered.
… und müssen deshalb auf sofortiger Lieferung bestehen.	… and must therefore insist on delivery being made promptly / as quickly as possible.
Da wir die Ware für den Herbstverkauf benötigen, erwarten wir die Auslieferung bis spätestens zum …	As we require the goods for our autumn sales we expect delivery to be made not later than …
Der genannte Liefertermin muss unbedingt eingehalten werden.	The delivery date mentioned must be strictly adhered to.
Wir bitten um Bestätigung, dass die Arbeiten bis zum … abgeschlossen werden können.	Please confirm that the work can be completed before the end of …
Lieferung bis zum … ist fester Auftragsbestandteil. Wir behalten uns das Recht vor, die Annahme zu verweigern, sollte die Auslieferung nach diesem Termin erfolgen.	Delivery of the goods before … is a firm condition of this order, and we reserve the right to refuse goods delivered after that time.
… den Auftrag zu stornieren, wenn die Lieferung nicht bis zum … erfolgt.	… to cancel the order if delivery is not made/effected by …
Liefern Sie die Ware bitte an unser Lager / unsere Niederlassung / unser Zweigwerk in …	Please supply the goods to our warehouse / branch (office) in …
Die Lieferung soll an folgende Adresse/Anschrift erfolgen: …	The goods are / The above order is to be sent to the following address: …

7 Buyer's forwarding and packing instructions

Wir benötigen die Ware dringend und bitten daher um Versand per Express.	Please send the goods (by) express as we need them urgently.
Wir bitten um Versand per Luftfracht.	Please forward the goods by air.
Der Versand soll per Bahn erfolgen.	Please arrange for delivery by rail freight / goods train.
… möchten wir Sie daran erinnern, dass pünktliche Lieferung nur per Luftfracht sichergestellt werden kann.	… and please remember that only airfreight will ensure prompt delivery.
Wir raten dringend, die Ware per Straße zu versenden, damit die zerbrechliche Sendung nicht ständig umgeladen werden muss.	We advise delivery by road to avoid constant handling of this fragile consignment.
Um unnötige Verzögerungen zu vermeiden, bitten wir um Versand per Linienfrachter.	Please ship/send/forward by scheduled freighter to avoid unnecessary delays.
Zur Vermeidung von Versandschäden muss die Ware unbedingt in festen Kartons verpackt werden.	To ensure that the goods are not damaged in transit we must stipulate strong boxes for packing.

8 Closing lines

Bitte führen Sie diesen Auftrag sorgfältig aus.	Please give this order your careful attention.
Wir erwarten den baldigen Eingang Ihrer Lieferung.	We look forward to receiving the goods promptly.
Über eine Auftragsbestätigung würden wir uns freuen. Teilen Sie uns auch bitte mit, wann wir mit der Lieferung rechnen können.	Kindly confirm our order and let us know when we can expect delivery.
Für die Rücksendung einer unterschriebenen Auftragskopie würden wir uns freuen.	Please sign the enclosed order form and return a copy to us by way of confirmation.
Wir würden uns freuen, wenn dieser Auftrag den Beginn einer intensiven Geschäftsbeziehung darstellen würde.	We hope that this will be the first of many orders we will be placing with you.
Weitere Aufträge werden folgen, wenn dieser zu unserer (vollen) Zufriedenheit erledigt/ abgewickelt wird.	We will submit/place further orders, if this one is completed/executed to our (full) satisfaction.
Wenn sich diese Ware entsprechend unseren Erwartungen absetzen lässt, werden wir in Kürze weitere Aufträge erteilen.	If the goods sell as well as we hope, we will be placing further orders in the near future.
Den Eingang Ihrer Versandanzeige/Auftragsbestätigung sehen wir gern entgegen.	We look forward to receiving your advice of dispatch / your confirmation/ acknowledgement.

Orders UNIT 5   61

C Practising language

1 Complete this letter with the appropriate terms from the list below. There are more items than you need.

> attention | brochure | cash discount | cash with order | find a ready market
> local market | not later than | prepare | quantity discount | quotation
> remittance | sales drive | sales outlet | terms and conditions | trial order
> trust | understand | your service

Dear Ms Jason

Thank you for your letter of 15 May and your informative … [1]. Your products seem very attractive and we are confident that they will … [2] here.

We have selected a number of items for our … [3] (see order form attached). You will … [4] that we would like both to test the acceptance of your products in the … [5] and also the quality and efficiency of … [6].

As stipulated in your … [7] payment will be made by … [8] to your account with the ANZ Bank in Brisbane. In view of the size of this order you will grant us a … [9] of 10 per cent on top of the 25 per cent trade discount. There is also a 2 per cent … [10]. Please ensure that the goods reach us … [11] 20 August as we are planning a special … [12] in the early autumn where your products will also be displayed.

We … [13] that our order will have your careful … [14] and look forward to receiving the goods.

Yours sincerely

2 Decide which is the most suitable term.

1 Thank you for your prompt *reaction/reply/response* to our mail.
2 We have carefully tested the *patterns/samples/specimens* of your herbal soaps.
3 Please find *added/enclosed/included* our trial order for plastic tool boxes.
4 If one of the *items/pieces/units* should be out of stock, we would appreciate being *advised/instructed/told* accordingly.
5 Information about possible *replacements/subsidiaries/substitutes* would be welcome.
6 We accept your *terms/conditions/rules* of payment and delivery.
7 We understand that payment within 7 days of *receipt/reception/recipe* of *bill/invoice/sales* voucher is subject to a 2 per cent cash *discount/rebate/reduction*.
8 *Delivery/dispatch/supply* should be made by 20 June at the *last/latest/latter*.
9 Please *assure/ensure/insure* that the goods are packed in *fast/firm/sturdy* cardboard boxes.
10 We look forward to *receipt/receive/receiving* your *acceptance/acknowledgement/advice* of order by return.

3 Put the sentences of this letter in the correct order.

Dear Ms Richardson

We saw your advertisement …
a and settle your invoices.
b and that you should make an effort to meet us.
c as our forwarding agents, Messrs. Grisham Bros., 120 Manor Road, London EC3Y 4XT,
d as soon as you can place the goods at their disposal.
e As we have not yet seen this product here in Australia,
f but we feel that as pioneers
g for Axis scanner pens in the July issue
h into the Australian market.
i It will not be necessary for you
j of the magazine Computer Monthly.
k Please get in touch with our agents
l that the scanner pen could be successfully introduced
m Therefore we should be glad
n to make special arrangements for export
o to receive a small trial shipment of 500 pens to test the market there.
p we are entitled to some further concessions
q we have every reason to believe
r will take charge of the goods
s Your trade discount of 15 per cent seems favourable,

We look forward to hearing from you.

Yours faithfully

4 How would you say it in English?

1 Wir erwarten die Lieferung der bestellten Ware bis spätestens zum 15. März.
2 Die in unserem heutigen Auftrag genannten Liefertermine müssen genau eingehalten werden.
3 Wir behalten uns das Recht vor, den Auftrag zu stornieren, wenn Sie nicht zusichern können, dass wir die Ware innerhalb von 4 Wochen zugesandt bekommen.
4 Für jeglichen Verlust, der aus einer Lieferverzögerung entsteht, müssen wir Sie haftbar machen.
5 Ware minderer Qualität schicken wir auf Ihre Rechnung und Ihr Risiko zurück.
6 Wir werden Ihnen in den nächsten Tagen eingehende Anweisungen für die Verpackung und Beschriftung zukommen lassen.
7 Sicherlich werden Sie uns zu gegebener Zeit über den genauen Liefertermin unterrichten.
8 Bitte teilen Sie uns mit, wann wir mit der Lieferung rechnen können.

5 Change the sections in *italics* to make sentences that you would say to your business partner. Avoid impersonal or passive structures. Use the phrases in brackets.

EXAMPLE: *The goods* are very attractive. (your swimwear …)
Your swimwear is very attractive.
We find your swimwear very attractive.

1. *It should be possible* to market the Euro-plugs here. (we are confident)
2. Though *the design is very acceptable,* / *a few alterations would be welcome.* (we approve of, we would like to ask you)
3. The prices and terms stated in the offer of 15 October *are quite acceptable.* (accept)
4. *The trade discount* is less than that granted by the competition. (you allowed us)
5. *There must be* a six month guarantee on the mobiles. (we expect, you will give us)
6. Our packing instructions *must be* strictly adhered to. (ensure)
7. *This order is placed* on condition that there will be no extra charges beyond those mentioned in the offer. (we place, you will not ask for)
8. Our agents *should be contacted* immediately. (we would advise you)
9. We reserve the right to reject the refrigerators *should they be delivered* later than 20 October. (if you fail)
10. Any consignment that does not correspond to the samples *will be rejected*. (reject, you submitted)

Listening comprehension

(7) 6 Listen to the dialogue on the disk and complete Peter's memo with the details agreed with Carsten.

MEMO

Date (today's date) …
Time (US -mid-morning) …

Phone call from/to: …

Problem: discrepancies between … and …

Order No.: …
Order item 3
Order item 7
Order item 9

Correction in documents:

D Letter writing

1 Write an accompanying letter for an order form.

Confirm the receipt of the catalogue and the offer for greeting cards for special occasions. You enclose the order form. In view of the size of the order (more than 5000 cards) you ask for an additional quantity discount of 5 per cent. As cards are available from stock you expect delivery to be made within two weeks of placing the order.

Addresses
Supplier: JPF Quality Printers, 15 Finnegan Square, Dublin, Ireland
Customer: Card Corner, 17 Old Canal Street, Glasgow G5 4PW

2 Write an email confirming a telephone order.

Schreiben Sie eine E-Mail und bestätigen Sie den telefonisch erteilten Folgeauftrag für jeweils 20.000 Diskettenlaufwerke (*disk drive*) und CD-ROM-Laufwerke (Bestellnummer QR 285 und DS 82). Es gelten dieselben Preise und Bedingungen wie beim vorangehenden Auftrag vom 27.6. Die Lieferung soll schnellstmöglich an das Werk in Leicester erfolgen. Die Rechnung soll an die Einkaufsabteilung (*purchasing department*) geschickt werden. Die Anschriften sind dem Lieferanten bekannt.

3 Write a summary of this offer.

Dear Mr Simpson

<u>OFFER FOR BOTTLING EQUIPMENT</u>

Thank you for your enquiry regarding the construction and supply of a bottling machine according to your drawings and specifications. We have carefully studied your technical requirements and can now inform you that we are in a position to design and build a machine according to the details you provided. Therefore we would be pleased to execute your order if we are awarded the contract.

The price will be €256,800.– FOB German seaport, seaworthy packing included. The delivery period will be about three months after receipt of your order. But you will understand that in case of strikes or other events of force majeure we must refuse to accept any liability for punctual delivery.

Payment is to be effected by irrevocable and confirmed documentary letter of credit to Dresdner Bank AG in Hanau. We will start production as soon as they advise us of the opening of the credit.

Our service team will set up the bottling machine in your plant and also assist with putting it into operation. If requested we will, of course, as an additional service also provide initial training for your engineers and machine operators.

This offer is firm for twelve weeks. For all our transactions, our general terms for the supply of machines according to ECE-188A apply. You will find a copy of the English translation enclosed for your convenience.

We trust that you will find this offer competitive and look forward to receiving your order.

Yours sincerely

Helmut Menger

Engineering Department

4 Reply to the offer above and place an order.

Nehmen Sie Bezug auf dieses Angebot und bedanken Sie sich dafür. Nach eingehender Prüfung der vorliegenden Angebote hat die Unternehmensleitung die Beschaffung der Abfüllanlage beschlossen. Der Auftrag wird gemäß den technischen Angaben in der Anlage erteilt. Dabei haben sich einige kleinere Änderungen gegenüber den zuvor übersandten Konstruktionsdaten ergeben. Deshalb gelten für diesen Auftrag nur die beigefügten Unterlagen. Verabredungsgemäß wird bei der Baltimore City Bank ein Antrag auf Eröffnung eines Akkreditivs gestellt. Näheres wird die Bank in Kürze mitteilen. Sie danken für das Angebot, das Service- und Bedienerpersonal zu schulen und schlagen vor, die Einzelheiten zu einem späteren Zeitpunkt zu klären. Bitten sie um eine kurze Auftragsbestätigung und Mitteilung, wann mit der Lieferung der Abfüllanlage gerechnet werden kann.

5 Write a letter from notes.

Sie arbeiten im Architekturbüro eines britischen Baukonzerns (Industrial Architects Ltd, 52 Great Russell Street, London EC1X 4PQ), der mit der Erstellung eines Hotelneubaus in Irland beauftragt ist. Sie haben verschiedene Angebote für Aufzugsanlagen verglichen. Nach entsprechender Prüfung des Angebots der Firma, Mittler & Kappel AG, Sonnborner Str. 73, 58349 Hagen, hat man sich auf Folgendes geeinigt: Lieferung und Installation von 3 Aufzügen für einen 10-geschossigen Bau, Tragkraft (*load-carrying capacity*) 800 kg.

> **Aufgabe**
> Schreiben Sie den Auftrag an die deutsche Aufzugsfirma:
> - Lieferung und Montage der kompletten Aufzugsanlagen
> - Mitteilung über den Zeitpunkt der Montage (*erection*)
> - Anzahlung von 10 % des Auftragswerts
> - Restliche Zahlung in 2 Raten bei Lieferung und nach Abschluss der Montage
> - Garantiezeit und -umfang
> - Wartung durch englische Firma?

6 Write a fax from notes.

Sie arbeiten in der Beschaffungsabteilung eines deutschen Lebensmittelimporteurs (Hamburger Früchtekontor, Kirchenbauerstr. 23, 21037 Hamburg). Während der internationalen Grünen Woche in Berlin im Januar haben Sie einige Produkte eines südafrikanischen Anbieters (Drews Food Imports and Exports Pty, 15 Pretoria Road, Durban, South Africa, Attn. Jan Sleuters) probiert und anschließend in Ihrem Unternehmen getestet. Bestätigen Sie per Fax die während der Messe in Aussicht gestellte Probebestellung.

> **Aufgabe**
> Schreiben Sie ein Begleitschreiben zu Ihrem Probeauftrag:
> - Dank für die freundliche Aufnahme am Messestand
> - Verweis auf beigefügten Probeauftrag
> - Bestätigung der mündlich vereinbarten Konditionen (Messerabatt auf den Listenpreis; Preis auf CIF-Hamburg-Basis; Rechnungsstellung in Euro)
> - Zahlung gegen Dokumente
> - Lieferung 4 Wochen nach Auftragserteilung
> - Bitte um Versandmitteilung

E Useful words

jds Anforderungen entsprechen	to meet sb's requirements
dem Muster entsprechen	to be up to / correspond to the sample, to match the pattern
Angebotsbedingungen	terms stated in the offer
zum Preis von	at a price of / priced at
pro Stück	each / per item
pro Verpackungseinheit/Gebinde	per unit
Auftrag erteilen	to place an order / to order
Auftragsformular	order form
Auftrag ausführen	to complete/handle/execute an order
auf der Grundlage von	subject to / on the basis of
nachstehend aufgeführt	listed/detailed below
Nachlass für Erstaufträge	initial order discount
Einführungsrabatt	introductory offer discount
Skonto, Barzahlungsrabatt	early payment discount / cash discount
schicken, jdn beliefern mit	to supply sb with
versenden	to send/despatch/forward/ship
Ware liefern	to supply goods
Ware anliefern/ausliefern	to deliver goods
baldige/sofortige/umgehende Lieferung	early/prompt delivery
bis zum ... liefern	to deliver goods by (+ date)
veranlassen, dass ..., dafür sorgen, dass	to arrange for sth to be done
Versand veranlassen, für den Versand sorgen	to arrange shipment
Lieferdatum, Liefertermin, Lieferzeitpunkt	delivery date
Liefertermin, Abgabetermin, Frist	deadline
Termin einhalten, Frist wahren	to meet the deadline
innerhalb der angegebenen Zeit/Frist	in the time / within the period stated
Frist versäumen, Frist nicht einhalten	to fail to meet the deadline
wir nehmen zu Kenntnis	we understand
zu jds. Lasten gehen	to be at sb's expense
gemäß unseren schriftlichen Anweisungen	as per our written instructions
Quartalsauszug, vierteljährlicher Auszug (Konto)	quarterly statement
langfristige Zahlungsziele	long-term credit facilities
sofortige Rechnungsbegleichung	cash settlement
nach Erhalt von	on receipt of
innerhalb von ... Tagen nach Erhalt von	within ... days of receipt of

Terms of payment

Vorauszahlung	payment in advance
Bezahlung bei Auftragserteilung	cash with order (CWO)
(gegen) Nachnahme	cash on delivery (COD)
Dokumente gegen Kasse	cash against documents (CAD), documents against payment (D/P)
Dokumente gegen Annahme (der Tratte) (Wechsel)	documents against acceptance (D/A)
Zahlung durch Verrechnungsscheck	payment by crossed cheque
Wechsel	bill of exchange (B/E)
(unwiderrufliches und bestätigtes) Dokumenten-Akkreditiv	(irrevocable and confirmed) documentary letter of credit (L/C)
Überweisung auf jds. Konto bei der ... Bank	transfer to sb's account with/at ... bank

6 Dealing with orders

Model letters: an acknowledgement of an order, advice of dispatch, delay in delivery

Useful phrases: acknowledgement of order; advice of dispatch (shipment of goods, packing instructions, marking instructions); refusing an order / making a new offer (non-availability, bad reputation, delay in delivery, inability to fulfil order)

Upon receipt of the order the supplier will, in the normal course of business, process the order from stock and dispatch the goods straightaway so that the goods reach the customer within a matter of days. This is the case with the vast majority of goods that we use or consume in our everyday lives. The buyer will then be sent the invoice; when it is paid the transaction is complete and no further exchange of 'messages' is required.

For goods which are not made for stock (e.g. items of furniture) there will be longer periods of delivery, as the supplier requires time to either make or buy in the goods. These goods are often produced to the customer's specifications. In such cases it is standard practice for the supplier to confirm that the order can be executed (**acknowledgement of order**) and to specify the expected time of delivery. When the goods are ready for dispatch the supplier informs the customer accordingly by sending an **advice of dispatch**. In this letter, the packing and forwarding instructions are confirmed and, if necessary, the supplier explains the details of delivery.

Problems may arise when certain goods are not in stock in sufficient quantities or even out of stock. In this case further communication is necessary to explain the situation and give reasons for a **delay in delivery**. The supplier may on this occasion decide to offer a suitable substitute to satisfy the customer. This, however, constitutes a new offer which the customer may refuse to accept. So the supplier will make every effort to make the replacement offer as attractive as possible.

In any case, the order and, when this is written, the order confirmation are binding for both the buyer and the seller. Any failure in the performance of the contract by either party may lead to complaints and, ultimately, to legal action. It is the seller's duty, of course, to supply goods in line with the contract of sale (the order), within the usual time and without any faults. The customer is expected to accept the goods upon delivery and after the customary inspection.

Model letters

1 An acknowledgement of an order

This order confirmation is written to inform the buyer about the expected time of dispatch of the goods ordered.

Whitmore Timber Products
L T D
Hilldean Estate   Farleigh   Hants   IS8 4DD

Brandis & Markstadt Import GmbH
Brüsseler Str. 75
28259 Bremen
Germany

17 February 20..

Dear Ms Steurer

Order for garden furniture

Thank you very much for your order no 23496, dated 12 February.

Your order is receiving our immediate attention. All the items are in stock, and we expect to be able to dispatch the goods to you by the end of next week. We trust that the consignment will reach you in good condition and turn out to your satisfaction.

Hoping that our products will find a ready market we look forward to receiving further orders.

Yours sincerely

Decide which expressions in the text can be replaced by the following.

1 are certain
2 available
3 of
4 now being processed
5 sell well
6 send off
7 shipment
8 you will be satisfied

Letter plan for an acknowledgement of order

- Refer to the order.
- State dispatch date.
- Mention attached invoice.
- Say you expect safe arrival of goods.
- (Offer service in case of future needs.)
- Close with a polite phrase.

2 Advice of dispatch

This letter is written to inform the customer of the expected arrival of the goods and confirm payment details.

Dear Mr Chong

ORDER FOR AGRICULTURAL MACHINES

We are pleased to advise you of the despatch of your order for agricultural machines which is being shipped by S.S. 'OCEAN TRADER', due at Pusan on August 15th.

The machines have been produced to your exact specifications and are securely packed in strong wooden crates. We are sure they will reach you in good order. The machines and especially the motors have been put through a lengthy and thorough test programme and carry our full guarantee. If you wish to raise any point of fitting or maintenance, our agent in Seoul, Engineering Services Ltd., will be pleased to advise you at any time. They also hold an adequate stock of spare parts.

As agreed we have handed over the shipping documents to the German HSBC office in Frankfurt, who have accepted our draft for the invoice amount.

We thank you for your order and hope to be of service again.

Yours sincerely

Decide which of the following points are covered by this letter.

1. advice of despatch
2. after-sales service
3. assembly
4. customised machines
5. damage of goods in transit
6. delay in delivery
7. documentation
8. end-of-line checks
9. payment
10. receipt of order
11. stock-keeping
12. wrapping instructions

Letter plan for an advice of dispatch

☐ Refer to any previous correspondence (order, enquiry about expected delivery date).
☐ Mention the current state of processing of order.
☐ Confirm the delivery instructions (marking, packing).
☐ Give any relevant details of forwarding arrangements.
☐ Mention the invoicing of charges if necessary.
☐ Close with a polite phrase.

3 Delay in delivery

This letter is written to inform the customer that the goods are out of stock and more time is required to fulfil the order.

Dear Ms Freytag

Order No. 7843/XP for woven fabrics
Thank you for your order of 15 July for woven fabrics in accordance with patterns submitted. But as our stocks have been cleared much faster than anticipated, we are not in a position to make delivery in less than a fortnight.

We apologise very much for the inconvenience we are sure this will cause you, but we hope you will understand that we were not able to predict the sudden rush of orders. You may rest assured that we will do our utmost to produce the fabrics you require as quickly as possible.

However, if your demand is so urgent as to necessitate immediate delivery, we are prepared to supply a material which in some respects is inferior, but perfectly satisfactory for most ordinary purposes, as the samples enclosed will show. This material is available in sufficient quantities.

We feel, however, that it would pay to wait until we have been able to replenish our stocks.

Perhaps you would be good enough to confirm your order subject to these conditions.

Complete the secretary's notes by listing the main points of the letter.

letter to Willkens
goods ordered not in stock
…

> **Letter plan for a new offer**
>
> ☐ Refer to the order.
> **Non-availability:**
>   ☐ State reasons for non-availability of product.
>   ☐ Apologise for the situation.
>   ☐ Offer an alternative/substitute.
>   ☐ (continue as in Offer).
> **Delay in delivery:**
>   ☐ Explain reason for delay in delivery.
>   ☐ Apologise for the situation.
>   ☐ Offer a solution.
>   ☐ (continue as in Offer).
> ☐ Close with a polite phrase.

B Useful phrases

1 Acknowledgement of order

Für Ihren Auftrag Nr. 338B, der heute bei uns einging, danken wir.	Thank you for your order No. 338B which we received today.
Der Auftrag wird bereits bearbeitet, und Sie können mit der Auslieferung innerhalb von drei Wochen rechnen.	We are now dealing with it and you may expect delivery within the next three weeks.
Sie dürfen davon ausgehen, dass wir unser Möglichstes tun werden, um den Liefertermin einzuhalten.	You may rest assured that we will do our utmost to keep to the delivery date.
Hiermit bestätigen wir den in Ihrem Schreiben genannten Liefertermin.	We confirm the delivery date stipulated in your letter.
Leider können wir auf Ihre Lieferbedingungen nicht eingehen.	Unfortunately, we cannot accept your terms of delivery.
Sie können versichert sein, dass wir alle Ihre Anweisungen genau ausführen werden.	You may rely on us to carry out your instructions in every detail.
Ihr Auftrag Nr. 6712/X wird gerade bearbeitet, so dass die Auslieferung voraussichtlich in der nächsten Woche erfolgen kann.	Your order No. 6712/X is now being processed and should be ready for dispatch by next week.
Wir können Ihnen heute mitteilen, dass Ihr Auftrag bereits zusammengestellt ist. Wir bereiten soeben den Versand nach Port Elizabeth vor.	We are pleased to say that we have already made up your order and are now making arrangements for shipment to Port Elizabeth.
Wir werden unser Möglichstes tun, um die Bearbeitung Ihren Auftrags / den Versand zu beschleunigen.	We shall do our utmost to expedite the completion of the order / to hasten delivery.
Sobald die Sendung abholbereit ist, werden wir Ihren Spediteur benachrichtigen.	As soon as the consignment is ready for collection we will notify your forwarding agent.
… hoffen wir, dass weitere Aufträge folgen. / Über weitere Aufträge würden wir uns freuen.	We trust that … will lead to further business. / … we may have the pleasure of serving you again soon.
… der Anfang / erste Schritt für die Begründung einer langjährigen und für beide Seiten nützlichen Geschäftsbeziehung ist.	… is the beginning of / the first step in the establishment of a long and mutually satisfactory business relationship.

2 Advice of dispatch

Shipment of goods

Die Ware ist praktisch versandfertig, daher erwarten wir Ihre weiteren Anweisungen.	The goods are nearly ready for dispatch, and we should be glad to have your instructions.
Hiermit teilen wir Ihnen mit / Wir können Ihnen nunmehr mitteilen, dass die Ware am ... hier abgeht.	We herewith inform you / We have the pleasure of informing you that the goods will leave our works on ...
Um häufiges Umladen zu vermeiden und eine schnelle Auslieferung sicherzustellen, haben wir die Ware heute per LKW an Sie abgesandt.	The goods have been dispatched by road to avoid frequent handling and to ensure speedy delivery.
Ihren Auftrag für ... haben wir sorgfältig ausgeführt. Die Ware wurde inzwischen an Ihre Anschrift versandt.	We have carefully executed your order for ... and forwarded the goods to your address.
Die Spedition hat heute Ihre Sendung auftragsgemäß bei uns abgeholt.	As per your instructions the freight/forwarding company has today collected your consignment.
Die Waren sind auf die SS ... verladen worden, die Sydney am ... verlässt und am ... in Tilbury, London eintrifft. Die Verschiffungspapiere befinden sich bereits auf dem Wege zu Ihrer Bank und können dort abgeholt werden.	The goods have been loaded on board SS ... sailing from Sydney on ... and arriving at Tilbury, London on ... . The shipping documents have already been sent to your bank for collection.
Die bestellte Ware wird am 9. August mit LH-Flug 6482 um 11.00 in München abgehen. Ankunft in Manchester um 12.15. Beiliegend übersenden wir Ihnen den Luftfrachtbrief und Kopien der Rechnung.	Your goods will be put on flight LH 4682 leaving Munich at 11.00 on 9 August and arriving Manchester 12.15. Please find enclosed the air waybill and copies of the invoice.
Wie vereinbart wird Ihre Ware per Bahn versandt. Sie kann am Bahnhof ... abgeholt werden. Dazu sollte der beigefügte Frachtbrief Nr. ... vorgelegt werden.	As agreed your order will be sent by rail/railroad. The goods can be collected at ... station. Enclosed is consignment note No. ... which should be presented on collection.
Wir hoffen, dass die Sendung in gutem Zustand bei Ihnen eintrifft.	We hope that the consignment will reach you in good condition.

Packing instructions

Alle Waren sind in festes wasserdichtes Material eingeschlagen und in leichten Kisten verpackt.	All goods are wrapped in strong waterproof material and packed in lightweight crates.
Alle Kisten sind mit einem festen und wasserabweisenden Material ausgeschlagen.	All crates have a hard-wearing and damp-resistant lining.
Stabiles Verpackungsmaterial schützt die Ware vor Erschütterungen.	Solid packing material inside the cases is used to protect the goods from vibration.

Die Ware wird in reichlich Füllmaterial verpackt, um Kratz- und Stoßschäden zu vermeiden.	The goods will be generously padded to avoid scratching and knocking against the container.
Die Ware ist in stabilen, mit Keilen verstärkten Kisten verpackt, die mit Draht/Metallbändern verschlossen sind.	The goods are packed in strong cases, cleated and wire-strapped/steel-strapped / bound with metal bands.
Die Chemikalien werden in stabilen Kunststoffflaschen/Korbflaschen geliefert.	The chemicals are supplied in stout plastic drums / in carboys.
Die Sendung besteht aus zwei Paletten mit einem Gewicht von jeweils 500 Kilo.	The consignment consists of two pallets, each weighing 500 kilos.
Die Ware können wir leider nicht in der von Ihnen gewünschten Form verpacken.	We cannot pack the goods in the way you requested.

Marking instructions

Zur Vermeidung von Verwechslung, Verzögerung oder Verlust sind die Kisten fortlaufend von 1 bis 20 nummeriert.	The crates have been numbered consecutively from 1–20 to avoid confusion, delay or loss.
Wir haben die Kisten nach Ihren Anweisungen gekennzeichnet und das Brutto- und Nettogewicht angegeben.	In accordance with your instructions we have marked the the cases and given the gross and net weight.
Wir haben die Behälter mit den Markierungen „Zerbrechlich!" und „Hier oben!" gekennzeichnet.	The containers haven been marked 'Fragile' and 'This side up'.

3 Refusing an order / Making a new offer

Non-availability

Leider müssen wir Ihnen mitteilen, dass wir diesen Artikel zur Zeit nicht auf Lager haben. Die nächste Lieferung trifft frühestens in sechs Wochen ein. Wir lassen Ihren Auftrag bis dahin liegen.	We are sorry to inform you that we are completely out of stock of this item, and it will be at least six weeks before we get our next delivery. We will hold your order until then.
Wegen der rückläufigen Nachfrage in den letzten Jahren haben wir die Herstellung dieses Artikels eingestellt.	We no longer manufacture this product as demand over the past few years has declined.

Bad reputation

Wir sind nur bereit, gegen bar zu liefern.	We would only be prepared to supply on a cash basis.
Wir liefern nur nach Erhalt Ihrer Vorauszahlung.	We can only supply on receipt of your advance payment.
Bei Neukunden ist unsere Zahlungsbedingung normalerweise Kasse gegen Dokumente.	Normally we deal with new customers on a cash against documents (COD) basis.

Wir müssen Sie daran erinnern, dass wir bei Erstaufträgen nur zwei Wochen Ziel gewähren.	We must remind you that we only allow two weeks' credit for first orders.

Delay in delivery

Für die Ausführung Ihres Auftrages benötigen wir etwa drei Wochen.	We require approximately three weeks to complete your order.
Wegen der starken Nachfrage haben wir nur geringe Mengen dieses Artikels auf Lager. Wir bearbeiten die Aufträge daher in der Reihenfolge ihres Eingangs.	As there is a heavy demand we have very few of these products in stock and are serving on a rota basis.
Leider haben wir nur ungenügende Mengen am Lager, um Ihren Bedarf zu decken. Der Versand wird sich deshalb um 14 Tage verzögern. Wir bedauern etwaige Unannehmlichkeiten.	Unfortunately we have insufficient quantities in stock to meet your requirements. The dispatch will therefore be delayed by a fortnight. We apologise for the inconvenience this may cause.
Da wir während der Werksferien nicht produzieren, können wir Ihren Auftrag zu dem von Ihnen gewünschten Termin nicht fertig stellen. Daher können wir Ihren Auftrag leider nicht annehmen.	As our plant is closing for the summer vacation we would not be able to process your order for the date you have given. Therefore regretfully we have to decline it.
Zu unserem Bedauern müssen wir Ihnen mitteilen, dass wir Ihren Auftrag nicht annehmen können, da wir zur Zeit voll ausgelastet sind. Aus diesem Grund können wir Ihnen keinen festen Liefertermin angeben.	We are sorry to say that we must turn down your order, as we have full order books and cannot give a definite date for delivery.
Wir sind unter keinen Umständen in der Lage, innerhalb der von Ihnen gesetzten Frist zu liefern.	Delivery could not possibly be promised within the time given in your letter.
Bis zur Auslieferung müssen zwei Monate veranschlagt werden, da wir die Rohstoffe beschaffen müssen und von unseren Lieferanten abhängig sind.	Two months must be allowed for delivery, as we ourselves have to get raw materials and rely on our suppliers.

Inability to fulfil order

Wir sind nur ein kleines Unternehmen und daher unter keinen Umständen in der Lage, einen Auftrag für 20.000 Stück auszuführen.	We are only a small firm and could not possibly handle an order for 20,000 units.
Wir sehen uns nicht imstande, mit unseren Anlagen 30.000 Stück pro Woche herzustellen.	Our factory does not have facilities to turn out 30,000 units a week.
Wir liefern diese Ware nur in Partien von 12 Dutzend aus und empfehlen, sich nicht an Hersteller sondern an den Einzelhandel zu wenden.	We only supply orders for these goods by the gross, but suggest you turn to a retailer rather than a manufacturer.
Wir verkaufen Materialien nur in Rollen. Geringere Mengen können wir nicht liefern.	Our factory sells materials only by the roll which cannot be cut up.

C Practising language

**1 Which item does not belong to the group?
Look at the Useful words on page 80.**

	a		b		c		d	
1	a	to dispatch	b	to send off	c	to ship	d	to store
2	a	crate	b	drum	c	lift	d	pallet
3	a	carrier	b	driver	c	forwarder	d	shipper
4	a	consignment	b	lot	c	party	d	shipment
5	a	filling material	b	packing material	c	plastic material	d	wrapping material
6	a	alternative	b	assembly	c	replacement	d	substitute
7	a	fragile	b	heavy	c	inflammable	d	poisonous
8	a	handle with care	b	keep dry	c	stand back	d	this way up
9	a	customs duty	b	freight charges	c	storage costs	d	transport costs
10	a	empty weight	b	gross weight	c	net weight	d	real weight

2 Decide in which of these types of letter you would expect the following terms and phrases.

a Acknowledgement of order	b Advice of dispatch	c Delay in delivery

1 carefully packed
2 pallets are returnable
3 circumstances beyond our control
4 deal with orders in strict rotation
5 delivery date stipulated in the order
6 goods await collection
7 keep to the delivery date
8 not in stock at the moment
9 packing instructions
10 pick up a consignment
11 ready for shipment
12 receipt of your order
13 replenish stocks
14 speed up the dispatch
15 the cases have been marked
16 the goods will be shipped

3 Find suitable beginnings for these sentences.

1 ... will reach you in good order and condition.
2 ... how the goods are to be transported.
3 ... must be paid to packing.
4 ... , the shipment will be delayed by at least two weeks.
5 ... having to inform you that we are completely out of stock of this item.
6 ... our apologies for the inconvenience this may cause you.
7 ... to learn that your goods have been dispatched today.
8 ... to ensure that the goods reach you by the stipulated date.
9 ... for not being able to send the ordered quantities by the date you require.
10 ... that we must turn down your order as the quantities are too small.

UNIT 6 Dealing with orders

4 Complete the sentences below. Use the ideas in brackets.

1. The bulk of your order is ready for shipment. But ...
   (*5 weitere Tage für die Produktion erforderlich*)
2. Please make arrangements to have ...
   (*Ware vom Werk abholen lassen*)
3. The production of your goods is nearing completion. ...
   (*bitte Versandadresse mitteilen*)
4. To date we have not yet received any information as to ...
   (*erwarteter Zeitpunkt für die Zusendung der Ware*)
5. You have exceeded the promised delivery date by more than three weeks. ...
   (*7 Tage Frist, sonst Auftragsstornierung*)
6. An oversight in the production schedule resulted in a delay in the processing of your order. ...
   (*Entschuldigung für die Unannehmlichkeiten*)
7. Unfortunately, the article No. 726495B is out of stock at the moment. ...
   (*Angebot eines gleichwertigen Ersatzartikels zu einem leicht günstigeren Preis*)
8. We are pleased to confirm our order for the substitute product. ...
   (*Bitte um Lieferung zum ursprünglich vereinbarten Termin*)

5 Express these ideas in idiomatic English.

1. Sie bedanken sich für den erteilten Auftrag. Nennen Sie das Auftragsdatum und ein Produkt.
2. Sie sagen, dass die bestellten Produkte und Mengen vorrätig sind und sofort geliefert werden können.
3. Teilen Sie dem Kunden mit, dass die Ware nach Kundenangaben angefertigt werden muss und deshalb mit einer Lieferung erst in 3 Wochen zu rechnen ist.
4. Informieren Sie den Kunden, dass die Ware wunschgemäß auf dem Luftwege ab Frankfurt versandt wird. Geben Sie weitere Einzelheiten an.
5. Sie müssen Ihren Kunden über eine Verzögerung in der Auslieferung der Ware informieren, da ein Artikel noch beschafft werden muss.
6. Sie sagen, dass die Ware als Sammelladung versandt und heute vom Spediteur abgeholt wird. Die Abrechnung der Transportkosten erfolgt durch den Spediteur.
7. Sie hoffen, dass die Ware in gutem Zustand beim Kunden eintrifft und bedanken sich für diesen Auftrag.
8. Sie bestätigen, dass Sie einen Wechsel mit 90 Tagen Laufzeit auf den Kunden ziehen auf der Basis Dokumente gegen Annahme.

Listening comprehension

 6 Listen to the dialogue on the CD and then do this exercise.

Write a short memo in German stating the main points of the answerphone message.

Dealing with orders UNIT 6

D Letter writing

1 Use these notes to write an advice of dispatch (email).

Refer to the order placed by the customer for pharmaceutical products. The goods are being shipped by air on Monday, 2nd June, on flight no. LH1497, arrival at Lagos airport at 17.35 local time. The cases are marked as per instructions received and also carry the consignee's full address. All the documents required for customs clearance have been sent by air mail. Payment is to be made as usual by documents against acceptance. Express the hope for a safe arrival of the goods and thank the customer for placing the order.

Addresses
Supplier: Medical Supplies for Africa Ltd., 16 Tower Lane, Romford Business Park, Romford RM4 7TR (george.mellors@med-supplies.co.uk)
Customer: Pharma Imports, 27 Badagry Road, Lagos (thomas.beedam@pharmaimports.com)

2 Use these notes to write a fax.

Teilen Sie ihrem Kunden per Fax mit, dass die Ausführung des Auftrags, für den Sie sich bedanken, sich um einige Tage verzögern wird. Ihre Werbekampagne hat zu einem unerwartet regen Bestelleingang geführt, so dass Sie nicht in der Lage sind, alle Bestellungen sofort aus Lagerbeständen auszuführen. Neue Ware ist bestellt und für die nächsten Tage zugesagt. Die Aufträge wird in strikter Reihenfolge des Eingangs erledigt. Sie haben selbst Maßnahmen ergriffen (Überstunden, Einschaltung eines Transportunternehmens), um die Auslieferung zu beschleunigen. Bitten Sie um Verständnis für diese Ausnahmesituation.

3 Write a letter from notes.

Als Sachbearbeiter/in der Orgatech GmbH, Grabenstraße 42, 80213 München, sind Sie für die Auftragsbearbeitung verantwortlich. Ihnen liegt der Auftrag eines englischen Großkunden, Office Systems Ltd, 35 Keele Road, Stafford, ST5 8CP vor. Der Auftrag ist durch ein Versehen liegen geblieben.

> **Aufgabe**
> Richten Sie ein Entschuldigungsschreiben an den Kunden und berücksichtigen Sie dabei folgende Punkte:
> - Auftragsbestätigung
> - Erklärung der Situation und Entschuldigung
> - Position Stahlschränke für Hängeablage (*filing cabinets*) nicht ab Lager lieferbar
> - Versuch Auslieferung direkt vom Hersteller zu erreichen erfolgreich
> - Lieferzeit somit um 7 Arbeitstage kürzer
> - Restauftrag in der Bearbeitung und umgehend versandfertig
> - Zum Ausgleich des Lieferverzugs Angebot einer günstigeren Zahlungsweise
> - Entschuldigung und entsprechend freundliche Schlussformel

4 Write a letter from notes.

Als Mitarbeiter/in der Exportabteilung der Firma Fugger & Söhne GmbH, Porschestr. 120, 70435 Stuttgart, benachrichtigen Sie Ihren Kunden, Hotel Supplies Corp., 3084 Harbor Drive, Cape Coral, FL 33917, U.S.A. über die Erledigung eines umfangreichen Auftrags für diverse Glasartikel für den Hotelbedarf. Sie teilen Einzelheiten zum Versand mit.

> **Aufgabe**
> Verfassen Sie eine Versandanzeige (Fax). Berücksichtigen Sie dabei folgende Punkte:
> - Bezug auf Auftrag
> - Ware heute vom Spediteur abgeholt
> - Verpackung in Holzkisten mit Kundenanschrift und Vorsichtsmarkierungen
> - Verschiffung voraussichtlich in einer Woche von Rotterdam
> - Weitere Einzelheiten vom Spediteur; von dort Rechnung über Transportkosten ab Rotterdam
> - Warenrechnung folgt auf dem Postwege
> - Hoffnung auf unversehrte Ankunft der Ware
> - Höfliche Schlussformel

5 Write an email preceding this fax.

> Dear Ms Shankar,
>
> Thank you for the email you sent yesterday. We offer our sincere apologies for the delay in the execution of your order.
>
> Through an oversight which we are unable to explain, because we normally deal with orders as they come in, your order was overlooked. But we are pleased to be able to tell you now that your goods are ready for dispatch and will be collected tomorrow morning for shipment by SS Voyager Queen, sailing from Antwerp on 22 May. The consignment should reach you in early June. Our forwarding agents will inform you about the details of the arrangements.
>
> We hope that this delay has not caused you any serious inconvenience and assure you that we will make every effort to improve our procedures to ensure prompt execution of orders at all times. Thank you for your patience.
>
> Yours sincerely,
>
> *Michelle Truong*
> Michelle Truong (Ms)

Verweisen Sie auf Ihre Bestellung vom 10.4. und das Begleitschreiben, in dem ausdrücklich auf eine Auslieferung bis zum 22.5. als einer Bedingung für die Auftragserteilung verwiesen wird. Vier Wochen nach Auftragserteilung haben Sie weder eine Bestätigung noch eine Versandanzeige erhalten. Bitten Sie um zügige Aufklärung des Sachverhalts und drohen Sie mit der Auftragsstornierung für den Fall, dass die Ware nicht sofort ausgeliefert werden kann.

6 Write a summary of the fax in Exercise 5.

E Useful words

Auftrag bestätigen	to confirm/acknowledge an order
Auftrag zurückweisen	to refuse/reject/turn down an order
Auftrag ausführen	to fill/fulfil/meet/execute/process an order
Auftrag fertig stellen	to make up/complete an order
Auftrag ausliefern	to deliver an order
Auftrag stornieren	to cancel an order
ab Lager liefern	to supply from stock
Handelsrechnung, Handelsfaktura	commercial invoice
Proformarechnung	pro-forma invoice
Versandpapiere, Verschiffungsdokumente	shipping documents
Luftfrachtbrief	air waybill, airway bill (AWB)
Seefrachtbrief, Konnossement	bill of lading (B/L)
Versicherungsschein, Versicherungszertifikat	insurance certificate
Versicherungspolice	insurance policy
Ursprungszeugnis	certificate of origin
Frachtbrief	freight/consignment note
Lieferschein	delivery/despatch/dispatch note
Versandanzeige	advice of dispatch, advice/dispatch note
Versandanzeige, Verschiffungsanzeige	shipping advice
Versandanweisungen	instructions for dispatch
Packliste	packing list
in zweifacher/dreifacher/vierfacher/fünffacher Ausfertigung	in duplicate/triplicate/quadruplicate/quintuplicate
Spediteur, Seespediteur, Spedition	forwarding/shipping agent
Versender, Absender; Spedition(sfirma)	shipper
Versender, Absender; Verfrachter	consignor
Empfänger	consignee
Transportfirma, Spedition, Frachtführer	carrier
Schifffahrtsgesellschaft, Reederei	shipping company
Straßenspediteur, (Güter)Spedition	road haulier, haulage company
Sammelladung zusammenstellen	to consolidate shipments
Sendung, Ladung, Lieferung, Partie	consignment, shipment
Sammelladung	grouped consignment
versenden, zum Versand bringen	to forward/despatch/dispatch/ship
transportieren	to carry
Fracht bezahlt	freight paid
ausschließlich Fracht	exclusive of freight
einschließlich Fracht	inclusive of freight
frachtfrei, Fracht bezahlt	carriage paid (C/P), freight prepaid
unfrei, per Frachtnachnahme, Fracht bezahlt Empfänger	carriage forward (C/F), freight collect
verzollt	duty paid
unverzollt	duty forward
Nettogewicht	net weight
Bruttogewicht	gross weight
Eigengewicht, Leergewicht	dead weight

als Luftfracht	as air freight
per Luftfracht	by air freight
per Bahn	by rail
mit dem Flugzeug, auf dem Luftweg	by air
mit dem Schiff, auf dem Seewege	by ship
mit Lastkraftwagen/LKW	by lorry/truck
per Straße	by road
Transitwaren	goods in transit

Caution marks

Vorsicht!	Caution!
Nicht werfen	Handle with care
Nicht fallen lassen	Do not drop
Keine Haken	Use no hooks
Vor Hitze schützen	Stow away from heat
Nicht an Deck verstauen	Do not stow on deck
Vorsicht Glas	Glass with care
Zerbrechlich	Fragile
Verderblich	Perishable
Feuergefährlich	Flammable
Vorsicht. Feuergefahr	Highly inflammable
Kühl aufbewahren	Keep cool
Vor Nässe schützen; Trocken aufbewahren/lagern	Keep dry
Hier oben	This way up
Hier öffnen	Open here
Hier anheben	Lift here
oben	top
unten	bottom

Packing containers and materials

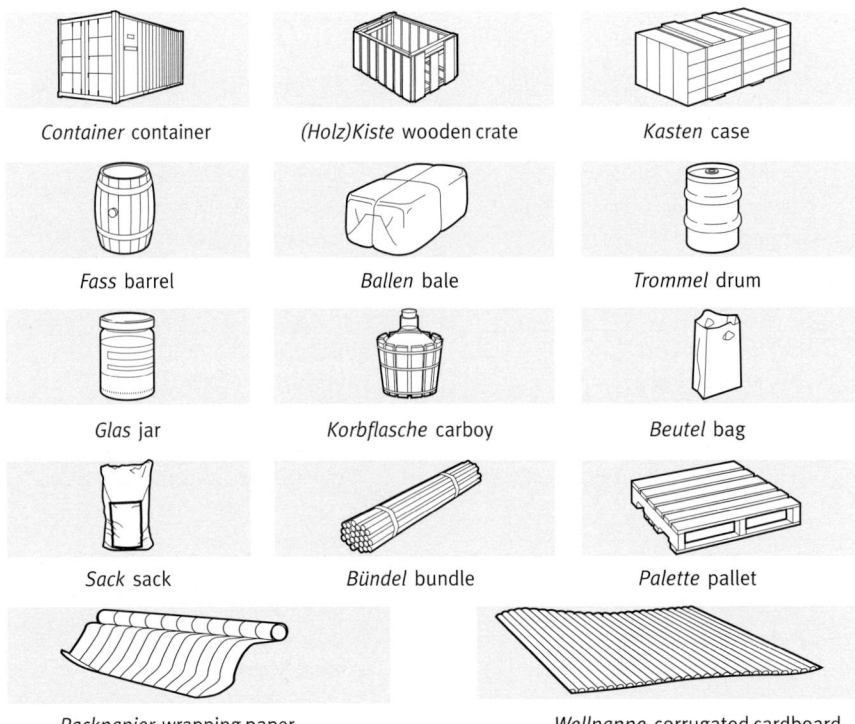

Container container   *(Holz)Kiste* wooden crate   *Kasten* case

Fass barrel   *Ballen* bale   *Trommel* drum

Glas jar   *Korbflasche* carboy   *Beutel* bag

Sack sack   *Bündel* bundle   *Palette* pallet

Packpapier wrapping paper   *Wellpappe* corrugated cardboard

7 Payment and reminders

Model letters: a pro-forma invoice, a quarterly statement, querying an invoice, a reply to an invoice query, a request for payment, a first reminder, a second (final) reminder, a reply to a first/second reminder

Useful phrases: invoices, statements of account, credit/debit notes; notification of payment; invoice queries; request for payment, reminders; delayed payment

Forms of invoicing and payment

Together with the delivery of the goods the customer will be sent a commercial invoice, often sent by separate post, indicating the details of the transaction and the total amount due. Payment has to be made in accordance with the terms of payment agreed.

A **pro-forma invoice** is made out if
- the customer is asked to pay in advance, or
- the customer wants information about how much he will be charged and for what, or
- the goods are sent on approval or consigned to an agent, or
- the importer requires advance information about the invoice amount to apply for an import licence or a documentary credit.

A **customs invoice** is prepared by the exporter for customs purposes both in the exporting and in the importing country. A **consular invoice** certifies that the prices charged by the exporter are the prices current in the exporting country.

In a well-established business relationship the partners are most likely to use **open account terms**. This means that the seller will send an invoice for the transactions after an agreed period of time, one month or a quarter, itemising the transactions during that period (i.e. goods supplied, remittances received as well as credit and debit notes) and charging the amount due for the period. **Debit and credit notes** may become necessary to adjust accounting errors: a debit note if the customer was undercharged and a credit note if the customer was overcharged or faulty goods and empty containers or pallets etc. have been returned. The buyer is expected to settle the outstanding amount as agreed, usually by bank transfer or cheque. In this case there is normally no discount for cash payment.

Payment transactions

Payment can be made in a variety of ways. The most common for two businesses in the same country are: cash; cash on delivery (COD); cheque; bank transfer; credit transfer; bank draft; bill of exchange (B/E). Invoices from foreign business partners are usually settled in the following manner: international giro; international money order; bank transfer; international banker's draft: bill of exchange (B/E); documentary credit/letter of credit (L/C). For further details refer to the glossary.

Reminders

There are various reasons why an account can become overdue. An invoice may simply have been forgotten or may have taken longer to process. In such a case the supplier will send a short reminder (**request for payment**) referring to the transaction and asking in very polite, often friendly terms for payment to be made. This is sometimes even linked to an advertising letter. In most cases such a 'gentle nudge' will suffice.

If payment is not received within a reasonable period of time a **reminder** (collection letter) will become necessary. Now the seller refers to previous correspondence in more detail, encloses a copy of the invoice and other relevant statements and gives a final date for payment. S/He may wish to know about the reasons for the delay in payment and, depending on the business relationship with the customer, possibly even offer an extension or some other compromise solution.

The **second and final reminder**, while being friendly in tone, will be quite insistent. And again all the details relating to the transaction and previous reminders are mentioned. The supplier makes clear in no uncertain terms that payment must be made and gives a final deadline. S/He may go as far as suggesting a revision of the terms of payment, withholding further supplies, turning the account over to a collection agency and even threatening to take legal action.

At the second and third stage, it is good business practice for the buyer to write and explain the **reasons for the delay** and apologise. If necessary, he can make a suggestion as to how the outstanding amount is to be settled when payment, for whatever reason, cannot be made in full just now or ask for an extension. It is obvious that once the credit period is exceeded the buyer is no longer entitled to the cash discount granted and the supplier may even charge interest until the account is cleared. The terms of payment and delivery usually account for these eventualities.

A Model letters

1 Forms of payment: a pro-forma invoice

In this accompanying letter for an invoice the seller requests payment before delivery.

Order No. 1895/V for plastic toys

Thank you for your order for plastic toys. We are pleased to enclose our invoice number FG 1754/04 for the plastics toys you ordered by email on 26 July.
All the goods are available from stock and will be dispatched to you as soon as we have received the invoice amount of € 8,627.50.
We hope our goods will find good sales in your market and look forward to doing business with you again.

Invoice No. FG 1754/04   **Your order No. 1895/V**

Quantity	Item	Unit price	Total in €
50	Tractor XM	€ 25.75	€ 1287.50
100	Scooter BA	€ 30.50	€ 3050.00
200	Duckie BMX	€ 6.75	€ 1350.00
500	Beach Set TX	€ 3.50	€ 1750.00
			€ 7437.50
		VAT @ 16%	€ 1190.00
	Terms: payable within 14 days of receipt	Total	€ 8627.50

Decide which is correct.

1 The order is for ...
   a metal toys   **b** plastic toys   **c** wooden toys.
2 The order ... placed by email.
   a is being   **b** will be   **c** was
3 The goods are ...
   a in stock   **b** out of stock   **c** produced for stock.
4 The goods are to be paid for ...
   a after delivery   **b** before dispatch   **c** when ordering.
5 VAT ...
   a does not apply   **b** is included   **c** must be added.

Letter plan for a pro-forma invoice

☐ Refer to the order.
☐ Mention the status of order processing/availability of goods.
☐ Mention the enclosed invoice.
☐ Ask for payment to be made.
☐ Close with a polite ending.

2 Forms of payment: a quarterly statement

Here a quarterly statement is sent with a cover letter to explain a new pallet charge and ask for the customer's understanding.

Account No. 10 35 74 – June statement

Please find enclosed our statement for the second quarter. You will note that we have credited you with the amount overcharged in the March statement of $245.75 and also debited you for the pallets which we used for our shipments to you.

You may recall our circular from the beginning of the year, where we explained the reasons for this change in policy: We are aiming to keep product costs down by using the existing pool of standard pallets which are now available here in Europe. And this must be in your interest as much as it is in ours. A deposit charge on standard Euro-pallets has become a widely established business practice here.

If the statement has been calculated correctly, we would be pleased to receive your payment in the usual manner. Thank you again for your continued custom.

List the main points of the letter.

Letter plan for a quarterly statement

- Refer to the enclosed statement.
- Mention any 'irregularities' in the accounting period (debits, credits, etc.).
- Add any other relevant information.
- Ask for the statement to be checked and transfer to be made.
- Close with a polite ending.

3 Forms of payment: querying an invoice

This letter is a customer query regarding a special reduction in price.

Dear Mr Dieck

ORDER FOR AGRICULTURAL MACHINERY

Thank you for the consignment of agricultural machinery which arrived here in good condition. We accepted the draft as agreed. On checking the invoice, however, we noticed with surprise that you have failed to take into account the special reduction of 5 per cent off your quoted prices that we had arranged for this order.

As we are planning to place another order in the near future we would suggest that you send us a credit note for this amount. We trust that this proposal will meet with your approval and look forward to hearing from you in this matter again.

Yours sincerely

Letter plan: querying the invoice

- Refer to the invoice.
- Describe the discrepancy (quantities/quality of goods, prices, discounts).
- Ask for the difference to be settled, make a suggestion.
- Close with a polite ending.

4 Forms of payment: a reply to an invoice query

This letter is in reply to the customer query. The seller apologises for a mistake.

> Dear Mr Chong
>
> ORDER FOR AGRICULTURAL MACHINES
>
> Thank you for your letter of 27 August. The special reduction we agreed for your order was indeed overlooked when we made out the invoice.
>
> We offer our sincere apologies for this oversight und hope it has not inconvenienced you unduly. Your cooperation in this matter is much appreciated, and we are only too glad to issue a credit note for €2,050.00 which will be taken into account when the invoice for your next order is made up. Once again many thanks for your understanding and we are looking forward to being of service again.
>
> Yours sincerely

You are the export manager. Write a short memo in German (!) to your colleague in the Accounts Department giving a brief account of this exchange of letters.

Letter plan: reply to a letter querying the invoice

- ☐ Refer to the query.
- ☐ Say what went wrong.
- ☐ Offer an apology.
- ☐ Explain how you intend to put the situation right.
- ☐ Close with a polite ending.

5 A request for payment

This sales letter also serves to remind the customer that payment is overdue.

Watertown Manufacturing Inc.

2739 Johnstone Street
Waterville SC 29301
Phone 0303-3334141
Fax 0303-3334142
e-mail info@watertown.manu.com

H & W Design Center
29 Socrates Wynd
New Perkin, ME 04578

Attn. Mr John Fairfax

June 24, 20..

Dear Mr. Fairfax:

Order No. 2785/XY for office equipment

Anticipating market trends. That is what success in state of the art design is about. The enclosed catalog is an indication of where we are going. Interested??
Just browse and see where you want to go. Let us know your requirements.
When you do, also take care to remember that the invoice for the am. order is still waiting for your attention. Overworked? Well, if and when you find the time. But don't leave it for too long. Why not just let us have your order and your payment at the same time? Think about it.

Truly yours,

C. Dombrowski

> **Letter plan for a request for payment** (Use very friendly language.)
>
> - ☐ Refer to the invoice.
> - ☐ (Express hope for safe arrival of the goods.)
> - ☐ Ask for the invoice to be paid.
> - ☐ Close with a polite ending.

6 Collection letters: a first reminder

This letter is to remind the customer that payment is overdue and to request payment.

Watertown
Manufacturing Inc.

2739 Johnstone Street
Waterville SC 29301
Phone 0303-3334141
Fax 0303-3334142
e-mail info@watertown.manu.com

H & W Design Center
29 Socrates Wynd
New Perkin, ME 04578

July 24, 20..

Dear Mr Fairfax:

Order No. 2785/XY for office equipment

Our letter and the catalog we sent you on June 24 may have failed to attract your attention. Unfortunately, our records show that your account with us is now more than 60 days overdue. We are very concerned that we have not yet heard from you. Nor has payment of our invoice WM 7464/03 for your order No. 2785/XY for office equipment been received, even though we have already sent you a reminder about this matter.

We are requesting that you send your payment to us immediately. In this way you can preserve your excellent credit record with us.

H & W Design Center has always been one of our best customers, and we value your business very much. If some special circumstances are preventing you from making payment, please call us now so that we can discuss the situation with you and find a mutually satisfactory solution. We look forward to hearing from you in this matter.

Truly yours,

C. Dombrowski

> **Letter plan for a first reminder** (Use friendly but firm language.)
>
> - ☐ Refer to the query.
> - ☐ Refer to the amount overdue (state order No.).
> - ☐ Mention the first reminder & enclose a copy of the invoice.
> - ☐ Express surprise at failure to observe payment terms.
> - ☐ Ask for an explanation & offer help.
> - ☐ Ask for payment & give a deadline.
> - ☐ (State consequences of non-payment.)
> - ☐ Regret necessity of this course of action.
> - ☐ Close with a polite ending.

7 Collection letters: a second (final) reminder

This letter is a final request for payment, amicable and yet firm in tone.

August 24, 20..

Dear Mr Fairfax:

Order No. 2785/XY for office equipment

This is the third time we have had to call your attention to your long-overdue account. So far we have neither received payment nor any communication regarding the delay in settling your account.
You will surely realise that good business relations are very much the result of a joint effort. I hope you will agree that we have done our share to make this business transaction a success. The time has come for you to meet your obligations now.
A check put in the post today or a bank transfer arranged upon receipt of this letter will settle the matter amicably.
If you feel that there are circumstances that prevent you from making payment now, you should talk to us immediately so that we can find a mutually acceptable solution.
You will no doubt understand that we will have no alternative but to turn the matter over to our legal advisers if we do not receive payment within the next seven days.
It is in your interest as much as it is in ours to avoid this unpleasant situation. So do not delay, act now.

Truly yours,

Answer these questions.

1. When does Carol Dombrowski send a catalog?
2. How long is the account overdue when Carol sends the first reminder?
3. How long is the account overdue when Carol sends the second reminder?
4. How does Carol expect to be paid?
5. What is Carol hoping for in addition to the settlement of the invoice?
6. Does Carol offer any help?
7. How can the credit record be preserved?
8. Who will the matter be turned to if H & W Design Center fails to settle the invoice?

Letter plan for a second (final) reminder

- ☐ Refer to the overdue account & state for how long.
- ☐ Refer to the previous reminders & enclose invoice & other relevant details.
- ☐ Refer to your own obligations and/or concessions granted in this case.
- ☐ Express disappointment at buyer's behaviour.
- ☐ Ask for an explanation & offer help with finding a solution.
- ☐ Ask for prompt payment & fix a deadline.
- ☐ Point out action that will be taken in case of non-payment (legal action, stopping further supplies, cash-only transactions).
- ☐ Close with a polite ending.

8 A reply to a first/second reminder

This letter is a very apologetic reply offering an explanation and proposing a solution.

Dear Ms Dombrowski:

<u>Our order No. 2785/XY for office equipment; your invoice WM 7464/03</u>

Thank you for your mail referring to the am. transaction and the patience shown. We offer our most sincere apologies for not settling our account and not contacting you earlier. Our company has been going through a very difficult period during which the very existence of H & W Design Center was at risk. We are happy to say that we can now look ahead with some confidence.

However, we would be glad if you were still prepared to come to a mutually satisfactory arrangement as regards the settlement of the am. invoice. We would propose to settle a third of the outstanding amount now, i.e. $ 7,500.00 and pay the balance of $15,000.00 in two equal instalments in October and November. This would greatly assist us in meeting our other commitments without straining our cash situation even further. You can be assured that with business picking up again a steady cashflow is guaranteed in the next quarter. A check for the amount of $7,500.00 is enclosed.

We look forward to receiving your approval to our suggestion and thank you once again for your understanding.

Yours truly,

J. Fairfax

Correct these statements.

1 Mr Fairfax has tried several times to contact Watertown Manufacturing Inc.
2 H & W Design Center has been very busy in recent weeks.
3 H & W Design Center was all but bankrupt.
4 Mr Fairfax is not very optimistic about the future.
5 Payment is to be stretched over a period of four months.
6 Mr Fairfax prefers to pay by bank transfer.
7 A cashflow problem is very likely in the next quarter.
8 The proposed solution requires managerial approval at H & W Design Center.

Letter plan for a reply to a first/second reminder

- ☐ Refer to transaction & correspondence received.
- ☐ Apologise for not replying earlier.
- ☐ State reasons for delay in payment.
- ☐ Explain steps taken to improve business and/or financial situation.
- ☐ Make suggestions for the settlement of the matter (full payment, part payments over a period of time, payment by bill of exchange etc.).
- ☐ Express hope for acceptance of proposal.
- ☐ (Another short apology.)
- ☐ Express hope for understanding of situation and close with a polite ending.

B Useful phrases

1 Invoices, statements of account, credit/debit notes

Beiliegend / Als Anlage übersenden wir (Ihnen) die Rechnung Nr. B 1991 über den Betrag von …	Please find enclosed our invoice No. B 1991 for … / Our invoice No. … is attached.
Die beiliegende Rechnung enthält die gegen Ihre Bestellung Nr. … gelieferten Waren.	The enclosed invoice covers the goods delivered against your order number …
Der Rabatt ist schon abgezogen worden.	The discount has already been deducted.
Der zu zahlende Gesamtbetrag beläuft sich auf …	The total amount payable is …
Wie Sie der Rechnung entnehmen, sind … zur Zahlung fällig.	From the invoice you will note that the amount due is …
Wir bitten um Überweisung des Rechnungsbetrags auf unser Konto.	Please credit our account with the invoice amount.
Bitte begleichen Sie den Betrag gemäß beiliegender/beigefügter Rechnung (durch Scheck oder Postüberweisung).	Please send us your remittance (cheque, postal/money order) for the amount of the invoice enclosed/attached.
Wir bitten um umgehende/baldige Begleichung unserer Rechnung / … baldige Überweisung des Rechnungsbetrags.	Prompt payment/remittance would be appreciated. / We ask you for an early settlement of our invoice.
Bei Begleichung innerhalb von 7 Tagen können wir 3% Skonto / einen Barzahlungsrabatt von 3% gewähren.	If payment is made within seven days, we are prepared to grant/allow 3% for cash.
Beiliegend übersenden wir den Kontoauszug per 31.7. / für das erste Quartal.	We enclose your statement as per 31 July / for the first quarter.

2 Notification of payment

Beiliegend übersenden wir Ihnen einen Scheck über den Betrag von …	Please find enclosed / We have pleasure in enclosing our cheque for …
Wir danken für Ihre Rechnung. Den Betrag von … haben wir heute auf Ihr Konto bei der … Bank überwiesen.	We received your invoice and have today transferred/remitted the amount of … to the … Bank for your credit / for the credit of your account.
Für die Zusendung der Proforma-Rechnung danken wir und teilen mit, dass wir heute eine Überweisung auf Ihr Konto bei der … Bank veranlasst haben.	We thank you for your pro-forma invoice and are pleased to inform you that we have arranged for a credit transfer to your account with … Bank today.
Wir haben die Überweisung der Summe von … veranlasst. Dabei wurde ein Skonto von 2% berücksichtigt. Unser Konto ist damit glatt gestellt / ausgeglichen.	We have arranged payment / the transfer of the sum of … , which clears our account after allowing for a discount of 2%.

Ihr Kontoauszug stimmt mit unseren Unterlagen überein. Daher haben wir unsere Bank beauftragt, zum vollen Ausgleich Ihres Auszugs den Betrag von … auf Ihr Postscheckkonto zu überweisen.	We are pleased to advise you that your statement of our account corresponds with our books. We have therefore instructed our bank to transfer the amount of … to your Giro Account in full settlement of your statement.
Wie vereinbart bitten wir Sie, für die oben erwähnte Rechnung mit 90 Tagen Sicht auf uns zu ziehen und uns die Tratte zur Annahme vorzulegen.	As arranged we kindly ask you to draw on our account at 90 d/s for your / the above-mentioned invoice and send us your draft for acceptance.

3 Invoice queries

Sie haben sich in Ihrer Rechnung Nr. … verrechnet. / Wir möchten Sie darauf hinweisen, dass Ihnen in Ihrer Rechnung Nr. … ein Fehler unterlaufen ist.	We must point out that there is an error in your invoice No. …
Gemäß Ihrer Rechnung gewähren Sie uns einen Handelsrabatt von nur 10%.	In your invoice you allow us a trade discount of only 10%.
Wir wären Ihnen dankbar, wenn Sie die Rechnung entsprechend berichtigen könnten.	We would be grateful if you could adjust the invoice accordingly.
Wunschgemäß haben wir den Handelsrabatt neu berechnet und übersenden Ihnen beiliegend unsere Gutschrift über den Differenzbetrag. Für den Fehler möchten wir uns entschuldigen.	As requested we have recalculated the trade discount and have enclosed our credit note for the difference. We apologise for the oversight.
Die Mehrwertsteuer wurde fälschlicherweise mit 7% statt mit 16% angesetzt. Der Unterschiedsbetrag beläuft sich auf £ 35,64 und wird in Ihrer nächsten Abrechnung ausgewiesen.	VAT should have been calculated at 16% and not at 7%. The difference amounts to £35.64 and will be shown in your next statement of account.
Bei Rechnung Nr. 574/E ist in unserer Buchhaltung leider ein Fehler unterlaufen. Wir möchten uns für dieses Versehen entschuldigen und um Begleichung des Differenzbetrages in Höhe von $421,35 bitten.	We should like to apologise for our mistake in invoice No. 574/E, which was due to an oversight in our accounting department. Would you please send us the balance of $421.35.

4 Request for payment, reminders

Wir wenden uns an Sie, da unser Auszug für Oktober noch nicht beglichen ist.	We are writing concerning our outstanding October account.
Leider müssen wir feststellen, dass Ihre Rechnung Nr. … noch offen ist.	We refer to our invoice No. … which has not been settled yet.
Wir müssen Sie daran erinnern, dass wir bei Erstaufträgen nur zwei Wochen Ziel gewähren.	We must remind you that we only allow two weeks credit for first orders.

Da Sie sonst Ihre Rechnungen immer pünktlich begleichen, gehen wir davon aus, dass Sie Rechnung Nr. ... übersehen haben.	As you usually clear your accounts promptly we assume you may have overlooked invoice No. ...
Wir möchten bei dieser Gelegenheit darauf hinweisen, dass ... und um umgehende Erledigung bitten.	May we remind you on this occasion that ... and ask you to clear your account as soon as possible.
Unser Schreiben ist bisher unbeantwortet geblieben. Eine Zahlung ist auch nicht eingegangen.	Since we wrote we have neither received a reply nor a remittance from you.
... müssen wir Schritte zur Einziehung des fälligen Betrags einleiten.	... we must take steps to collect the amount due.
In Beantwortung unseres Schreibens vom ... sagten Sie den Ausgleich Ihres Kontos bis zum ... zu.	In your reply to our letter of ... you promised clearance of the account by ...
Wir bitten um den umgehenden Ausgleich Ihres Kontos. Andernfalls erläutern Sie uns bitte die Gründe für die Zahlungsverzögerung.	We would like to have your remittance by return or, failing that, your reasons for not clearing your account.
Wir müssen nunmehr darauf bestehen, dass Sie Ihre Rechnung innerhalb von 7 Tagen begleichen.	We must now insist on your clearing your account within the next seven days.
Sollte Ihre Zahlung nicht bis zum ... eingehen, sehen wir uns leider gezwungen, die Angelegenheit unserem Anwalt zu übergeben.	Unless you send us your remittance by ... we see no alternative but to hand over the matter to our solicitors.

5 Delayed payment

Wir hatten die Absicht, unsere Rechnung wie versprochen zu bezahlen, aber ...	We had intended to clear our account as promised, but ...
Leider waren wir nicht in der Lage, unser Konto für das letzte Quartal auszugleichen.	We regret that we were unable to settle our account for the last quarter.
Wegen des Konkurses eines unserer wichtigsten Kunden ...	... because of the bankruptcy of one of our main customers.
Wir dürfen Ihnen versichern, dass unsere derzeitige schwierige Situation nur von vorübergehender Natur ist. Daher wären wir für eine Verlängerung der Zahlungsfrist um 4 Wochen sehr dankbar.	We can assure you that our present difficulties are purely temporary. Therefore we would appreciate your granting us an extension of credit for four weeks.
Unter den gegebenen Umständen möchten wir Sie bitten, die Zahlungsbedingungen zu überprüfen. Unser Vorschlag geht dahin, die Hälfte des offenen Betrags sofort zu zahlen und den verbleibenden Betrag in zwei gleichen Monatsraten.	Under the circumstances we would ask you to revise our terms of payment. We would propose to pay half the outstanding amount now and the remainder in two monthly instalments.
Wir danken für Ihr Entgegenkommen in dieser Angelegenheit.	We thank you for accommodating us in this matter.

C Practising language

1 Choose the right expression to complete this letter.

It is with *amazement/astonishment/regret/sorrow* [1] that we note that you appear to have ignored our letter of 17th November, drawing attention to a(n) *negative/open/opening/outstanding* [2] balance of £14,610.53 on your account.

You will recognise that, as this sum is more than two months *due/overdue/payable/unpaid* [3], we are at least entitled to some expression of your intentions in the matter.

Your *failure/inability/incapacity/unwillingness* [4] to pay causes us particular *difficulties/inconvenience/problems/trouble* [5], as the prices of the goods were cut so low as to leave only the narrowest margin of profit. The delay in payment threatens to turn this small profit into a loss.

We therefore enclose a duplicate *bank statement/income statement/statement of account/statement of charges* [6] and must ask you to *credit/debit/pay/settle* [7] your overdue account without delay. We expect payment to be made *at/before/by/on* [8] 15th March at the very latest.

Should you fail to balance your account we shall be forced to turn the matter over to a *cashier/cashing company/collecting company/collection agency* [9]. This can certainly not be in your interest. We therefore look forward to receiving your *immediate/prompt/quick/soon* [10] remittance.

2 In which of the following types of letter would you use the sentences below?

a	First reminder	c	Reply to reminder
b	Second or final reminder	d	Query about the invoice

1. Business in this sector is rather slack at the moment.
2. If your remittance is already on its way, please disregard this notice.
3. New marketing initiatives are beginning to pay off.
4. Our invoice No. 26783 may have escaped your attention.
5. Payment of the remainder will then be made in two months.
6. Please check whether the trade discount has been correctly calculated.
7. Settlement of our invoice 3XO/476 is now four weeks overdue.
8. There may have been a keying error with regard to item 6 of invoice 2000A.
9. Unfortunately you have failed to react to our previous letter asking you to clear your outstanding account.
10. We all rely on customers paying promptly.
11. We apologise for not replying to your request for payment.
12. We found that you did not credit us for the returns.
13. We must ask you to clear your outstanding account by 26 June at the latest.
14. Your prompt payment would be greatly appreciated.

3 **Rearrange these sentences in their proper order for a reply to a statement of account.**

Dear Ms Fraser

- a Activities in our field of enterprise are at a low ebb, and payments to us have fallen into arrears.
- b But as you will appreciate we are reluctant to dispose of our assets until such a drastic step becomes really necessary.
- c By doing so now we would incur a heavy loss.
- d Some of our regular customers have temporarily suspended orders, and this has resulted in our firm having some financial difficulties.
- e Thank you for your letter of 15th October requesting us to settle the above account amounting to $7,500.00 by return of mail.
- f Therefore we would ask you for an extension of credit in order to await an improvement of the business climate.
- g To show our goodwill we have instructed our bank to transfer $3,000.00 to your bank account as part payment of the outstanding amount.
- h We can assure you, however, that we have sufficient resources to meet all our obligations.
- i We hope for your understanding of our situation and look forward to your approval to our proposal.
- j We regret not having been able to pay your July statement as promptly as usual.
- k You will doubtlessly be aware of the current business situation.

Yours sincerely

4 **Combining sentences. Link the part sentences 1–8 with the appropriate section a–j to form meaningful sentences. There are more items than you need.**

1. Going through our books we note that ...
2. Unfortunately, we have reason to call your attention to our invoice No. 4561 ...
3. We kindly ask you ...
4. We have experienced considerable losses ...
5. Unless payment is received by 15 July, ...
6. In view of the difficulties outlined above ...
7. You will be pleased to learn that, according to our books, ...
8. We apologise for the delay in settling our account ...

- a ... due to the business failure of one of our major customers.
- b ... how you wish to pay.
- c ... how you would like to settle the outstanding amount.
- d ... there is an outstanding balance of $12,500.00.
- e ... to remit the amount outstanding within a fortnight.
- f ... we hope that you will grant us an extension of 30 days.
- g ... we will have no alternative but to start legal action.
- h ... which has not been settled yet.
- i ... which is entirely due to an error in our bookkeeping department.
- j ... your invoice was paid on 12 September.

5 Express these ideas in idiomatic English.

1 Sie beziehen sich auf Ihre Lieferung vom 28.3. und müssen leider feststellen, dass der Betrag von $1,385.75 noch nicht beglichen ist. Vielleicht hat der Kunde das Zahlungsziel (14 Tage nach Rechnungserhalt) übersehen. Sie bitten um schnelle Überweisung.

2 Sie gehen davon aus, dass der Kunde die Ware in gutem Zustand erhalten hat. Nachdem Sie alle Anstrengungen unternommen haben, um pünktlich zu liefern, müssen Sie jetzt feststellen, dass der Kunde seine Vertragspflichten nicht ganz so ernst nimmt. Bisher haben Sie noch keinen Zahlungseingang feststellen können.

3 Verdeutlichen Sie Ihrem Kunden, dass Sie selbst gegenüber Ihren Lieferanten Zahlungsverpflichtungen zu erfüllen haben und deshalb die Zahlungsziele nicht unbegrenzt verlängern können.

4 Sagen Sie Ihrem Kunden, dass Ihre bisherigen Versuche, den Kunden zur Begleichung der Rechnung Nr. KN 74832 vom 23.1. zu veranlassen, fehlgeschlagen sind. Machen Sie klar, dass Sie nunmehr gewillt sind, ein Inkassobüro einzuschalten, um den ausstehenden Betrag einzutreiben, wenn die Zahlung nicht bis zum 27.4. eingeht.

5 Geben Sie ihrem Kunden zu verstehen, dass Sie durchaus bereit sind, mit ihm über eine Verlängerung der Zahlungsfrist zu verhandeln, wenn Sie die Ursachen für den Zahlungsverzug kennen. Über einen Vorschlag zur Begleichung des seit 60 Tagen offenen Rechnungsbetrages, würden Sie sich freuen.

6 Entschuldigen Sie sich bei Ihrem Lieferanten dafür, dass Sie auf die bisherigen Mahnschreiben nicht reagiert haben. Wegen der zur Zeit schwierigen Geschäftslage hatten Sie ebenfalls Schwierigkeiten, offene Beträge von einigen Ihrer Kunden einzutreiben. Inzwischen ist der offene Betrag zur Zahlung angewiesen. Danken Sie für die Geduld.

6 Saying you are sorry in English.

1 Es tut mir sehr Leid, wenn ich Sie verletzt habe.
2 Entschuldigung, aber hätten Sie mal ein Blatt Papier für mich?
3 Entschuldigen Sie vielmals. Aber ich habe Sie wirklich nicht gesehen.
4 Entschuldigen Sie mich bitte für einen Augenblick. Ich muss noch eben ein dringendes Telefonat führen.
5 Bitte entschuldigen Sie mein Zu-spät-Kommen. Aber ich hatte noch ein dringendes Gespräch mit dem Abteilungsleiter.
6 Können Sie mich bei Frau Schneider entschuldigen. Ich kann leider nicht zur Sitzung kommen.
7 Wir möchten uns für den Zahlungsverzug entschuldigen.
8 Wir möchten uns aufrichtig entschuldigen, dass wir in dieser Angelegenheit nicht eher geschrieben haben.

Listening comprehension

 7 Listen to the dialogue on the CD and then do the exercise.

Write an email in German (!) to the bookkeeping department of ABC Reisen, summarise the telephone conversation and ask for action to be taken immediately.

D Letter writing

1 Write a summary of this letter.

Stoltemeyer GmbH

Donaustraße 34　　Tel. 07130/65 72 61
D-74345 Löwenstein　Fax 07130/65 72 62

Carghill Ltd
17 Hamilton Drive
Durham
DH15 5WL
ENGLAND

28 Feb. 20..

Dear Ms Clarion

Our invoice No 36897

Three months ago you received your consignment of office furniture, and we trust that you are pleased with the design and finish of the articles you ordered.

Unfortunately, our invoice No. 36897 for this consignment has not been settled yet, although we sent you two letters informing you of the fact that payment of our am. invoice was overdue. You may remember that we accommodated you in every possible way to ensure that the goods ordered reached you in time for the opening of your new premises in Furnitureland.

We would therefore be grateful if you would complete your part of the sales contract and ask you to settle your account as soon as possible. We expect your payment by 15 March at the very latest. Should you fail in remitting the outstanding amount or offering a satisfactory explanation for the delay in payment we shall, unfortunately, have no alternative but to turn the matter over to our solicitor. It is in your interest as much as it is in ours to avoid such a step.

We look forward to hearing from you.

Yours sincerely

Doris Bast

Doris Bast
(Manager, Accounts Dept.)

---

2 Write a reply to the letter in Exercise 1 above.

> **Aufgabe**
> Beantworten Sie dieses Schreiben unter Berücksichtigung der folgenden Punkte:
> - Bestätigung des Eingangs
> - Angemessene Entschuldigung
> - Erklärung für den Zahlungsverzug (Personalwechsel, Störungen in der Rechnungsabwicklung)
> - Probleme beseitigt und die Zahlung veranlasst
> - Hoffnung auf weiterhin gute Geschäftsbeziehung
> - neuer Auftrag anbei

3 Write a letter from notes.

Als Mitarbeiter/in der Rechnungsabteilung Ihres Unternehmens Gestner & Co KG in 70432 Stuttgart, Esslinger Str. 23 schicken Sie Ihrem säumigen Kunden (Cumbersand LTD, Unit 15, Meadowbank Business Park, Stirling, FK15 4UT) eine letzte Mahnung über den ausstehenden Betrag von €24.975,50.

> **Aufgabe**
> Verfassen Sie eine Mahnung unter Berücksichtigung der folgenden Punkte:
> - Erinnerung an Auftrag Nr. 76554 und Rechnung vom 22. Sept.
> - Zahlungseingang 3 Monate nach Rechnungsversand bisher nicht zu verzeichnen
> - Zwei Zahlungserinnerungen unbeantwortet
> - Ursprüngliches Zahlungsziel 30 Tage
> - Letztmalige Zahlungsaufforderung
> - Zahlungseingang innerhalb von 10 Tagen erwartet, sonst gerichtliche Schritte
> - Angemessener Schluss

4 Write a reply to this letter.

> Invoice for car parts
>
> We note with regret that our previous request for the payment of our invoice No 47894(K) does not seem to have reached you. The amount of €32,575 is still outstanding and more than 2 months overdue.
>
> We would ask you to clear your account promptly. You will realise that we have done everything in our power to assist you in your business efforts by granting generous discounts and speeding up delivery at no extra charge. Therefore we feel that we are entitled to a speedy settlement of our invoice.
>
> An explanation would be much appreciated, and we look forward to hearing from you by return.

Addresses
Supplier: Daniel Sauer, MobilTech KG, Daimlerstr. 424, 70421 Stuttgart
Customer: Jane O'Leary, Runcis & Partners, 115 Woolsington Rd, Ponteland, Northumberland, NE14 6WR

> **Aufgabe**
> Beantworten Sie dieses Schreiben unter Berücksichtigung der folgenden Punkte:
> - Bestätigung des Eingangs sowie des ersten Mahnschreibens
> - Bezahlung von 50% des Rechnungsbetrags inzwischen veranlasst
> - Vorschlag Restbetrag in 2 weiteren Raten mit jeweils 4 Wochen Abstand zu zahlen
> - Grund: schwierige Geschäftssituation in der Branche sowie überraschender Totalausfall eines Hauptkunden
> - Hoffnung schwierige Absatzsituation mit erweiterter Produktpalette zu beheben – Auftragsbestand zeigt Erholungstendenz
> - Bitte um Verständnis und Dank für Geduld

5 Write a letter from notes.

Als Sachbearbeiter/in in der Wunder Software GmbH, Grafenwald 20, 40213 Düsseldorf, sind Sie für die Bearbeitung des Zahlungsverkehrs verantwortlich. Ihnen liegt die Zahlungsaufforderung des englischen Lieferanten Snyders Ltd, 35 Stafford Road, Newcastle-under-Lyme, Staffs ST5 4XY, vor. Die Rechnung ist bereits mehr als 6 Wochen überfällig.

> **Aufgabe**
> Schreiben Sie eine Antwort unter Berücksichtigung der folgenden Punkte:
> - Zusicherung der zügigen Begleichung der ausstehenden Summe von €25,550.00 durch sofortige Banküberweisung in Höhe von €10,000.00
> - Vorschlag Restbetrag von €15,550.00 in zwei gleichen Raten von €7,775.00 in 4 bzw. 8 Wochen zu bezahlen
> - Verweis auf langjährige gute Geschäftsbeziehungen
> - Zahlungsverzug begründet durch nahezu gleichzeitigen Zahlungsausfall von zwei bedeutenden Abnehmern
> - Geschäftsaussichten insgesamt aber positiv, Werbeanstrengungen führen zu regem Neugeschäft

6 Write a reply to this letter.

> **Your order No. 45963/98**
>
> We note with regret that you appear to have ignored our letter of 22 December, drawing your attention to the outstanding balance of £14,695.60 on your account. You will recognise that, as this sum is two months overdue, we are at least entitled to some expression of your intentions in this matter. Your failure to pay causes us particular inconvenience, as the prices for your goods were cut as low as to leave only the narrowest margin of profit. The delay in payment threatens to turn this small profit into a loss. We therefore enclose a duplicate statement of account and must ask you to meet this obligation without delay.
> We look forward to hearing from you by return.

Addresses
Supplier: Chris Warren, James Warren + Sons, 24 Chester Street, Birmingham, B 15 6SO
Customer: Oliver Wusthaus, Wanderer + Co KG, Bockenheimer Allee 34, 14189 Berlin

> **Aufgabe**
> Beantworten Sie dieses Schreiben unter Berücksichtigung der folgenden Punkte:
> - Bedauern über den Zahlungsrückstand
> - Grund: Absatzschwierigkeiten wegen allgemein schlechter Geschäftslage in der Branche und ausstehende Zahlungen von mehreren wichtigen Kunden
> - Mahnschreiben vermutlich wegen fehlerhafter Anschrift und der Weihnachtspause erst verspätet eingegangen
> - Banküberweisung inzwischen veranlasst
> - angemessene Entschuldigung

UNIT 7 Payment and reminders

E Useful words

Irrtümer und Auslassungen vorbehalten	errors and omissions excepted (E&OE)
Rechnung ausstellen	to make out an invoice
Rechnung ausstellen; berechnen, in Rechnung stellen	to invoice
Zollrechnung, Zollfaktura	customs invoice
Konsulatsrechnung, Konsulatsfaktura	consular invoice
Kontoauszug	statement of account
Monatauszug, Quartalsabrechnung	monthly/quarterly statement
Konto mit periodischer Abrechnung	open account facility
(Frist)Verlängerung, Verlängerung der Zahlungsfrist	extension of credit
um Verlängerung des Zahlungsziels bitten	to ask for an extension
Kreditverlängerung gewähren	to extend a credit
Zahlungsverzug	delay in payment
in Verzug sein/kommen	to default
Saldo, Restbetrag; Differenzbetrag	balance
Gesamtbetrag	(sum) total
Rechnungsbetrag	invoice amount
zum Ausgleich Ihres Kontoauszuges	in settlement of your statement
zum vollen Ausgleich	in full settlement
fälliger/offener Betrag	amount due/outstanding
Verfalltag, Fälligkeitsdatum, Fälligkeitstermin	due date, date of maturity
Rechnung begleichen, Konto ausgleichen	to clear/settle an account
offen stehende/überfällige Rechnung	overdue account
(Rück)Erstattung, Rückzahlung	refund
Gutschriftanzeige	credit note/memo
Belastungsanzeige	debit note/memo
Gutschrift	credit entry
Lastschrift	debit entry
Konto belasten mit	to debit an account with
dem Konto gutschreiben	to credit an account with
Überweisung	remittance, (credit) transfer
Überweisender, Geldsender	remitter, transferor
Zahlungsempfänger, Überweisungsempfänger	remittee, transferee
Zahlungsempfänger	payee
Restbetrag, verbleibender Betrag	remainder
Tratte zur Annahme	draft for acceptance
Banküberweisung	bank/banker's transfer
Sichttratte, Sichtwechsel	sight draft
auf 90 Tage Sicht	at 90 d/s (days sight)
Zahlungserinnerung, Erinnerungsschreiben	reminder
Mahnschreiben, Mahnung	collection letter
Inkassobüro	collection agency
Rechnungsbetrag eintreiben	to collect an account
auf dem Rechtsweg/Klageweg	by legal means
gerichtliche Schritte	legal steps
(Rechts)Anwalt	solicitor

Complaints

Model letters: a delay in delivery, a complaint about inferior goods, a reply to a complaint

Useful phrases: complaints (opening lines, oversupply and undersupply, variation in quality, wrong goods and defects, bad packing, request for remedy, further action); settling complaints (opening lines and general, oversupply and undersupply, variation in quality, wrong goods and defects, bad packing)

Reasons for complaints

Complaints may arise from a delay in delivery, incorrect quantities, variations in quality, wrong, faulty, damaged or substandard goods or, faulty packaging and damage in transit. The complaint needs to be supported by credible evidence to substantiate the claim that is made. Therefore the buyer will give a detailed report of what s/he finds wrong with the consignment. Reference to the order and/or the information (catalogue, any other form of goods description, samples) on which the order was based may have to be made.

Settling complaints

If the claim is justified a solution needs to be found that is satisfactory to the customer while not being too costly for the seller. One obvious solution is to send replacements and take the faulty items back. If the goods are still in a marketable condition the buyer may agree to keep the goods subject to a reduction in price. This compromise solution is the preferred arrangement especially in the export trade, as the cost of transport and related charges are enormous. If the buyer decides that the goods are of no use, the seller cannot but take them back at his cost and risk and offer a refund of the purchase price.

With ever more sophisticated packaging materials and means of transport, damage to or loss of goods in transit has become an infrequent occurrence. However, if such a damage does occur, the freight forwarder and/or the insurance company need to be contacted to establish the reasons for the incident.

The seller investigates the complaint and puts the matter right if s/he is to blame. In his/her reply to the buyer the seller explains the reasons for the mistake that has occurred, apologises and offers a solution taking into account that he will want to preserve the goodwill of the customer. If the claim is not justified the seller needs to consider his business relationship with the customer and decide whether it is good policy to accommodate the customer, to try and reach a compromise solution or to reject the claim outright.

In the interests of the business relationship the language used is an important point to consider when a complaint becomes necessary and a reply is being drawn up (irrespective of whether the complaint is accepted or rejected). The complaint and the reply should be couched in polite and factual language and the apology should be sincere. A rejection must be well-founded without putting the blame on the customer if the business relationship is to be maintained.

Model letters

1   A delay in delivery

In this email the customer complains about the delay in the delivery of a consignment of carpets.

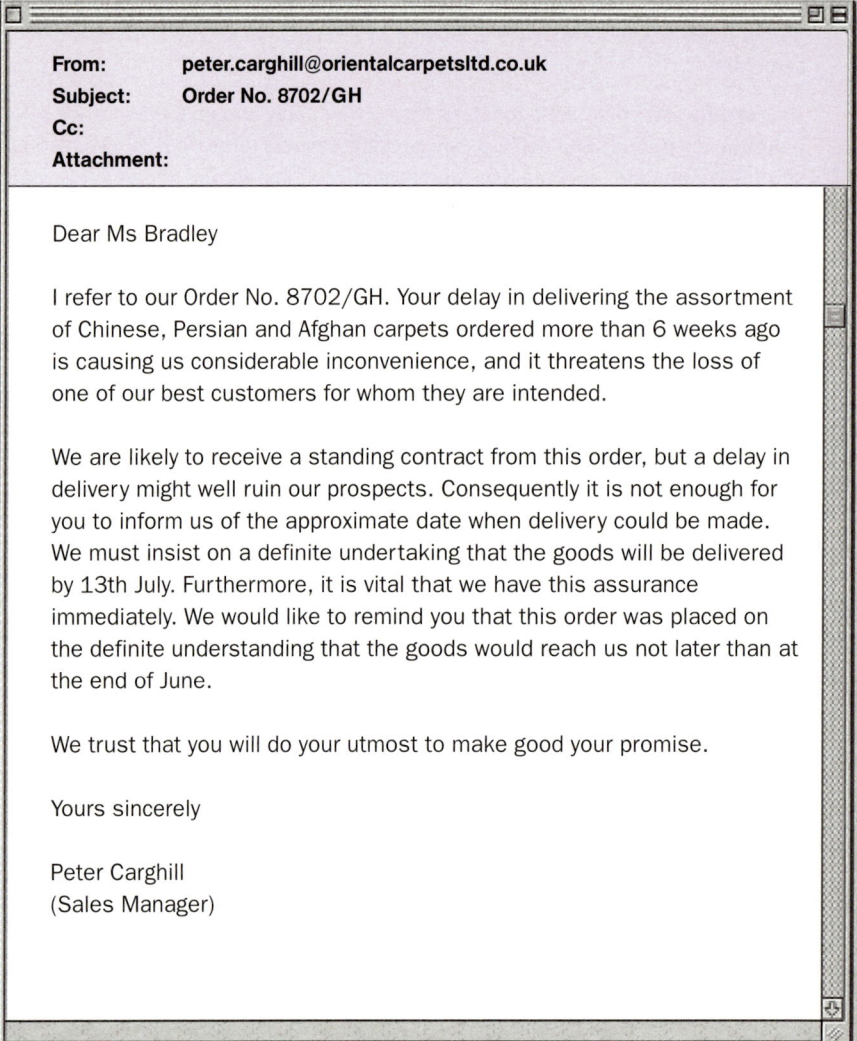

From: peter.carghill@orientalcarpetsltd.co.uk
Subject: Order No. 8702/GH
Cc:
Attachment:

Dear Ms Bradley

I refer to our Order No. 8702/GH. Your delay in delivering the assortment of Chinese, Persian and Afghan carpets ordered more than 6 weeks ago is causing us considerable inconvenience, and it threatens the loss of one of our best customers for whom they are intended.

We are likely to receive a standing contract from this order, but a delay in delivery might well ruin our prospects. Consequently it is not enough for you to inform us of the approximate date when delivery could be made. We must insist on a definite undertaking that the goods will be delivered by 13th July. Furthermore, it is vital that we have this assurance immediately. We would like to remind you that this order was placed on the definite understanding that the goods would reach us not later than at the end of June.

We trust that you will do your utmost to make good your promise.

Yours sincerely

Peter Carghill
(Sales Manager)

Correct these sentences.

1   The delivery is six weeks overdue.
2   The carpets were lost in transit to one of the best customers.
3   The customer expects a standing order.
4   The customer's business prospects are ruined.
5   The customer needs to know the approximate time of delivery.
6   The information is needed by 13 July.
7   The carpets should have arrived after the end of June.

2 A complaint about inferior goods

This letter is a complaint about poor quality. The customer asks for replacements to be sent.

Dear Ms Bradley

Order No. 8702/GH

Thank you for arranging for our consignment of carpets to be delivered by the agreed date of 13th July. After carefully examining the carpets supplied, we were surprised and disappointed, however, at the quality of the carpets. They certainly do not match the samples you sent us. The Persian carpets do not seem to be hand-made as described in your catalogue. Nor does the wool used seem to be of the advertised top quality. The Chinese and Afghan carpets show an irregularity of pile that makes them impossible to sell. Therefore we cannot help feeling there must have been some mistake in making up our order. It seems to us that you supplied us with seconds rather than the top quality material we had ordered.

You will understand that we have no choice but to ask you to take back the whole consignment and replace the carpets by materials of the quality ordered. If this is not possible, then I am afraid we shall have to ask you to cancel our order altogether.

At this stage we refer to our email of 28th June in which we complained about the delivery being late. The current state of affairs aggravates the situation even further by making it impossible for us to keep our promise to supply our customer by 20th July. It is therefore all the more important that you act swiftly to replace the merchandise. You will understand that in these circumstances we expect not only to be given an explanation but also to be granted some compensation for the inconvenience incurred.

Please let us know by return when we can expect the new consignment and also what you intend us to do with the carpets we have just received.

We look forward to hearing from you promptly.

Yours sincerely

Complete these sentences.

1. Oriental Carpets Ltd are disappointed about …
2. The carpets do not … sent earlier.
3. … for the Persian carpets is not of first-rate quality.
4. It seems that … were supplied.
5. Oriental Carpets Ltd intend to return …
6. … if the goods cannot be replaced.
7. The current situation makes it impossible for Oriental Carpets Ltd …
8. Oriental Carpets Ltd expect to be given both an …

Letter plan for a complaint

- ☐ Refer to the order & goods received.
- ☐ Describe the problem giving details of what is wrong, enclosing evidence
- ☐ Ask for an explanation.
- ☐ (Return goods to seller or offer to keep the goods.)
- ☐ Point out consequences for your company.
- ☐ Ask for matter to be put right (compensation, reduction, new consignment).
- ☐ Close with a polite ending.

3 A reply to a complaint

This letter is a reply to the letter on page 101. The seller offers an explanation, but refuses to supply replacements.

Dear Mr Carghill

Order No. 8702/GH

It is with regret that we note from your letter of 15th July that our consignment of Persian, Chinese and Afghan carpets did not turn out to your satisfaction.

We have, in the meantime, looked into the matter very thoroughly, also comparing the samples we sent you to carpets similar to those that you have now received. Our tests have shown that your claim of inferior quality is unfounded.

You will realise that in our trade samples of goods can only give an indication of the quality and texture of the material. It is in the very nature of hand-woven materials like Persian carpets that no single item is identical with another. The irregularity of the pile of the Afghan and Chinese carpets is due to the materials used and is likely to disappear once the carpets have been fully unpacked and displayed in the carpet salesroom.

If after reading our comments you still feel that the carpets supplied are not up to the standard you require we quite prepared to take them back with the costs and risk of the return consignment to be borne by you. But we are sorry to have to say that we cannot send you any replacements, as you have been supplied with the best material we have available.

The delay in delivery is entirely due to the fact that the consignment of which your carpets were a part was more than three weeks late in arriving here in Britain. And we therefore cannot be held responsible, especially as we did everything to speed up customs clearance and delivery to your premises. We discussed this on the phone.

To show our goodwill, however, we would be prepared to extend the period of payment for this consignment by 4 weeks and hope that this meets with your approval.

We look forward to your next order which will have our usual prompt attention.

Find expressions in the letter for the following.

1 We are sorry to read …
2 … you are dissatisfied with …
3 We have analysed the problem.
4 What you say is not correct.
5 If the goods are not good enough for you …
6 You will be responsible for the costs and risks …
7 transport to our warehouse
8 to allow sb. to pay later

Letter plan for a reply to a complaint

- ☐ Acknowledge receipt of complaint.
- ☐ Apologise for mistake and inconvenience.
- ☐ Say you are looking/have looked into the problem.
- ☐ (Ask for time to finish your investigation.)
- ☐ State the result of your investigation (you are at fault/not at fault).
- ☐ Suggest a solution if at fault (replacements, reduction etc.).
- ☐ (Apologise again.)
- ☐ Close with a polite ending.

B Useful phrases

1 Complaints

Opening lines

Ihre Sendung von … ist bei uns eingegangen. Leider haben wir Anlass zur Beschwerde über …	Thank you for your shipment of … . Unfortunately, we have reason to complain about …
Ihre Lieferung von … traf heute hier in scheinbar gutem Zustand ein. Bei Öffnung / Beim Öffnen der Packstücke/Kisten stellten wir jedoch fest, dass …	The consignment of … arrived here today in apparent good order and condition. However, on opening the packages/cases we found that …
Leider gibt/geben der/die/das … Anlass zu einer Beanstandung.	We are writing to complain about …
Leider haben wir Anlass, uns über die gestern eingegangene Sendung zu beschweren.	The consignment received yesterday has, unfortunately, given cause for complaint.
Wir müssen Ihnen leider mitteilen, dass die genannte Sendung nicht zu unserer Zufriedenheit ausgefallen ist.	We regret to inform you that the above-mentioned consignment has not turned out to our satisfaction.
Bei Durchsicht Ihrer Sendung vom … mussten wir leider feststellen, dass unser Auftrag nicht richtig ausgeführt wurde.	On checking your consignment of … we find/note that our order has not been handled/processed correctly.
Bei der Erledigung unserer Bestellung ist offenkundig ein Fehler unterlaufen.	There has obviously been an error in the execution of our order.

Oversupply and undersupply

Wir haben festgestellt, dass Sie nicht entsprechend der Auftragsmenge geliefert haben. / Leider haben Sie nicht … geliefert.	We found that / Unfortunately, you did not send/supply the quantities ordered.
Zu unserem Bedauern / Leider mussten wir feststellen, dass Sie für unseren Auftrag Nr. … bei weitem nicht die volle Bestellmenge/Auftragsmenge geliefert haben.	We regret to find that your delivery of our Order No. … was considerably short.
Die Angaben in der Packliste für Kiste Nr. … und in der Rechnung stimmen nicht überein.	There is a discrepancy between the packing list of case No. … and your invoice.
Sie haben bei dieser Sendung 150 Liter zu wenig geliefert.	You have short-shipped this consignment by 150 litres.
Statt der bestellten Mengen sandten Sie wie folgt …	Instead of the quantities ordered you sent us the following …
Wir müssen Ihnen leider mitteilen, dass … Stücke von Position … zu viel/wenig geliefert wurden.	We are sorry to report an oversupply / a shortage of … pieces of item …

Bei Überprüfung der Waren stellten wir fest, dass verschiedene Posten fehlten, obgleich sie in der Rechnung aufgeführt waren.	On checking the goods received we found that several items were missing, although they appeared on the invoice.
Die nachstehend aufgeführten Posten fehlen.	The following items are missing.
Beigefügt finden Sie eine Liste der fehlenden Artikel.	A list of the missing articles is enclosed.

Variation in quality

Die Qualität der Waren hat unsere Erwartungen nicht erfüllt / unseren Erwartungen nicht entsprochen.	The quality of the goods did not come up to / meet our expectations.
Die Qualität Ihrer Waren weicht beträchtlich von der Ihrer Musterstücke ab / entspricht nicht der Ihrer Musterstücke.	The quality of your goods varies considerably from / does not correspond to that of your samples.
Wir haben Qualitätsware bestellt und lehnen die Annahme minderwertiger Ware ab.	We ordered goods of superior quality and refuse to accept inferior merchandise.
Wenn Sie uns nicht eine beträchtliche Ermäßigung einräumen, schicken wir die minderwertige Ware zurück.	We will therefore return the inferior merchandise unless you allow us a substantial reduction.
Ihre Lieferung entspricht nicht Ihrem Angebot. Daher lehnen wir Annahme der gelieferten Ware ab.	Your delivery does not correspond with your offer. We therefore refuse to accept the goods supplied.
Die Artikel scheinen von einer anderen Bauart zu sein.	The items appear to be of different construction.
Die zugesandten Waren entsprechen nicht dem Muster, das die Grundlage für unseren Auftrag war.	The goods sent do not correspond with / are not up to the sample on the basis of which we ordered.

Wrong goods and defects

Aufgrund eines Versehens sind uns offenkundig falsche Waren zugegangen.	Evidently some mistake has been made and the wrong goods have been delivered.
Ihre Lieferung / Die gelieferte Ware von ... entspricht nicht unserem Auftrag Nr. ... / stimmt nicht mit unserer Bestellung überein.	Your shipment / The goods delivered of ... does/do not correspond to our order No. ... / are not what we ordered.
Die Artikel waren in der falschen Farbe / in den falschen Größen.	The items were in the wrong colour/sizes.
Offensichtlich ist in Ihrer Versandabteilung ein Fehler unterlaufen, denn wir haben Ware erhalten, die laut Rechnung für einen anderen Kunden bestimmt ist.	A mistake must have occurred in your shipping department. We were sent goods which, according to the invoice, were intended for another company.
Der Inhalt der Kisten stimmt nicht mit der Versandanzeige überein.	The contents of the crates do not agree with the delivery note.

Bad packing

Leider müssen wir Sie darauf aufmerksam machen, dass die soeben eingegangene Sendung sehr schlecht verpackt war.	We regret having to draw your attention to the fact that the consignment just received was very badly packed.
Die Verpackung in der Kiste war unzureichend. Das hatte zur Folge, dass der Inhalt hin- und herrutschen konnte.	The packing inside the case was insufficient with the result that there was some shifting of the contents.
Die Kartons sind anscheinend sehr sorglos / nicht sachgemäß behandelt worden.	The cartons appear to have been very roughly handled.
Wegen mangelhafter/unzureichender/ungenügender Verpackung waren einige Kisten bei Ankunft nass/defekt. Bitte senden Sie uns umgehend Ersatz.	Because of / due to poor/insufficient/ inadequate packing the contents of some of the cases arrived wet/broken. Please let us have replacements by return of post.
Wir bitten Sie, in Zukunft mehr Sorgfalt auf die Verpackung zu verwenden.	In future please pack the goods more carefully.

Request for remedy, further action

Wir lassen einen Teil der / die ganze Sendung / alle während des Transports beschädigten Artikel an Sie zurückgehen.	We are returning part of the consignment / the whole consignment / all of the articles damaged en route.
Die überzähligen/fehlerhaften Stücke/Posten schicken wir umgehend / zu Ihren Lasten zurück.	The surplus/faulty items will be returned immediately / at your expense.
Wir sind nur dann bereit, die zuviel gelieferte Menge zu behalten, wenn Sie uns einen größeren Preisnachlass/Rabatt gewähren/einräumen.	We are willing to accept the excess quantity only if the price is considerably reduced / only at a considerable discount.
Wir sind nicht gewillt, die zusätzliche Menge zum ursprünglichen Preis zu behalten.	We are not willing to keep the additional quantity at the original price.
Sie werden sicher verstehen, dass wir die fehlenden Stücke/Artikel dringend benötigen.	You will appreciate that we are urgently awaiting receipt of the missing items.
Wir gehen davon aus, dass Sie uns eine Gutschrift für die nicht gelieferte Menge ausstellen.	We trust that you will let us have a credit note for the short-shipped quantity.
Bis wir weitere Anweisungen von Ihnen bekommen, halten wir die falsch adressierte Sendung zu Ihrer Verfügung.	Awaiting your further instructions we will hold the wrongly addressed consignment at your disposal.
Teilen Sie uns bitte mit, was wir mit der fehlgeleiteten Sendung tun sollen.	Please let us know what you wish us to do with the misdirected consignment.
Wir hoffen, dass Sie in Zukunft solche Fehler vermeiden werden.	We hope that you will avoid similar errors in future.
Dies hat uns erhebliche Unannehmlichkeiten verursacht / Schwierigkeiten mit einer Anzahl unserer Kunden bereitet.	This has caused us considerable inconvenience / difficulties with a number of customers.

2 Settling complaints

Opening lines and general

Wir danken Ihnen für den Hinweis auf den Irrtum unserer Buchhaltung.	We would like to thank you for informing us of our accounting error.
Wir können Ihnen zu diesem Zeitpunkt noch keine Erklärung geben. Aber wir versichern Ihnen, dass wir die Angelegenheit prüfen und Ihnen in Kürze wieder schreiben werden.	While we cannot give you an explanation at present, we can promise you that we will be looking into the matter and writing to you again shortly.
Könnten Sie uns bitte zu Prüfzwecken einige Einzelstücke der Posten zurücksenden, die Ihnen nicht gefallen?	Would you please return samples of the items you are dissatisfied with so that we may test them.
Wir bedauern Ihnen mitzuteilen, dass wir die Waren unter den gegebenen Umständen nicht zurücknehmen können.	We regret to inform you that under the circumstances we cannot take the goods back.
Um Ihnen entgegenzukommen, werden wir die Ware auf unsere Kosten ersetzen.	We shall replace the goods at our expense for your convenience.
Wir können die Verantwortung für den Schaden nicht übernehmen.	We cannot accept responsibility for the damage.
Wir schlagen vor, dass Sie die Angelegenheit der Versicherungsgesellschaft melden.	We suggest that you report the matter to your insurance company.
Um der Angelegenheit nachgehen zu können, brauchen wir einen Bericht vom Spediteur mit Angabe der Schäden.	In order to follow up the matter we require a report from the forwarding agents listing the damage.

Oversupply and undersupply

Nach unseren Unterlagen ist keine überschüssige Lieferung erfolgt. Wir möchten Sie deshalb bitten, Ihren Auftrag zu überprüfen.	Our records show no surplus delivery. May we therefore suggest that you examine your order?
Nach sorgfältiger Prüfung der Angelegenheit stellen wir fest, dass Ihre Beschwerde wegen zu viel gelieferter Ware gerechtfertigt ist, und wir möchten uns wegen der dadurch verursachten Unannehmlichkeiten entschuldigen.	After careful investigation/examination of the matter we found that your complaint about excess delivery is justified. Please accept our sincere apologies for the inconvenience caused.
Die Liefermengen stimmen genau mit den in ihrem Auftrag genannten Mengen überein. Wir sind daher der Meinung, dass Ihre Mängelrüge wegen unvollständiger Lieferung jeglicher Grundlage entbehrt.	The quantities delivered correspond exactly with the amounts stated in your order. Therefore we feel that your complaint about incomplete delivery is not justified.
… müssen wir feststellen, dass Ihre Beschwerde wegen unvollständiger Lieferung gerechtfertigt ist. Unser Spediteur hat einige Kisten nicht geladen. Wir haben diese inzwischen an Ihr Lager in … aufgegeben.	… we accept your claim of incomplete delivery. Our forwarding agent forgot to load several cases which we have in the meantime despatched to your warehouse in …

Variation in quality

Ihre Beschwerde über fehlerhaftes Material nehmen wir mit Bedauern zur Kenntnis.

We are sorry to receive your complaint about faulty material.

Ihre Beschwerde über die minderwertige Qualität der Ware können wir nicht anerkennen, da diese genau dem Muster entspricht, das wir Ihnen vor Auftragserteilung zugesandt haben.

We cannot accept your complaint about the inferior quality of the goods as they correspond exactly to the sample supplied before ordering.

Der Fehler ist möglicherweise auf einen Maschinenfehler zurückzuführen, der uns entgangen ist. Wir haben zwischenzeitlich die Überprüfung aller unserer Maschinen veranlasst.

The fault may be due to a fault in one of the machines which has escaped our attention. As a result we are having all our machines tested.

Wrong goods and defects

Fälschlicherweise haben wir Sie mit Ware beliefert, die für einen anderen Kunden bestimmt war. Wir danken für Ihre Bereitschaft, die Ware weiterzuleiten.

By mistake we supplied you with goods that were intended for another customer. We appreciate your willingness to re-consign the goods.

Diese Schwierigkeit tritt nur selten auf, aber wir kümmern uns um die Angelegenheit.

It is quite uncommon for this problem to arise, but it is now being dealt with.

Wenn Sie die irrtümlich gelieferte Ware behalten wollen, sind wir bereit, Ihnen einen Preisnachlass von ... % zu gewähren.

Should you wish to keep the wrongly delivered goods, we would be willing to grant you a reduction in price by/of ...%.

Wir danken für Ihr Entgegenkommen ...

We appreciate your offer to ...

Wir hoffen, dass Sie dieser Regelung zustimmen können.

We trust this will meet with your approval.

Bad packing

Ihre Beschwerde wegen ungeeigneter Verpackung ist gerechtfertigt. Wir werden zukünftig festeres Verpackungsmaterial verwenden.

Your complaint for improper packing is justified. We will use stouter packing material in future.

Die Verpackungsfirma kann sich Ihrer Meinung nicht anschließen, dass es sich um Mängel beim Packmaterial handelt. Sie vertritt die Auffassung, dass die Kisten nicht mit der gebührenden Sorgfalt behandelt wurden.

The packers do not agree that there is any defect in the material used and maintain that the cases must have been subjected to rough handling.

Die Kisten wurden wie sonst üblich gepackt. Von anderen Kunden sind uns ähnliche Beschwerden bisher nicht zugegangen. Wir sind daher der Ansicht, dass uns für den von Ihnen beschriebenen Schaden keine Schuld trifft.

All the cases were packed in the usual manner. As we have not had similar complaints from other customers we feel that we cannot be held responsible for the damage described in your letter.

C Practising language

1 Find the proper adjective in the box below to go with the nouns. There are more adjectives than you need.

| broken | considerable | contractual | current | dirty | faulty | improper |
| incomplete | late | poor | rough | sincere | substandard | wrong |

1 apologies
2 arrival
3 china
4 consignment
5 goods
6 handling
7 inconvenience
8 material
9 obligations
10 packing
11 quality
12 quantity

2 Choose the most suitable word to complete these sentences.

1 The change in quantity has *attracted/escaped/given/taken* your notice.
2 We *find/hold/keep/make* you responsible for any loss arising from late delivery.
3 You will realise that we will *ask about/claim/demand/require* damages for the loss *enforced/incurred/maintained/occurred*.
4 The delivery note and your invoice do not *coincide/match/tally/work out*.
5 Your complaint for improper packing is *correct/just/justified/true*.
6 The cases have been subjected to rough *handling/movement/processing/transport*.
7 The *alternative/replacement/spare/substitute* goods for the faulty consignment were dispatched this morning.
8 We would advise you to take up the matter with the *appropriate/correct/respective/right* authorities in your country.

3 Add the missing parts to complete this letter.

> We have recently received a number of complaints from customers about your board markers. The mark... are clear... not giv... satisfaction and i... some ca... we ha... had to refu... the pur... price.
> The mar... our cust... have be... complaining ab... are pa... of the bat... of five thou... supplied to o... order No 5897 of 14th June. This or... was pla... with yo... representative, Gwyn Jones, on the ba... of sample mar... left by h... . We ha... ourselves compa... the perfor... of the... samples wi... that of a num... of the mar... returned t... us a... there is lit... doubt th... many of th... are fau... ; some of th... leak and ot... fail t... write wit... making blot... or ru... out ve... quickly.
> The compla... received rela... only t... markers fr... the bat... referred to. Mar... supplied bef... these ha... always be... satisfactory. We a... therefore wri... to a... you t... accept t... return o... the unso... balance amoun... to so... 3500 a... to repla... them wi... mark... of the qua... our earl... dealings wit... you ha... led u... to exp... .
> In vi... of th... refunds w... had t... make o... some occa... and the inconven... the infer... quality o... your prod... has cau... we kin... ask y... for so... reduction i... price f... our ne... consignment.

4 Complete the sentences below.

1 … we found that several items were missing. (*beim Auspacken*)
2 In the meantime we are holding the consignment … (*warten auf Anweisungen*)
3 Enclosed you will find a photograph … (*zeigt den Umfang des Schadens*)
4 Your comments regarding this matter … (*sehr erwünscht*)
5 In future … execution of our order. (*mehr Sorgfalt*)
6 … but to ask you for replacements for the faulty items. (*leider keine andere Wahl*)
7 … we are returning them to you carriage forward. (*Ware beschädigt und daher unverkäuflich*)
8 In the meantime you may rest assured that we will do everything … (*einvernehmliche Regelung der Angelegenheit*)

5 Put these ideas into appropriate English.

1 Entschuldigung für die aufgetretenen Materialschäden. Nach Ihrer Einschätzung auf unsachgemäße Behandlung bei der Verladung zurückzuführen. Klärung der Angelegenheit mit Ihrer Spedition.
2 Ungewöhnlich hohe Ausschussquote (*reject rate*) in der Produktion wegen mangelhafter Qualität des kürzlich gelieferten Plastikmaterials. Bitte um Prüfung der beigefügten Materialprobe. Rückäußerung erbeten. Frage der Entschädigung.
3 Bestätigung des Beschwerdeschreibens vom 28.6. Prüfung ergab, dass die Ware ordnungsgemäß verpackt war. Annahmebestätigung auf Lieferschein ohne besonderen Hinweis auf Lieferschaden. Bitte um Prüfung der Angelegenheit im eigenen Hause.
4 Prüfung ergab, dass die Beschwerde leider berechtigt war. Entschuldigung für Unannehmlichkeiten. Dank für Vorschlag, die Ware gegen eine Ermäßigung zu behalten. Angebot einer Preisminderung um 10% für die schadhaften Artikel.
5 Nach Rücksprache mit dem Versand ist Ware in gutem Zustand abgegangen. Geschildertes Problem tritt eigentlich nur bei unsachgemäßer Lagerung (*not to store properly*) auf.

6 Try and improve the style and tone of these sentences.

1 The goods arrived too late to be of any use. Therefore we are sending them back.
2 There is nothing wrong with the woollen fabrics.
3 We refuse to settle your invoice until you have looked into our complaint.
4 We need the replacement goods immediately because our customers are waiting.
5 We cannot understand how such a silly mistake could happen and are very sorry.
6 We promise to pay more attention to your orders in future.
7 We refuse to accept these goods because of bad workmanship.
8 The goods arrived more than three weeks late. Therefore we must demand compensation.

Listening comprehension

7 Listen to the dialogue and then do the exercise.

Take the part of Bianca Ritter and write a summary of this telephone conversation in German (!) to the head of the purchasing department.

D Letter writing

1 Write a letter of complaint preceding this reply.

> Dear Ms Barnard
>
> **Orders for audio-visual equipment**
>
> Thank you for your letter of 28 August in which you complain about our order handling processes. Orders are normally dealt with as they come in without reference being made to previous orders by the same customer. So it may well happen that two or more orders placed by the same customer at very short intervals may be processed by different members of staff in our sales and accounting departments.
>
> This is why your orders of 30th and 31st July were treated as separate orders. As the order value in either case was too low to qualify for the quantity discount we grant on orders exceeding a value of €5,000.00, you were not allowed the discount you had expected. We can fully understand your disappointment and apologise for the inconvenience caused. We would hope on the other hand that you will realise that with the volume of orders we deal with it would be impracticable for us to introduce schemes to detect situations as the one described by you.
>
> To accommodate you in this matter we have decided to grant you the quantity discount you have been asking for and your account has been credited accordingly as you will see from the next quarterly statement. To avoid such an unfortunate situation in future we would like to ask you to consolidate your requirements so that you can benefit to the fullest extent from the discounts available.
>
> Thank you for your understanding.
>
> Yours sincerely

2 Write a letter from notes.

Bei der Lieferung vom 1. Februar an die Firma Stanley and Sons (23 Winston Street, Nottingham, NG5 4PA) haben sich Probleme ergeben. Der Kunde beanstandet die Verarbeitung (*finishing*) der gelieferten Einheiten für Einbauküchen (*fitted kitchen*). Außerdem weichen die Farbtöne von früheren Lieferungen ab. Da es sich um einen umfangreichen Auftrag handelt und für eine Reihe von Kunden feste Liefer- und Einbautermine zugesagt sind, ist die Angelegenheit dringend.

> **Aufgabe**
> Als Mitarbeiter/in der Firma Sauter GmbH (Löhner Straße 61–63, 33102 Paderborn) beantworten Sie die Mängelrüge. Sichern Sie eine rasche Bearbeitung zu. Farbabweichungen und Mängel wegen umfangreicher Endkontrollen ungewöhnlich. Wegen des Auftragsvolumens schlagen Sie einen Besuch eines Mitarbeiters vor, damit die Beanstandung vor Ort geprüft und eine Lösung gefunden werden kann. Machen Sie einen Terminvorschlag.

3 Write a letter from notes.

Die Firma Xunil Inc. (3100 Oakwood Plaza, 14359 N. Harbour Street, Los Angeles CA 96559) hat einen umfangreichen Auftrag für die Lieferung von diversen Softwareprogrammen für den deutschen Markt ausgeführt. Bei der Öffnung der Sendung wird festgestellt, dass die Programmbeschreibungen den verschweißten (*sealed*) Packungen nicht beiliegen.

> **Aufgabe**
> Als Mitarbeiter/in der Firma PC Welt, Schützenstr. 25, 74074 Heilbronn, verfassen Sie eine Mängelrüge an den amerikanischen Lieferanten. Stellen Sie die Angelegenheit dar. Aus Ihrer Sicht ist es zweckmäßig sowie Zeit und Kosten sparend, die Verpackungen hier zu komplettieren. Nach Ihren Erkundungen beläuft sich der Aufwand auf ca. €3,75 pro Softwarepaket. Dieser Betrag müsste von Xunil übernommen werden. Bitten sie um Zustimmung zu diesem Vorschlag und Nachlieferung der fehlenden Programmbeschreibungen. Ein Alternativvorschlag von Xunil ist ebenfalls willkommen.

4 Write a reply to this letter.

> Dear Ms O'Sullivan
>
> Short-shipped goods
>
> We note with regret that the consignment of cotton shirts dispatched on 15 February to our order No. 29/2025 was delivered to us in a very unsatisfactory state. It was clear that two of the cases (Nos. 2 and 7) had been tampered with. On checking the contents we found that case No. 2 contained only 372 and case No. 7 375 instead of the 400 cotton shirts invoiced for each.
> Before reporting the matter to the railway authorities we would be glad if you would confirm that each of the cases did, in fact, contain the invoiced quantity when they left your premises. At the same time we would ask you to replace the missing 53 items with others of the same quality.
> You will no doubt be claiming compensation from the railway authorities, and we shall be glad to assist you with any information you will require to do so. Meanwhile we are holding the cases and contents for inspection.
> We look forward to hearing from you in this matter.
>
> Yours sincerely

> **Aufgabe**
> Beantworten Sie den Brief unter Berücksichtigung der folgenden Punkte:
> - Bestätigung der Mängelrüge
> - Angemessene Entschuldigung
> - Kisten bei Versand vollständig (vgl. Packzettel)
> - Kisten in gutem Zustand an Spediteur übergeben (vgl. Spediteurübernahmebescheinigung)
> - Warenversand auf Kundenwunsch eingeleitet
> - Dank für Unterstützung bei der Aufklärung des Vorfalls

5 Write a summary of this letter.

Bremer & Söhne
Uferstr. 39 • D-30463 Hannover

John Brown Ltd
17 Hamden Towers
York
YO7 4VY
England

Dear Mr Darling

Our order No. 5627V for office equipment

Thank you for the consignment of office furniture which arrived today and especially for the speedy execution of our order. Unfortunately we find reason to complain.
On unpacking the container in our warehouse we found that some of the items on one side of the container were moist and damaged (steel frames bent, dented and scratched in places). We also discovered that at least four of the filing cabinets had serious scratches on the side and also on the top surface. Furthermore five of the roll-fronted cabinets had broken roller guides, possibly due to rough handling. The container, incidentally, did not show any signs of having been broken into.
For your information we enclose photos of the damaged items, because we could imagine that you may want to take up the matter with your insurance company or your freight agent.
Much to our surprise we only received 40 office desks instead of the 60 that we had ordered. As we have firm orders for all the items in question we would ask you to send replacements for the damaged and short-shipped items as soon as possible, so that we can supply our customers without undue delay.
As we have no use for the damaged items we would want to return them and therefore ask for your instructions.
We would be interested to know what may have been the reasons for this faulty consignment and look forward to hearing from you in due course.

Yours sincerely

Stephen Sörensen
(Import Manager)

6 Write a reply to the letter in Exercise 5 above.

Aufgabe
Beantworten Sie dieses Schreiben unter Berücksichtigung der folgenden Punkte:
- Bestätigung des Eingangs
- Angemessene Entschuldigung
- Dank für hilfreiche Fotos
- Untersuchung eingeleitet
- Ware vor Verlassen des Werks in ordnungsgemäßem Zustand
- werksseitige Verpackung in Ordnung?
- Ersatzstücke versandbereit, Ankunft in 3–4 Tagen zu erwarten
- berichtigte Rechnung beigefügt
- Rechnungsbegleichung erst nach Eingang dieser Sendung erforderlich
- Information über Untersuchungsergebnis später
- Beschädigte Waren werden durch Spediteur abgeholt

E Useful words

entstandener Verlust	loss incurred
Schadensersatzanspruch	claim for compensation
um Entschädigung bitten, auf Entschädigung bestehen	to ask for / insist on compensation
Verlust decken/ausgleichen	to cover a loss
Rückerstattung	reimbursement
verspätete Ankunft, verspätetes Eintreffen	late arrival
Nichtlieferung	non-delivery
zu wenig geliefert (Minderlieferung, Fehlmenge)	short-shipped, short-delivered, undelivered
schlechte Verarbeitung, fehlerhafte Arbeit	poor workmanship
Oberfläche(nbeschaffenheit)	finish
Überprüfung, Durchsicht	checking
übereinstimmen	to tally
Differenz, Unterschied, Unstimmigkeit, Abweichung	discrepancy
Waren minderer Qualität	second-rate goods
Verderb	deterioration
(natürlicher) Verschleiß	wear and tear
Haltbarkeitsdatum	expiry/use-by / best before date
fehlerhaft, schadhaft	defective
Verrutschen der Ware	shifting of contents
schwer/leicht beschädigt	badly/slightly damaged
durch Hitze/Wasser/Feuer / unsachgemäße Behandlung beschädigt	damaged by heat/water/fire / rough handling
während des Transport beschädigt	damaged en route / in transit
zerkratzt	scratched
eingedellt	dented
angeschmutzt	soiled
Flüssigkeitsverlust, Auslaufen	ullage
Durchsickern	seepage
Lecken, Leckage, Schwund	leakage
(geringfügiger) Diebstahl	pilferage
sich entschuldigen, um Entschuldigung bitten	to apologise, to offer one's apologies
wir bitten um Entschuldigung (für)	please accept our apologies (for)
um eine Erklärung bitten	to ask for an explanation
Angelegenheit untersuchen	to investigate the matter
Angelegenheit mit ... besprechen	to take the matter up with
Vertragsbedingungen	terms of the contract
vertragliche Verpflichtungen	contractual obligations
auf die Einhaltung des Vertrags drängen	to hold sb to a contract
Vertragsbruch	breach of contract
Ersatz, Ersatzstück, Ersatzlieferung	replacement
zuviel berechneter Betrag, Überforderung	overcharge
zuwenig berechneter Betrag, Unterforderung	undercharge
Ausgleich, Erstattung	compensation
gütlich regeln/beilegen	to settle amicably
Irrtum wiedergutmachen	to redress an error

9 Credit enquiries

Model letters: a request for credit information, a cautious/negative reply to a request for information, a positive reply to a credit enquiry

Useful phrases: asking for information; making a positive reply; making a cautious/negative reply; confidentiality and reliability of information; declining information

Generally commercial sales transactions are based on trust unless specific payment terms such as cash with order (CWO), cash against documents (C/D), cash on delivery (COD) etc. have been agreed. Routinely, payment will be made within a certain period after delivery. In technical terms the supplier grants the buyer credit until payment has been received.

To reduce the risk of non-payment the supplier will resort to **credit enquiries** when
- business on a larger scale is being negotiated with a new business partner,
- the (new) buyer demands longer periods of payment,
- the buyer demands special forms of payment (bill of exchange).
- the buyer demands open account terms (i.e. payment at certain intervals, once a month or once a quarter).

The advantages of buying on credit to the buyer (less capital tied up in goods, payment out of sales proceeds) must be weighed against the disadvantages for the seller (risk of bad debts, capital tied up in goods already sold). On the other hand open account terms are advantageous for both parties in that they reduce the volume of paperwork and are cost-saving, when there are frequent transactions.

It is standard practice for the seller to ask the buyer to quote trade references where information may be obtained (usually business partners who are likely to give a favourable reference). In industrialised countries there is also a well-established network of commercial credit agencies which suppliers may approach and which collect information from businesses (press reports, company reports, information provided by companies on a voluntary basis etc.). To comply with data protection legislation, agencies can only reveal data that are not publicly available when the company in question agrees to this being done. Such information is sensitive and both parties are aware that it has to be treated as confidential.

Credit enquiries UNIT 9

A Model letters

1 A request for credit information

This letter is a credit enquiry to a business partner because the amount involved is very high.

King George Dock   75 Harbour Road   Hull HU3 7GD

Leicester Timber Traders Ltd
14 Hinckley Street
Leicester
LE2 6GX

Attn. Ms J McKerrars

26 March 20..

Dear Ms McKerrars

Request for information

We have been asked by Messrs. John Smith & Sons, 97 Riley Street, Wigston, LE5 4DS, to forward a shipload of timber for which they propose to pay by means of a three month bill. As the amount involved is far in excess of £10,000, we are naturally reluctant to allow credit without some assurance as to their credit standing.
Mr Smith has informed us that you would be willing to inform us on this point. If so, we should greatly appreciate your advice, and would be pleased to assist you similarly at any time. You may rest assured that any information you can provide will be treated as strictly confidential.
We look forward to hearing from you shortly.

Yours sincerely

Tom Pitman

Tom Pitman
General Manager

List the main points of the enquiry.

Letter plan for a request for information

- ☐ Refer to the company.
- ☐ State reason for request for information.
- ☐ State what information is required.
- ☐ Promise to render a similar service.
- ☐ Promise to treat information as confidential.
- ☐ Close with a polite ending.

2 A cautious/negative reply to a request for information

This is a cautious reply to the enquiry on the previous page.

> Request for information
>
> In reply to your inquiry of 26 March we recommend a policy of caution. Though Mr. Smith is an excellent businessman with a wide circle of customers, the volume of his operations hardly warrants an allowance of credit to the extent mentioned. There is little doubt that he is acting in the utmost good faith. But we ourselves would not recommend accepting the conditions he suggests.
> We hope that we have been of assistance to you, and that you will recognise the importance of keeping this communication strictly private.
>
> Yours sincerely

Give a brief summary of the content of the letter above.

Letter plan for a reply to a request for information

- ☐ Refer to the request for information/credit enquiry.
- ☐ (State your business relationship with the company in question.)
- ☐ State what information you have (volume of business, payment habits).
- ☐ Make a suggestion as to how the seller should proceed.
- ☐ (State that you will not be held liable for information provided.)
- ☐ Close with a polite ending.

3 A positive reply to a credit enquiry

This letter is a positive reply to request for information.

> Request for business information
>
> Thank your for your letter of 17 April requesting information about the company whose name is given on the attached slip. We have been dealing with them for a number of years now. As far as we are aware the company enjoys a very good reputation in the industry, both among its customers and competitors. Their business activities are quite considerable and the company has been growing steadily ever since we started business relations with them.
> As regards their payment habits, we do not hesitate to state that our invoices were usually settled very promptly. In the beginning we asked for payment to be made on a documents against acceptance basis, but after only a year we agreed to their request to allow them to pay within a fortnight of receipt of invoice.
> From our point of view there seems to be no reason for not starting a business relationship with them. You will realise, however, that we cannot assume any responsibility for the information provided above. It goes without saying that this information is strictly confidential.
> We trust that our views have been of assistance and hope that you will develop a good working relationship with the company in question.
> Yours sincerely

List the main points of this credit information.

B Useful phrases

1 Asking for information

Wir sind von … an Sie verwiesen worden.	We have been referred to you by …
Die auf dem beigefügten Blatt genannte Firma hat uns Ihren Namen als Referenz angegeben.	The firm mentioned on the enclosed/ attached slip has given us / quoted your name as a reference.
… hat um langfristige Zahlungsziele gebeten und bezieht sich auf Sie als einen ihrer Lieferanten.	… has applied to us for credit terms and refers to you as one of their suppliers.
Da wir mit dieser Firma zuvor noch keine Geschäfte getätigt haben, …	As we have not done business with this firm before …
Mit … haben wir eine neue Geschäftsbeziehung. Die … hat einen umfangreichen Auftrag erteilt.	… is a new business contact and has placed a sizeable/large order.
Sie hat uns gebeten, ihnen längerfristige Zahlungsziele einzuräumen.	They have asked us to grant them extended credit terms.
Wir wären Ihnen dankbar, wenn Sie uns über die betreffende Firma Auskunft erteilen könnten.	We would appreciate any information / your giving us information about the firm in question.
Gern wüssten wir, ob wir ihrer Meinung nach dieser Firma einen Kredit in Höhe von … einräumen können.	We would like to know if, in your opinion, we should allow them a credit of …
Wir wären Ihnen sehr dankbar, wenn Sie uns Ihre Ansicht über die Zahlungsfähigkeit / den Ruf der genannten Firma mitteilen würden.	We should be much obliged if you could let us have / give us your opinion as to the solvency/reputation of the firm mentioned.
Die Gesellschaft … hat uns gerade einen größeren Auftrag erteilt.	The company … has just placed a sizeable order with us.
Aus diesem Grunde wären wir dankbar für Auskünfte über ihre Zuverlässigkeit / finanzielle Lage / langfristigen Geschäftsaussichten.	Therefore we should be grateful for (any) information on their reliability / financial position / long-term prospects.
Wir wären Ihnen dankbar für Informationen zum Ruf dieser Firma im Inland und im Ausland.	We would be grateful for information about this company's reputation both at home and overseas.
… ob Sie die Firma in dieser Höhe für kreditwürdig halten?	… whether you consider the firm good for such an amount of credit.
Wir versichern Ihnen / Sie dürfen versichert sein, dass Ihre Auskunft mit größter Verschwiegenheit / streng vertraulich behandelt wird.	We (may) assure you that your information will be treated in strict confidence / strictly confidentially.
In dieser Angelegenheit sichern wir Ihnen größte Vertraulichkeit zu.	We assure you of our complete confidentiality in this matter.

Wir sind gern bereit, Ihnen ggf. einen gleichen Dienst zu erweisen.	We are ready to render you a similar service if the occasion arises.
Wir danken Ihnen im Voraus für Ihre Auskunft und sind zu (ähnlichen) Gegendiensten selbstverständlich stets gern bereit.	We thank you very much in advance for your information and shall, of course, always be pleased to reciprocate / be ready to render you a similar service.

2 Making a positive reply

Diese Firma ist uns seit mehr als sechs Jahren bekannt.	We have known this company for more than six years.
Wir stehen seit einer ganzen Reihe von Jahren mit dieser Firma in geschäftlicher Verbindung, die sich für uns als ebenso angenehm wie nutzbringend erwiesen hat.	We have had business relations / We have been doing business with this firm for a good number of years which have proved both agreeable and profitable to us.
Gern erteilen wir Ihnen eine positive Auskunft über die genannte Firma.	We welcome the opportunity to report favourably on the company mentioned.
Sie zählen zu unseren regelmäßigen Kunden.	They are regular customers of ours.
Die in Ihrer Anfrage genannte Firma genießt (in Geschäftskreisen / in der Branche) einen ausgezeichneten Ruf.	The firm mentioned in your enquiry enjoys an excellent reputation (in business/trade circles).
Unserer Meinung nach sind die Inhaber vertrauenswürdige Geschäftsleute.	In our opinion, the owners are trustworthy businessmen.
Die finanzielle Lage / Vermögenslage dieser Firma wird als gut angesehen / gilt als gut / ist offensichtlich sehr gut.	The financial position of this firm is looked upon as / is considered / seems sound/ good.
Die Firma verfügt über beträchtliche finanzielle Mittel.	They have considerable resources/funds at their disposal.
Die Firma ist ihren (Zahlungs)Verpflichtungen uns gegenüber immer pünktlich nachgekommen.	As far as we are concerned the company has always fulfilled/met its obligations/ commitments punctually/promptly.
Unserer Auffassung nach ist diese Firma völlig zuverlässig.	In our view this company is absolutely/ completely reliable.
Soweit uns bekannt, besteht kein Risiko, Waren bis zum Wert von ... zu schicken.	To the best of our knowledge, there is no risk in sending goods to the value of ...
Wir sind sicher, dass Sie diesen Kredit ohne Bedenken einräumen können.	We feel sure that you can allow/grant this credit without hesitation.
Die betreffende Firma ist kreditwürdig/sicher für einen Kredit bis zu dem erwähnten Betrag.	The firm in question is safe (good) for credit up to the amount mentioned.
Wir würden nicht zögern, dieser Firma einen Kreditrahmen von £... einzuräumen.	We would not hesitate granting this company credit up to £...

3 Making a cautious/negative reply

Wir wissen aus zuverlässiger Quelle, dass ...	We have learnt from reliable sources that ...
Wir bedauern, Ihnen mitteilen zu müssen ... / Leider müssen wir Ihnen mitteilen ...	We regret (having) to tell you ...
Unsere Erfahrungen mit dieser Firma sind leider nicht immer zufrieden stellend gewesen.	Our experience with this firm has not always been satisfactory.
In den letzten Monaten sind die Zahlungen schleppend eingegangen.	During the last few months there have been repeated delays in payment.
Sie sind uns noch ... schuldig.	They still owe us ...
Unsere Rechnungen vom letzten Quartal des vergangenen Jahres sind noch offen.	They have still not settled our invoices from the fourth quarter of last year.
Allem Anschein nach befinden sie sich in einer schwierigen finanziellen Lage.	It seems they are in a difficult financial position.
Deshalb raten wir Ihnen zur Vorsicht.	Therefore we would advise you to act with caution / to be cautious.
Wir sind der Meinung, dass es nicht ratsam wäre, dieser Firma Kredit zu gewähren.	We think it would not be advisable to grant this firm credit.

4 Confidentiality and reliability of information

Selbstverständlich erteilen wir diese Auskunft unverbindlich und streng vertraulich / mit der größten Diskretion.	It is understood that this information is given in strict confidence and without any responsibility on our part.
In Beantwortung Ihrer Anfrage vom ... übersenden wir Ihnen hiermit die gewünschte Auskunft. Wir können hierfür jedoch keinerlei Verpflichtung übernehmen.	In response to your query of ... we are sending you the desired information, but cannot assume any obligation with regard to it / but without any obligation on our part.
Wir bitten Sie nachdrücklich, diese Information vertraulich zu behandeln.	This information is given on condition that it will be treated confidentially.

5 Declining information

Diese / Die in ihrem Schreiben genannte Firma ist uns unbekannt.	This firm / The firm mentioned in your letter is unknown to us.
Wir sind leider nicht in der Lage, Sie in dieser Sache zu beraten.	We feel that we are not in a position to advise you in this matter.
Wir bedauern, dass wir die von Ihnen erbetene Auskunft nicht geben können.	We regret that we are unable to give the information which you request.
Wir kennen die Firma nicht lang genug, und müssen Sie deshalb an ... verweisen.	We have not known the company long enough and must therefore refer you to ...

C Practising language

1 Match the terms 1–8 to a–j. There are two more items than you need.

1	allow credit	a	as strictly confidential
2	be obliged	b	be grateful
3	business prospects	c	business outlook
4	do business	d	financial situation
5	financial resources	e	funds
6	in business circles	f	grant credit
7	in strict confidence	g	in the trade
8	render a similar service	h	reciprocate
		i	reliable
		j	transact business

2 Choose the correct verb from the list below to complete the sentences and put the verbs in the appropriate tense.

> ask for | do | enjoy | establish | grant | inform | know | manage | name |
> offer | qualify for | recommend | settle | take on | understand

1 We … that your firm … to act as referee for the firm mentioned above.
2 Please … us how this company … its financial obligations.
3 The company … more business than it can handle.
4 We (not) … that you … them the credit they …
5 In the past the company always … its invoices promptly in order … the cash discounts.
6 The company … only a few months ago.
7 They … a good reputation in trade circles for as long as we … them.

3 Use appropriate expressions of caution, personal opinion, confidence to complete the sentences. There may be more than one correct answer.

> as far as we are concerned | as far as we know | in our opinion | in our view | is looked upon as | is regarded as | is said to be/have | it seems | rumours are circulating | to the best of our knowledge | we are pleased to confirm | we can assure you | we have heard | we think | we would suggest

1 … that this company always settled their invoices promptly.
2 In the trade this firm … a very reliable business partner.
3 … that the company is having difficulties in meeting its financial obligations.
4 … the firm is quite safe for a credit of €25,000.
5 … this firm is financially sound.
6 … that they have repeatedly approached suppliers to ask for an extension of credit.
7 … it would be advisable to act with caution in these particular circumstances.

4 Spot the 20 mistakes in this letter.

> Dear Ms Simpson
>
> We referred to the company mentioned in your letter of 24 March and are pleased to state that this firm is a medium-sised business which is well-known in the aera and highly respectable. They have been established in Bishop Auckland for more than twenty-fife years. As far as we know their business has been growing stedily and they have recently moved to much larger premices. We have little or no information about their fiancial standing.
> We ourselves have know been doing business with them for over ten years, invoice-baced initally, but with the gross of business we switched to quarterly-account terms. Also they have not as a rule taken advantage of cash discount, they have always settled their accounts promtly on the due dates. The credit we have alowed the firm has at times been well above the £10,000 you mention in your letter. On the basis of the aforsaid we think that you will not be running an unduly risk when granting them the credit they have asked for.
> We hope that this information will be usefull to you and ask you to treat it as strictly confidental.
>
> Yours sincerly

5 Say it in English.

1 Verweisen Sie auf den Namen eines potenziellen Kunden auf einem beigefügten Zettel. Dieser Kunde stellt einen größeren Auftrag in Aussicht, möchte aber ein längeres Zahlungsziel eingeräumt bekommen.
2 Sagen Sie, dass Ihre üblichen Zahlungsziele bei Neukunden Zahlung nach Rechnungserhalt sind. Erst nach einer längeren Geschäftstätigkeit gewähren Sie andere Zahlungsmodalitäten.
3 Bitten Sie um Informationen über die genannte Firma, insbesondere über Geschäftsumfang, Zahlungsverhalten und, soweit möglich, Kapitalausstattung.
4 Sie sichern eine vertrauliche Behandlung jeglicher Informationen zu und sind selbstverständlich zu Gegendiensten bereit. Bedanken Sie sich im Voraus für die Auskunft.
5 Beziehen Sie sich auf die Bitte um Auskunft und sagen Sie, dass Sie diese gern geben, da Sie mit der genannten Firma schon seit vielen Jahren erfolgreich zusammenarbeiten.
6 Teilen Sie mit, dass sich die Firma aus kleinen Anfängen recht gut entwickelt hat und von einer Geschäftsführung geleitet wird, die die sich bietenden Marktchancen zu nutzen versteht.
7 Sagen Sie auch, dass das Unternehmen nach Ihrer Information über eine gesunde Kapitalstruktur verfügt und ihre Rechnungen immer pünktlich unter Ausnutzung der eingeräumten Skonti bezahlt.

Listening comprehension

6 Listen to the dialogue on the CD and then do the task.
Write a summary in German of the telephone conversation for Ann's German boss.

D Letter writing

1 Write a credit enquiry from the notes below.

> financial standing | large initial order | new customer | reliability |
> James Sharpe Giftware Inc., 81 Clair Street, Rumney, New Hampshire 06222, U.S.A |
> payment patterns | quoted as a reference | reciprocate |
> reputation in trade circles | request for generous payment terms |

2 Write a summary of the letter below.

> Gentlemen:
>
> We refer to your credit enquiry about James Sharpe Giftware Inc. and are pleased to inform you that we have been doing business with this company for quite a number of years now, and the volume of business has been increasing steadily. You will probably be aware that the core of the business is mail order with the over-the-counter trade only playing a minor role.
>
> In the last few years the company has been expanding into the e-commerce sector which seems the natural thing to do for a catalog company, but also involves some risks as we have seen from reports in the media. To what extent the sustained development of this type of activity will soak up capital remains to be seen, especially in the difficult economic environment at present.
>
> We have no information about their financial standing, but are pleased to report that in their dealings with us there has never been any problem. In view of the volume of business they are placing with us we have agreed to open-account terms with quarterly settlement. They have always settled their invoices when due. In our judgment you would be safe to grant them the kind of credit they are asking for.
>
> This information is given without any liability on our part, and we trust you will treat it with discretion. We wish you every success in your dealings with this company.
>
> Sincerely yours,

3 Write a request for information from these notes.

Portland Pen Co. Inc., 99 Vannah Ave, Portland, Maine 01556 wendet sich an Sven Rasmussen, Verkaufsleiter bei Business Equipment Inc., 1450 E. Las Olas, Fort Lauderdale FL 33444, um Informationen über einen neuen Kunden einzuholen.

United Office Supplies in 55 Mileta Ave, Burlington, Mass 01777 stellen regelmäßig größere Aufträge in Aussicht und möchten zur Verwaltungsvereinfachung möglichst quartalsweise abrechnen, wie sie dies auch bei ihren anderen Lieferanten tun.

Für den Verkaufsleiter von Portland Pen Co., Inc. bereiten Sie eine unterschriftsfähige Kreditanfrage an Business Equipment Inc. vor, die als Referenz angegeben war.

4 Write a letter from notes.

Die Firma Stürmer Maschinentechnik GmbH, Darmstadt hat der Midland Pumps Ltd, 55–57 Carlisle Street, Coventry, CV4 2HE, einen Erstauftrag über €16.750,00 mit der Bitte um dreimonatiges Zahlungsziel erteilt. Als Referenz ist u. a. Altenbrunner Maschinenbau GmbH & Co., Dieselstr. 18, 68723 Schwetzingen, angegeben. Midland Pumps richtet ein Schreiben an Firma Altenbrunner mit der Bitte um vertrauliche Auskunft, insbesondere im Hinblick auf die Zahlungsgepflogenheiten von Stürmer Maschinentechnik, da es sich um einen umfangreichen Erstauftrag handelt.

> **Aufgabe**
> Verfassen Sie für den Geschäftsführer der Firma Altenbrunner Maschinenbau GmbH unter Berücksichtigung folgender Punkte ein Antwortschreiben an Midland Pumps Ltd.:
> - seit mehreren Jahren gute Geschäftsbeziehung mit Stürmer Maschinentechnik GmbH
> - Aufträge etwa dreimal jährlich jeweils ca. €3.000,00 bis €5.000,00
> - Zahlungseingang bisher problemlos, Ausnutzung von Skonti
> - letzte 3 Rechnungen allerdings erst nach mehreren Mahnungen beglichen
> - Einzelheiten über finanzielle Situation nicht bekannt
> - wahrscheinlich branchenbedingte schwierige Geschäftslage, deshalb evtl. zu großer Lagerbestand
> - laut Informationen Kreditanträge von zwei Banken abgelehnt, aber Bankenkredite an Mittelständler (*small and medium-sized enterprises*) zur Zeit ohnehin problematisch
> - Vorschlag: auf Barzahlung bei Lieferung bestehen
> - keine Gewähr für Auskunft, vertrauliche Behandlung

5 Write a letter from notes

Der Textilhersteller Wattex GmbH, Bochumer Str. 16, 44866 Bochum hat von dem britischen Textilhändler Britaintext Ltd, 47 East Drive, Huddersfield, HD8 1RT eine Bitte um eine Kreditauskunft bzgl. seines neuen Kunden Sieler & Co KG, Flensburger Str. 27, 24340 Eckernförde erhalten, der einen ersten umfangreichen Auftrag mit einem Warenwert von €4.500,00 auf 60 Tage Ziel erteilen möchte.

> **Aufgabe**
> Beantworten Sie die per Fax erbetene Auskunft ebenfalls per Fax unter Berücksichtigung folgender Punkte:
> - Sieler & Co KG eine alteingesessene Firma, offenkundig Familienbetrieb, aber erst seit einigen Monaten Ihr Kunde
> - bisher Geschäftsvolumen vergleichsweise bescheiden
> - Größe des Auftrages überrascht
> - Geschäftsabwicklung insgesamt problemlos, Ausnutzung der Barzahlungsrabatte
> - vorgesehener Kreditrahmen recht groß
> - Kapitalausstattung nicht bekannt
> - Vorschlag: sicherere Zahlungsbedingungen
> - Bitte um Vertraulichkeit

6 Write a reply to this email.

> A new customer of ours, Henze Waermetechnik GmbH in Rostock have asked for open account facilities and mentioned your name as a reference. At the moment we are somewhat reluctant to agree to their request as we have only just begun trading with them. We would be glad if you could provide some information on the scope of their business activities, their reputation and their payment behaviour. It goes without saying that any information you can give us will be strictly confidential. We thank you for your help in this matter and look forward to hearing from you.

Aufgabe
Beantworten Sie diese Kreditanfrage unter Berücksichtigung folgender Punkte:
- Bisher nur geringer Kontakt mit dem Unternehmen
- Junges Unternehmen mit schnellem Wachstum
- Gründer selbst aktiv und offenkundig recht erfolgreich
- Ursprünglich lokal aktiv, jetzt Ausweitung in die Region
- Gerätepark auf dem neuesten Stand
- Keine Informationen über Finanzstatus, angeblich umfangreiche Bankkredite
- Längerfristige Zahlungsziele bevorzugt
- Vorsicht zweckmäßig
- Keine Gewähr für Richtigkeit der Informationen

7 Write a reply to this letter.

> Information about Bremer Import-Export GmbH
>
> Gentlemen:
> Your name was given to us as a reference by the company mentioned above and we would like to ask you to let us have any information available about that company. As a trading company we import German food products and export American food products on a large scale.
> We are currently negotiating an important export contract for Californian wines with them. As the order volume is likely to be substantial we are, of course, interested in getting as much information about our prospective trading partner as possible. We would be particularly keen to know about their business practices, their credit standing and their payment habits.
> Your information will, of course, be treated in the strictest confidence and we shall be pleased to reciprocate if the occasion arises.
> We thank you in advance for your assistance in the matter and we look forward to hearing from your soon.

Aufgabe
Beantworten Sie dies Schreiben unter Berücksichtigung folgender Punkte:
- Langjährige Geschäftsbeziehung
- Geringer aber ständig wachsender Umsatz
- Offenkundig erfolgreich arbeitendes Unternehmen
- Dem Vernehmen nach Aktivitäten mit verschiedenen Großkunden
- Korrekt im geschäftlichen Umgang
- Rechnungsbegleichung prompt unter Ausnutzung der Skonti
- Keine Gewähr für Richtigkeit der Informationen

E Useful words

potenzieller Kunde	prospective customer
langjähriger Kunde	long-standing customer
Geschäftsverkehr	business dealings
zuverlässige Auskunft	reliable information
Auskunft einholen	to take up a reference
Ruf	reputation
Zuverlässigkeit	reliability
Auskunftei	credit reference/status agency
Auskunft über ihre Kreditwürdigkeit und Zuverlässigkeit	information on the credit status and reliability
Geschäftsgebaren	business conduct
Finanzmittel	financial resources, means
Zahlungsverpflichtungen	financial obligations
Zahlungsfähigkeit	ability to meet financial obligations
finanzielle Lage, Vermögenslage	financial standing/status
Kreditwürdigkeit	credit standing/status, creditworthiness
ohne Stellung von Sicherheiten	without security
offenes Zahlungsziel, Kontokorrentbedingungen	open account terms
Zahlung bei Rechnungserhalt	payment on invoice
Anzahlung	payment on account
langfristiges Zahlungsziel	deferred payment terms
Bitte um Kreditgewährung	request for credit
einer Bitte entsprechen	to comply with a request
Kreditrahmen, Kreditlinie	credit line
Kredit/längerfristiges Zahlungsziel einräumen	to allow/grant credit
Gegendienste leisten, Gefälligkeit erwidern	to reciprocate
Zahlungsgewohnheiten	payment performance/habits
Zahlungsverhalten	payment pattern
Konkurs	bankruptcy
konkurs, pleite	bankrupt
Zahlungsfähigkeit	solvency
zahlungsfähig, liquide	solvent
Insolvenz, Zahlungsunfähigkeit	insolvency
zahlungsunfähig, illiquide	insolvent
Konkurs anmelden	to file for bankruptcy
vertrauliche Auskunft	confidential information
streng vertraulich	strictly confidential, in the strictest confidence, with the strictest discretion
unverbindlich	without obligation
ohne Gewähr	without liability

Looking for a job

Model letters: a British-style letter of application, a British-style CV, an American-style letter of application, an American-style CV, an unsolicited application

Useful phrases: introduction – source of information and application; information about qualifications; motivation and reasons for application / job change; closing paragraph (enclosures, invitation for an interview)

Information about job vacancies can be obtained from a variety of sources: job advertisements (daily/weekly papers and some specialist magazines), job exchanges on the internet and company websites, employment/recruitment agencies (esp. in English-speaking countries), government-run offices (in Britain the "Jobcentre"), word of mouth information from personal contacts, career centres in educational establishments or company notice-boards.

It is quite common for British and American companies to roughly indicate the salary that can be expected (often in the short form of c.€20K, i.e. in the range of €20,000 per annum excluding benefits). Very often a telephone number and the name of a contact person (frequently just the first name) at the end of the advertisement allows candidates to get additional information about the job and to ask for an application form.

Job applications are mostly sent in reply to an advertisement offering a particular job (**solicited application**). But job seekers do also take the initiative and send an **unsolicited application** hoping their qualifications will be considered when a vacancy arises.

The application documents include the **letter of application** and possibly the **application form**, the **CV** (**curriculum vitae**) and relevant **documents** and **testimonials**. These make up the candidate's profile which are his/her most important 'selling tool' at the first stage of the selection process, i.e. until the selectors have made up a shortlist of candidates they want to interview.

Letter of application/cover letter

Together with the CV, the letter of application (or cover letter) is the candidate's most important "selling tool" and needs to convince the reader of his/her qualifications and suitability for the job advertised. Therefore it must be well presented (layout, font), well structured (paragraphs, logic of thought and language), convincing (genuine interest) in order to arouse interest (content) and lead to action (short-listing of candidate).

The text itself must not be too long (15 to 20 lines), ideally arranged in three to four paragraphs covering the following points:

1. source of information and application
2. job-specific qualifications
3. motivation and/or suitability for the job
4. availability for the interview and contact.

CV (curriculum vitae)

The CV provides full information about the candidate: personal background, education, qualifications, experience and skills, interests. The information is usually presented in tabular form under the following or similar headings: personal data, education, job training and experience, further qualifications and skills, interests.

In English-speaking countries, the CV is not signed or dated. A photo is usually omitted. For reasons of possible discrimination Americans are not obliged to reveal age, sex, family status, skin colour or religious belief when applying for a job in their country. Americans arrange the information in reverse chronological order and also usually state their career goal below their personal data (name and address).

As candidates get older and work experience takes up more space, the section on the candidate's education will tend to become shorter. In Anglo-American CVs, references are mentioned either by saying that these can be supplied upon request or by giving the names and addresses of two referees who are prepared to say something about the candidate's character, abilities and qualifications. The 'Interests' section provides some indirect information on the applicant's personality (social skills, team orientation etc.) and obviously requires careful consideration as regards the 'image' certain activities of the candidate may project.

As in the cover letter the information should be presented with the reader very much in mind. This goes for content (the CV should be comprehensive, but not state every detail) and length. There are no hard and fast rules as to the layout.

**Temporary Bilingual Senior Secretaries
City £Excellent**

We have a number of superb opportunities for first class Bilingual Senior Secretaries. Working for this major U.S. Bank, your organisational skills and experience at Director level (preferably within the banking industry) will be utilised fully. With fluency in either French, German or Spanish (ideally mother tongue), excellent communication skills and the ability to work under pressure, you will be keen to secure a long term assignment. Proficiency in W4W, shorthand 100 wpm, and copy typing speed of 60 wpm are essential and will be rewarded with excellent rates of pay by this professional organisation. Call 020 7638 7003

SENIOR SECRETARY/PA
Required for small, friendly, hectic Interior Design office. Needs to be flexible, have initiative and work well under pressure. Must have shorthand, German and/or French an advantage. Send CV to: Nina Campbell, 9 Walton Street SW3 3JD

TELESALES MARKETING
(FULL AND PART TIME)

We are market leaders in our field with a current customer database of 2000 companies. We are looking for experienced telesales people (6 months minimum) with a proven track record to work either full time 9.30 a.m. to 5 p.m. or flexi part time hours. If you also have good communicative skills and are computer literate, write or give me a call to find out more about this excellent opportunity and to arrange an interview.
Sales Director, Fireplace Factors Ltd., Design House, Walnut Tree Close, Guildford GU1 4UQ. Tel. (01483) 568777

In the three advertisements above find out:

1 what the requirements are,
2 what the job is,
3 what the company says about itself,
4 what the compensation is,
5 how you can apply.

Abbreviations in job advertisements

bens	benefits
c.	circa
HQ	headquarters
HR	human resources
IT	information technology
pa	per annum
PA	personal assistant
W4W	word for windows
wpm	words per minute

A Model letters

1 A British-style letter of application

Here is Ingmar Kösters' letter of application to Bowman International plc for a job as Key Account Manager.

> Ingmar D. Kösters
> 27 Church Street
> Waterlooville
> Hants
> PO14 5BT
>
> Bowman International plc
> HR Dept.
> Kilburn High Road
> London NW6 7JR
>
> 27 August 20..
>
> Dear Sir or Madam
>
> **Application for post of Key Account Manager (Europe)**
>
> In response to your recent job listing on your website, I am sending you my personal profile as an attachment. I hope you will consider my application for the post of Key Account Manager (Europe).
>
> With a degree in Business Administration from Cologne University and more than 3 years experience in sales functions (1 year with a Portsmouth-based manufacturing company) I feel I fully meet your requirements. In my current function as account manager, I am responsible for developing existing business contacts abroad. As a native German with considerable exposure to an English-speaking environment, I also have some knowledge of French and Spanish.
>
> In the position you advertise on your website I would like to develop my potential as a successful customer relationship manager and establish new business contacts, thus contributing to the continued growth of your company.
>
> My track record to date is well documented in my personal profile. If there is any further information you may require to shortlist me as one of the possible candidates for the advertised post you can contact me under ingmarkoesters@cellnet.com or 07802 345123.
>
> I would welcome the opportunity of a personal interview and look forward to hearing from you.
>
> Thank you for your time and consideration.
>
> Yours faithfully
>
> *Ingmar D. Kösters*
>
> Enclosure

List the main points of this letter.

2 A British-style CV

Study Ingmar's CV and find out how it is different from CVs that you have seen.

Ingmar D. Kösters
27 Church Street
Waterlooville
Hants PO14 5BT
Tel: 07802 345123
ingmarkoesters@cellnet.com

Career objective:	Responsible position in sales/customer relationship function with international customer base
Personal data:	Born 19 September 19.. German national Single
Qualifcations:	Abitur (A-level equivalent) with Mathematics and English as main and German and History as subsidiary subjects (average grade: 2.3) (1993) Course in Economics at Cologne University 1994–2000 Exchange student at Leeds University 1996–1997 Diploma examination in Business Administration with Marketing, Finance and Controlling as felds of specialisation (fnal grade: 2.7) (2000)

Work experience	2-3 month practicals with
	  – Schubert GmbH in Cologne 1994 (general office work)
	  – Mayer & Co KG in Neuss 1995 (distribution)
	  – Fowler Ltd in Bradford 1997 (logistics & warehousing)
	  – Baines & Sons Ltd in Leeds 1998 (sales)
	2000-2002 Sales clerk at Preuss Maschinen GmbH, Düsseldorf, responsible for customer group based in Germany & Benelux countries
	2002 to present Account Manager at Marine Engineering Ltd in Portsmouth, responsible for development of French customer base

Military service:	1993-1994 in German Air Force
Other skills:	Languages: German (native) English (near native) French (fairly fluent) Spanish (fair) PC-literate (common software applications) Clean driving licence
Interests:	Foreign languages and cultures, travelling, ball sports

References available upon request

Find the information in the CV.

1 Describe in which field Ingmar would like to work.
2 Say in which field he specialised during his studies.
3 List the areas in which he obtained some practical experience.
4 Say in which areas he worked with customers.
5 List his language skills.

3 An American-style letter of application

Jennifer Pelham applies for the post of a bilingual secretary. She uses a combination of a cover letter and an executive briefing.

JENNIFER PELHAM
5698 SOUTHMORE ROAD, PEORIA HEIGHTS, ILLINOIS 61234
e-mail: pelhamjenny@aol.com   Tel.: 0866-665 9330

24 March 20..

P. D. Staples
Recruitment Officer
International Packaging Inc.
124 W. Lincoln Ave
Detroit, MI 48226-0876

Dear Ms Staples:

I am writing in response to your recent advertisement in the Morning Herald soliciting résumés for the post of bilingual secretary/PA. Please accept this letter and accompanying résumé as evidence of my interest in applying for that position with your company.

My enclosed résumé clearly shows I have qualifying skills and abilities compatible with this position. Briefly, they are:
– A formal university education augmented and refined by specialised secretarial training,
– Considerable industry-related experience in a similar capacity in a German-language environment,
– A proven record of success achieved through diligence, hard work, attention to detail, and my belief in a consistent application of the fundamentals, and
– A sincere desire to contribute to the continued growth and success of your company.

After you have had the opportunity to review my résumé I would like to meet with you to discuss how effectively I can contribute. Should you have any questions before scheduling an appointment I may be reached through the number listed above.

Thank you very much for taking the time to review my résumé and for your kind consideration. I look forward to speaking with you in the near future.

Sincerely,

Jennifer Pelham

Jennifer Pelham
Enclosures

4 An American-style CV

JENNIFER PELHAM
5698 SOUTHMORE ROAD, PEORIA HEIGHTS, ILLINOIS 61234
e-mail: pelhamjenny@aol.com   Tel.: 0866-665 9330

PROFESSIONAL PROFILE
- Extensive exposure to foreign language environment (German and French) in European industrial companies
- Bi-lingual through parentage (German mother)
- University education in foreign languages
- Sophisticated secretarial skills acquired in further education and enhanced in field work
- Highly developed communication and PC skills
- Team worker with self-starting qualities, pleasant personality, hard-working, well organized

CAREER DEVELOPMENT

Senior Secretary   2003 to present
at international desk of Wing Publications, Belleville, Ill
handle multiple office responsibilities, arrange meetings, deal with general administration, time management, keep appointments diary, maintain contacts with contributors/authors, deal with national and international correspondence, do occasional translation and interpreting work

Secretary   2001 to 2003
in busy sales department at Swanson and Taylor Inc., Belleville, Ill
deal with general office work, copywriting, proofreading of sales literature, do some translation work for German language publications

Foreign-language secretary   1999 to 2001
in project development dept. of major German engineering company
handle international correspondence (English-German-French), deal with some translation work of basic technical matter, process customer enquiries and draft sales letters, general office work

EDUCATION AND ACTIVITIES
Bachelor of Arts in German (Major) and French (Minor), Minnesota State University   1999
Au-pair work in Paris   1999 to 2000
(Certificat pratique de la langue française: Mention: bien)
Belleville College Diploma (1 yr Secretarial Training)   2000 to 2001
Team leader in Belleville Youth Club   since 1998

References available upon request

Study Jennifer Pelham's cover letter and CV and list the differences to the British CV.

Letter plan for a solicited application

- Refer to the advertisement / State source of information.
- Say which position you are applying for.
- Briefly list your relevant qualifications and experience.
- State why you are applying for the post and what 'added value' you have to offer.
- Refer to the enclosures.
- Say how you can be contacted.
- Express your hope for an invitation for an interview.
- Close with a polite ending.

5 An unsolicited application

Steve Donovan takes the initiative and applies for a position in marketing.

Dear Ms Fitzpatrick

APPLICATION FOR VACANCY IN INTERNATIONAL MARKETING

Recently I have been researching the leading local companies engaged in foreign trade activities. My search has been for companies that are respected and innovative in their field and show growth potential. I have covered the relevant websites in the internet, local and regional press, the Chamber of Commerce and the jobcentre. Your site provided highly interesting information about the activities of your company. So I followed it up with the Chamber of Commerce where I was also given your name.

If you are planning any appointments in marketing in the near future I would like you to consider my application. I am a fully-qualified marketing graduate from Nottingham University and have two years experience in the marketing department of a major group in the logistics sector. Prior to my appointment as marketing specialist I did a twelve month traineeship with this company covering the following areas: sales, controlling, human resources and marketing. Business contacts in my job involve a high degree of exposure to foreign business partners, the majority of them from the Continent.

Being a self-driven proactive person and an experienced team player I would like to develop, test and implement strategies that will contribute to above average business growth. For further details please refer to the enclosed CV.

I hope that my qualifications and experience will be of interest and look forward to examining any of the ways you feel my background and skills would benefit J. Allan Exports Ltd. Thank you for your time and consideration. You can reach me at 0191 223 3344 or by e-mail under steviedonovan@cellnet.com to initiate contact. I look forward to your reply with interest.

Yours sincerely

Steve Donovan

Steve Donovan
Enclosure

Complete this checklist.

Source of information: ...
Education: ...
Work experience: ...
Export-related qualifications: ...
Present employer: ...
Contact: ...

Letter plan for an unsolicited application

- ☐ Say why you are applying with the particular company and for what kind of post.
- ☐ State that you wish your application to be considered irrespective of a vacancy being available.
- ☐ All other points as in the standard cover letter.

B Useful phrases

1 Introduction – Source of information and application

Ihrer Anzeige vom … in … entnehme ich, dass Sie … suchen / eine freie Stelle für … haben.	From your advertisement of … in the … I see that you have a vacancy for a(n) …
Unter Bezugnahme auf Ihre Anzeige in der heutigen Ausgabe von … möchte ich …	Referring to / With reference to your advertisement in today's issue of … I would like …
Ihre Stellenanzeige im / in … für … habe ich mit großem Interesse gelesen.	It was with great interest that I read your advertisement in the … for …
Auf Ihrer Internet-Seite habe ich gesehen, dass Sie die Stelle einer/eines … zu besetzen haben.	From your company website I note that you are inviting applications for the post of …
Auf Ihrer Webseite habe ich Ihr Stellenangebot gesehen.	I am responding to your recent job listing on your website.
In der Internet-Jobbörse habe ich mit Interesse gesehen, dass …	From the Internet job exchange I note with interest that …
Mit diesem Schreiben möchte ich mich um die Stelle als Projektleiter bewerben, die Sie heute in der / im … ausgeschrieben haben.	I am writing to apply for the post of project manager, as advertised in today's issue of …
Für die Stelle als … möchte ich mich bewerben.	I wish to apply for the post of …
Ich suche eine Stelle auf dem Gebiet …	I am looking for a post in …
Hiermit möchte ich mich nach der Möglichkeit einer Mitarbeit in Ihrer Firma erkundigen.	I am writing to inquire about the possibility of working for your company.
Ich bin an einer Tätigkeit als … interessiert und wüsste gern, ob Sie eine entsprechende Stelle anzubieten haben.	I would be interested to learn/know whether you have a vacancy for …
Nach Abschluss meines Studium der … suche ich nun nach einer Trainee-Stelle in der …-Branche.	Having graduated from … with a degree in … I am now looking for a traineeship in the … industry.

2 Information about qualifications

Aus dem beigefügten Lebenslauf ersehen Sie, … / Wie Sie aus dem beigefügten Lebenslauf ersehen, …	As you will see from the enclosed curriculum vitae / résumé … / From the enclosed curriculum vitae / résumé you will see …
Ich bin mit dieser Arbeit sehr vertraut.	I have considerable experience of this kind of work.
Ich glaube, dass ich die Anforderungen dieser Stelle erfüllen kann.	I feel that I can meet the requirements of this post.

..., dass ich die erforderliche Ausbildung und Kompetenz für die Stelle als ... mitbringe.	... I have the necessary training and qualities needed for the post of ...
Ich bin gegenwärtig bei einer Exportfirma beschäftigt.	I am currently working for an export firm.
Zur Zeit arbeite ich als Projekt-Koordinator bei ..., die auf ... spezialisiert sind.	At present, I am working as a project co-ordinator at ... that specialises in ...
Während der letzten fünf Jahre war ich bei ... als ... beschäftigt.	For the past five years I have been employed with ... as a ...
Seit drei Jahren bin ich bei ... beschäftigt und habe wertvolle Erfahrung in ... gesammelt.	I have been working at ... for three years now and gained valuable experience in ...
Ich war verantwortlich für ...	I was responsible for... / in charge of ...
Ich bin in ... qualifiziert.	I have a diploma / qualifications in ...
Ich habe Prüfungen in ... bestanden..	... where I passed the following examinations: ...
..., wo ich... als Hauptfach studierte mit ... als Nebenfach.	... where I studied ... as my main subject / my major and ... as my subsidiary subject / my minor.
Ich wurde zu ... befördert.	I was promoted to ...
Ich wurde als Fremdsprachensekretär/in ausgebildet.	I was trained as a bilingual secretary.
Fünf Jahre lang habe ich in einer ähnlichen Funktion gearbeitet.	I have been working in a comparable job for five years and have ...
Es gehört zu meinen Aufgaben, jährlich acht Projekte zu betreuen.	I am responsible for overseeing approximately eight projects each year.
Ebenso wichtig ist es, dass ich mit Menschen gut auskomme, engen Kontakt zu Kunden pflege und ...	As important, I need to work well with people – liaising with clients and ...

3 Motivation and reasons for application / job change

Ich möchte meine Fremdsprachenkenntnisse anwenden.	I wish to make use of my knowledge of languages.
Gern möchte ich neue Verantwortung in einer anspruchsvollen Stellung übernehmen.	I am eager to take on new responsibilities in a challenging post.
Ich bin sehr daran interessiert, meine Kenntnisse auf dem Gebiet / im Bereich von ... zu vertiefen.	I am keen to broaden my knowledge in the field of ...
Bisher habe ich Kunden vor Ort betreut. Ich möchte mich nun weiter entwickeln und für Kunden auf nationaler und internationaler Ebene tätig sein.	I am looking to progress from working on local accounts to those of a national and international nature.

Die ausgeschriebene Stelle gibt mir Gelegenheit dazu.	Your job offers me the opportunity to do this.
Gern übernehme ich Verantwortung und freue mich auf die Herausforderung durch neue Situationen.	I like responsibility and enjoy the challenge of new situations.
Ich möchte für ein größeres Unternehmen mit internationalen Beziehungen arbeiten.	I wish to work for a larger organisation with international connections.
… , um meine Berufschancen zu verbessern.	… to improve my career prospects.
Ich suche eine Stelle mit mehr Verantwortung.	I am looking for a position with more responsibility.

4 Closing paragraph (enclosures, invitation for an interview)

In der Anlage habe ich die Zeugnisse von … und die im Lebenslauf angeführten Referenzen beigefügt.	Enclosed are copies of testimonials by … and the references given in the résumé.
In der Anlage finden Sie die Namen von zwei Personen, die bereit sind, Auskunft über mich zu geben.	The names of two referees/references are given below.
Bei Bedarf gebe ich Ihnen gern weitere Auskünfte. / Für weitere Fragen stehe ich Ihnen gern zur Verfügung.	I should be pleased/happy to provide you with any further information / any other details you may require.
Beigefügt / In der Anlage finden Sie ein Exemplar meines Lebenslaufs, aus dem Sie weitere Einzelheiten über meine Qualifikationen / meinen bisherigen Werdegang entnehmen können.	You will find enclosed/attached a copy of my curriculum vitae which will give you further particulars / more complete details of my qualifications / career to date.
Über eine Einladung zu einem Vorstellungsgespräch würde ich mich (sehr) freuen.	I would greatly appreciate being given the opportunity of an interview.
Bei dieser Gelegenheit könnte ich Ihnen dann meine Qualifikationen näher erläutern.	… when I can explain my qualifications more fully.
Für ein Vorstellungsgespräch stehe ich jederzeit zur Verfügung.	I can come to an interview / to be interviewed at any time.
Falls Sie mich zu einem Vorstellungsgespräch einladen möchten, …	Should you wish to invite me for an interview …
Ich bitte Sie, meine Bewerbung wohlwollend zu prüfen/berücksichtigen.	I hope that you will consider my application favourably.
Ich bitte Sie, meine Bewerbung und Korrespondenz streng vertraulich zu behandeln, bis …	I ask you to treat my application and correspondence as strictly confidential until …
In Erwartung einer günstigen/positiven Antwort / In der Hoffnung auf eine günstige/ positive Antwort verbleibe ich …	Hoping for / Anticipating a favourable reply, I remain …

UNIT 10 Looking for a job

C Practising language

1 Match the terms in box A with the appropriate definitions in box B. There are more items than you need.

A
1 ability to enter data into the computer
2 able to do basic maths
3 able to work with a computer
4 current stage of development in technology
5 description of the work content
6 list of persons working in rotation and their periods of work
7 motivation to achieve sth.
8 non-cash parts of the pay package (company car, business class travel)
9 person with a university degree
10 required as a condition for sth.
11 speaking a language very well
12 taking the initiative

B
a computer-literate
b drive
c fluent
d graduate calibre
e job profile
f keyboard skills
g negotiating skills
h numerate
i perks
j prerequisite
k proactive
l rota
m state-of-the-art
n telephone manners

2 Fill in the prepositional phrases below.

advertisement for | candidate for that post | capable of communicating | during my studies | for a number of years | for my present employer | for quite some time | from the attached documents | in a foreign market | in a team-oriented environment | looking for a new challenge | manager for software products | of my abilities | to the opportunity | visits to European and Asian customers

Gentlemen:

Your ... [1] an international sales ... [2] in yesterday's issue of New York Times attracted my attention and I would like to be considered as a ... [3]. I believe that I have the relevant qualifications and experience to meet your requirements.
As you will see ... [4] I have been working in an international environment ... [5]. ... [6] of Information Technology at Texas A & M I attended classes in German and French and am ... [7] quite well in these languages. My work ... [8] involved regular contacts with and frequent ... [9].
Having worked as a product manager ... [10] I am now ... [11] in the field of IT products. As I have always felt comfortable ... [12] I feel that I am capable and experienced enough to lead a small team of sales staff ... [13].
I would be quite happy to provide any further information you may require and look forward ... [14] of an interview where I would hope to convince you ... [15].

Sincerely yours,

3 Link the incomplete sentences 1–8 with the appropriate section a–j to form meaningful sentences. There are two more items than you need.

1 It is with great interest that …
2 Having just completed my training as foreign language secretary at the Carshalton College …
3 As will see from the enclosed CV …
4 During my three month practical at the Logica office in Leatherhead …
5 I am confident that with my experience in door-to-door selling …
6 I attended courses at the Boston Academy for Adult Education …
7 After graduating from high school I spent two years working in France and Germany …
8 I hope that you will find my qualifications and skills useful for your business …

a … and look forward to being invited to an interview.
b … I can make a useful contribution to the success of your telesales team.
c … I hold a general degree in French and German from Thames University.
d … I read your advertisement for the post of account manager in today's issue of the Yorkshire Post.
e … I was able to further develop my secretarial and administrative skills.
f … I wish to apply for the advertised post of PA to the export manager.
g … in order to get some practical marketing experience in an English-language environment.
h … and as a result I am now fairly fluent in both languages.
i … to further upgrade my computer literacy and keyboarding skills.
j … where I enrolled for a course in business administration.

4 Arrange the sentences of this cover letter in the right order.

Dear Madam, dear Sir

a Although the university course was largely literature-oriented, I feel that it has greatly enhanced my analytical and linguistic skills.
b As part of the course I spent my third year as a Socrates exchange student in Bochum and Orléans where I also attended classes in Business German and Business French.
c During my four year course at Strathclyde University I read German and French Language and Literature and I graduated with a Joint Honours degree in both these subjects.
d Enclosed you will find my complete personal profile and also two references.
e I note with interest from the careers office at Strathclyde University that you are recruiting graduates with an honours degree in foreign languages.
f I am available to come for an interview at any time and look forward to hearing from you.
g I am sure that the trainee programme described on your website will provide me with the necessary business background and help me to contribute more effectively to the tasks of an international organisation such as yours.
h I would like you to consider my application for one of these posts.
i If there is any further information you require do not hesitate to contact me under 01372 584321.
j In my holidays I gained some practical experience working for companies in my home town so I am familiar with the basic secretarial duties.

Yours faithfully

UNIT 10 Looking for a job

D Letter writing

1 Use the information below to write a British-style CV.

- 2 years secretarial college in Slough, diploma
- 5 years comprehensive school, O-levels in English, French, History, Geography, Maths
- born 31 March 1980, single, British

e-mail katevince@btconnect.com

Interests: Travelling, Jazz, Aerobics

July 1998–August 2000 junior secretary at Ride and Drive Surrey Ltd, Slough

Kate Vince, 3 Newlands Drive, Slough, Berkshire SL3 5DX, Tel. 01753 678912

September 2000–August 2003 Secretary at Thew, Arnott & Co, Ltd., Wallington/Surrey

Since September 2003 secretary/PA at Newsquest Ltd, North Cheam/Surrey

Skills: good keyboarding (70 wpm), shorthand (100 wpm), computer-literate, good communication skills

2 Use the information below to write an American-style CV.

Rearrange the information found below, add a time schedule and provide a suitable layout to complete the CV.

> Additional References and related data available on request
> **Education:** B.A. Economics, Montana State University (3 years); M.A. Business Administration, Michigan, State University (2 years), Major: Marketing, Minor: Media Studies
> Kathleen B. Ferrer, 75 South Union Ave, Colorado Springs, CO 80218, (719) 666 7020
> **Objective:** Business Administration, graduate seeking a position in a major company where I can augment my knowledge of theory with practical experience and gain understanding and expertise in the area of marketing policy and distribution. Outstanding young woman, intelligent, capable and hard-working ... well respected by her peers, a team member, a natural leader who has my personal recommendation (Head of Human Resources at Philip Stuyvesandt)
> **Personal & interests:** Languages: French - fair; Spanish - beginner. Personality: friendly, communicative, team-oriented. Interests: Reading, travelling, swimming, charity work.
> **Professional experience:** Work placement with Master Sweets Inc. (3 months) - back office support for field sales team, telephone contacts, data gathering, preparing charts, compiling statistics, data analysis, comprehensive use of PC; work placement with Philip Stuyvesandt (3 months) - public relations dept.: assisting with preparation for fair displays, editing & proof-reading sales literature, contacts with printers and layouters, copywriting, extensive use of diverse software applications
> **Selected references:** professional in manner and approach; ... well educated, articulate; committed and goal-focused (Head of department at Master Sweets Inc.)

3 **Study this advertisement and write a cover letter for your application. Use the information in Exercise 1.**

> ☞ **PA TO MANAGING DIRECTOR of Surrey-based Marketing Company**
>
> Supportive right hand is required to assist in reorganising all aspects of the company.
> Large volume of marketing to world wide client base requires care and attention to detail. The company is involved in a competitive business that is run in an informal yet professional manner.
> Computer literacy will be an asset. However a caring and quality conscious approach is essential.
> The successful applicant will be rewarded with an excellent remuneration package. Please reply to Box No. 9218, PO Box 3553, Virginia Street London E1 9GA enclosing full CV.

4 **Write a cover letter.**

Use the information in Ex. 2 on page 138 to write a cover letter for an application for a graduate traineeship with an American employer. Add any details that may seem important to you.

5 **Study this advertisement and write a letter of application and a CV.**

> Wir sind ein internationales, in den USA börsennotiertes Unternehmen für Outsourcing Services der IT-Bereiche. Zu unseren Aktivitäten gehören unter anderem technische Übersetzungen sowie Software-Lokalisierung. Für unsere expandierende Niederlassung in Leuven (Großraum Brüssel, Belgien) suchen wir einen
>
> # Technischen Übersetzer (m/w) Englisch — Deutsch
>
> Sie sind deutscher Muttersprachler und haben eine sprachverwandte Ausbildung (Übersetzer, Anglist, Germanist o. ä.) abgeschlossen und kennen sich mit PC-Produkten gut aus. Kenntnisse in der Anwendung von Übersetzungsprogrammen (z.B. Trados) sind ein Pluspunkt. Sie sprechen fließend Englisch und haben Spaß an einer Tätigkeit im Ausland.
> **Wir bieten Ihnen:**
> – eine interessante vielseitige Tätigkeit, in der Sie tagtäglich mit Sprache und den brandneuesten PC-Produkten zu tun haben,
> – ein junges, dynamisches Team und eine offene, stimulierende Arbeitsumgebung,
> – Jobsicherheit und Aufstiegsmöglichkeiten in einem renommierten und aufsteigenden Unternehmen mit internationaler Präsenz,
> – ein angemessenes Gehaltspaket mit guten Sozialleistungen.
>
> Interesse? Dann senden Sie bitte umgehend die üblichen Bewerbungsunterlagen in englischer Sprache an: Soykes Belgium.
> Attn. Ms Deirdre Williams. Staatsbaan 5C1, 3210 Lubbeek, Belgien.
> Sie finden uns auch im Internet unter **www.soykes.com**

In your letter of application also mention the following points:
- graduate in English and French (Mainz-Germersheim)
- several stays abroad
- extensive part-time work for translation agency
- interest in PC applications and software development

E Useful words

Bewerbungsunterlagen, Bewerbungsmappe	personal profile
Lebenslauf	CV (curriculum vitae), résumé or resume, personal data sheet (PDS)
Familienname	family name, surname
Vorname	given/first/Christian name
Mädchenname	maiden name
Geburtsdatum	date of birth
Geburtsort	place of birth
geboren am	born on
Familienstand	family status
ledig	single
verheiratet	married
verwitwet	widowed
geschieden	divorced
Anschrift, Adresse	address
mit Sitz in London, in London ansässig	based in London, London-based
Erziehung, schulischer Werdegang	education
Bildungsgang; Schulbildung, Hochschulbildung	educational background
Primarstufe	primary education
Vorschule	infant school
Grundschule	junior/primary school
Sekundarstufe	secondary education
weiterführende Schule (Hauptschule, Realschule, Gymnasium)	secondary/high [US] school
Gesamtschule	comprehensive school
Schule / einen Kurs besuchen	to attend school / a course
von der Schule abgehen	to leave school
Abschlusszeugnis	school leaving certificate
zentrale staatliche Prüfung zum Abschluss der Sekundarstufe I	GCSE examination (general certificate of secondary education) [GB]
Abschlussprüfung bestehen (Sekundarstufe I)	to pass one's GCSEs [GB]
Abiturprüfung	*etwa:* A-level exam(inations)
Abitur/Reifeprüfung bestehen	*etwa:* to pass one's A-levels
Schulabschluss erreichen, Schule beenden	to graduate from high school [US]
Hauptfach, Leistungskurs	main subject, major [US]
Nebenfach, Grundkurs	subsidiary subject, minor [US]
Note	mark, grade
Zeugnis	certificate, report (*Schule, Hochschule*)
Bescheinigung, Zeugnis	testimonial, certificate (*Arbeitgeber*)
Hochschulbildung	higher/tertiary education
Universität	university
Fachhochschule	polytechnic [GB]
Fachschule; Akademie, Institut; (kleine) Universität, Kolleg	college
im Fach Wirtschaftswissenschaften sein Examen machen	to graduate in economics
Abschluss mit dem Hauptfach ... machen	to major in [US]

Abschluss mit dem Nebenfach ... machen	to minor in [US]
Hochschulabsolvent/in	graduate
Student/in in den ersten 3/4 Studienjahren	undergraduate
Student/in in einem weiterführenden Studiengang	post-graduate
erster akad. Grad (in Geisteswissenschaften)	B.A. (Bachelor of Arts)
erster akad. Grad (in Natur- oder Ingenieurwissenschaften)	B.Sc. (Bachelor of Science)
Magister (Geisteswissenschaften)	M.A. (Master of Arts)
Magister (in Natur- oder Ingenieurwisschenschaften)	M.Sc. (Master of Science)
Sekretärinnenschule	secretarial college
Berufsschule, Berufskolleg	vocational school
Berufsausbildung	vocational training
Berufsbildungsabschluss	vocational qualification
Weiterbildung, Fortbildung	further training
berufliche Fort-/Weiterbildung	in-service training
betriebliche Weiterbildung	in-house/in-company training
Berufsausbildung; Volontariat; Trainee-Ausbildung; Ausbildungsplatz (für kaufm. Berufe)	traineeship
Auszubildende/r, Azubi; Trainee, Volontär/in	trainee
Ausbildungsplatz im gewerblichen Bereich	apprenticeship
Lehrling, Auszubildende/r	apprentice
eine Lehre/Ausbildung machen	to serve an apprenticeship
Praktikum	internship, clerkship, practical
praktische Erfahrung, Berufserfahrung	job/work experience
beruflicher Werdegang, Berufslaufbahn	professional career
Berufs-, beruflich	occupational
Beruf (mit akad. Ausbildung)	profession
freiberuflich tätig sein	to work freelance
Freiberufler/in	freelancer
selbstständig sein	to be self-employed
Teilzeitarbeit	part-time work
Teilzeit/halbtags arbeiten	to work part-time
voll/ganztags arbeiten	to work full-time
Zeitarbeit	temping
Zeitarbeiter/in	temp
Zeitarbeit machen	to temp
Stellenvermittlung	employment agency
Arbeitsamt	*etwa:* job centre
Arbeitsvertrag	employment contract
Probezeit	probationary period
freiwillige Sozialleistungen (des Arbeitgebers)	fringe benefits
Vergütung	pay package
Gehalt	salary
Lohn	wage
bezahlter Urlaub	paid holiday
Urlaubsanspruch	holiday entitlement
Jahresurlaub	annual vacation [US]
Arbeitszeit	working hours
Wochenarbeitszeit von 37 Stunden	37 hour working week

Glossar

A

acceptance 1 *Annahme* 1. Annahme eines Angebots oder einer Ware/Leistung. 2. Annahme einer Tratte (**draft**), eines gezogenen Wechsels durch den Bezogenen (**drawee**), der sich damit zur Zahlung verpflichtet und somit Wechselschuldner (Akzeptant: **acceptor**) wird. 2 *Akzept* angenommener Wechsel.

account 1 *Konto* Bankkonto. 2 *Abrechnungskonto für einen Kunden*

account payable *zur Zahlung fälliger Betrag*

account (of) sales *Verkaufsabrechnung* Aufstellung des Vertreters an den Lieferanten über verkaufte Ware mit Angabe der erzielten Preise, des Reinerlöses (**net earnings**) nach Abzug von Fracht, Provisionen und sonstigen verkaufsbezogenen Kosten.

account terms *periodische Abrechnung* Kundenkonto, das bei Lieferungen belastet und periodisch abgerechnet wird.

advice note 1 *Versandanzeige* Mitteilung des Verkäufers an den Käufer, dass die bestellte Ware abgeschickt wurde. 2 *Benachrichtigung* Mitteilung über die Ausführung eines Auftrags (Dienstleistungsbereich, z. B. Bank).

after-sales service *Kundendienst* Dienstleistungen des Verkäufers nach dem Verkauf, z. B. Wartung (**maintenance**), Ersatzteillieferung (**delivery/supply of spare parts**).

after sight *nach Sicht* cf. **bill of exchange**.

against all risks (a.a.r.) *gegen alle Risiken* Versicherung gegen alle Risiken des Verlusts (**loss**) oder der Beschädigung (**damage**).

agency *Agentur, Vertretung* Vertragsverhältnis zwischen Vertreter (**agent**) und Auftraggeber (**principal**), in dem Art und Umfang der Vertretung sowie die Provision (**commission**) geregelt sind.

air waybill (AWB) *Luftfrachtbrief* Beförderungsdokument (**transport document**) für den Gütertransport auf dem Luftwege. Der Luftfrachtbrief dient als: 1. Nachweis für den Abschluss eines Beförderungsvertrages (**contract of carriage**) und den Empfang der Güter zur Beförderung; 2. Versandliste (**shipping list**); 3. Frachtrechnung (**freight note**); 4. Zollpapier für die Ausfuhr, Einfuhr und Durchfuhr (**transit**) von Gütern; 5. Auslieferungsbestätigung (**proof of delivery**). Er wird vom Spediteur in mindestens drei Exemplaren für den Luftfrachtführer (**air carrier, airfreight forwarder**), für den Empfänger und für den Versender (als Nachweis der Annahme der Güter) ausgefertigt.

arbitration *Schlichtung* Verfahren zur Beilegung von Streitigkeiten (**dispute**) außerhalb des Rechtsweges. Die Schlichter (**arbitrator**) werden von beiden Parteien bei Vertragsabschluss einvernehmlich benannt. Der Schiedsspruch (**award**) ist verbindlich.

at warehouse *bis Lager* Preisstellung, bei der der Warenpreis die Beladung (**loading**) und Lieferung zum Kundenlager einschließt.

average *Versicherungsschaden* Bezieht sich auf Risiken beim Schiffstransport, die sowohl das Transportmittel (große Havarie: **general average**) als auch die Ladung (kleine Havarie: **particular average**) betreffen.

B

B2B (business to business) Transaktionen jedweder Art zwischen Unternehmen.

B2C (business to consumer) Transaktionen zwischen Unternehmen und Endverbrauchern.

back order *unerledigter Auftrag*

balance *Saldo* Betrag der sich aus der Verrechnung von Gutschriften (**credit**) und Lastschriften (**debit**) ergibt, cf. **current account**.

bank/banker's draft *Banktratte/Bankscheck* Scheckziehung (**drawing**) einer Bank auf eine andere Bank bei gleichzeitiger Belastung des Kontos des Bezogenen (**drawee**).

bankruptcy *Insolvenz* Zahlungsunfähigkeit eines Unternehmens.

bar code *Strichcode*

bill *Rechnung* Gebräuchlich insbesondere für die Abrechnung von Dienstleistungen (Versorgungsunternehmen, Telefon etc.), cf. **commercial invoice**.

bill of entry *Zolleingangserklärung* Erklärung des Importeurs zur zollmäßigen Abfertigung (**customs treatment**) der Einfuhrware.

bill of exchange (B/E) *Wechsel* Der Wechsel ist ein übertragbares Zahlungspapier (**negotiable instrument**) und stellt eine Zahlungsaufforderung (**draft**) des Gläubigers/Ausstellers (**drawer**) an den Schuldner/Bezogenen (**drawee**) dar, eine bestimmte Geldsumme an eine bestimmte Person (Wechselnehmer: **payee**) oder an deren Order zu zahlen. Der Wechsel muss folgende Bestandteile enthalten: 1. Ort und Datum der Ausstellung (**place and date of issue**); 2. Bezeichnung als Wechsel; 3. Verfallzeit (**maturity**); 4. Name des Wechselnehmers; 5. Anweisung zur Zahlung einer bestimmten Summe; 6. Name des Bezogenen; 7. Zahlungsort (**place of payment**); 8. Unterschrift des Ausstellers. Der Wechsel kann an fremde Order (**specified person**) oder eigene Order (**bearer**) ausgestellt werden. Man unterscheidet zwischen Sichtwechsel (**sight bill**), zahlbar bei Vorlage (**payable at sight**), Datowechsel (**time bill**) mit einer Laufzeit von z. B. 30, 60, 90 Tagen nach Sicht und Tagwechsel (**date bill**) mit Fälligkeit an einem bestimmten Tag. Der Wechsel kann vom Inhaber bis zur Fälligkeit (**maturity**), d.h. bis zum Einzug, aufbewahrt werden oder an einen Gläubiger zur Begleichung einer Rechnung/Schuld weitergegeben werden oder aber einer Bank zur Diskontierung (**discounting**) übergeben werden. Die Weitergabe erfolgt durch Übertragungserklärung (Indossament: **endorsement**) auf der Rückseite.

bill of lading (B/L) *Konnossement* Im Gegensatz zu den übrigen Transportdokumenten hat das Konnossement Wertpapiercharakter und verkörpert den Besitz der Ware. Es ist ein Traditions- oder Dispositionspapier (**document of title**). Die Schifffahrtsgesellschaft (**shipping company**) händigt die Ware nur gegen Vorlage (**presentation**) des Originalkonnossements aus. Es wird in der Regel vom Kapitän des Schiffs bzw. dem Reeder (**shipowner**) in Sätzen (**set**) mit drei Originalen ausgestellt und stellt eine Empfangsbestätigung (**confirmation of receipt**) der Ware durch den Verfrachter (**carrier**) dar, die den Anspruch auf Auslieferung der Ware im Bestimmungshafen (**port of destination**) gewährt, und ist zugleich Nachweis über den bestehenden Frachtvertrag (**document evidencing the contract of carriage**). Das An-Bord-Konnossement (**on-board B/L**) bestätigt die Übernahme der Ware an Bord und ebenso wie das Verschiffungskonnossement (**shipped-by B/L**) die Verschiffung der bezeichneten Güter durch den Verfrachter. Das Empfangskonnossement (**received-for-shipment B/L**) bestätigt die Übernahme der Ware durch den Verfrachter zur Verladung. Letzeres kann durch einen handschriftlichen Zusatz in ein An-Bord-Konnossement (**on-board bill**) verwandelt werden. Das Durchkonnossement (**through B/L**) ist ein Verladedokument (**freight/shipping document**), bei dem der Aussteller die Auslieferung der Ware an den Konnossementinhaber (**holder of the bill**) verspricht, wobei der Transport bis zum Bestimmungshafen unter Benutzung mehrerer Verkehrsmittel erfolgt. Das Konnossement wird in der Regel als Orderkonnossement (**order B/L**) ausgestellt und kann somit durch den Empfänger durch einfaches Indossament (**endorsement**) übertragen werden. Das Konnossement sollte als rein (**clean**) gezeichnet sein, d.h. keine Klauseln oder Ergänzungen enthalten, die den Zustand der Verpackung oder der Ware ausdrücklich als mangelhaft (**foul/unclean/ dirty**) bezeichnen, da Banken Verladedokumente dieser Art bei Zahlung zurückweisen können. Das Konnossement wird heute zumeist in elektronischer Form ausgestellt. Dies ist in den Incoterms (cf. **Incoterms**) berücksichtigt.

bill of sale 1 *Abtretungsurkunde* Sicherungsübereignung (**collateral assignment**), durch die der Schuldner (**debtor**) dem Gläubiger (**creditor**) zur Sicherung einer Schuld das Eigentum an einer beweglichen Sache überträgt. Nach Tilgung der Schuld (**payment of the amount due**) fällt das Eigentum an den Schuldner zurück. **2** *Kaufvertrag* Kaufvertrag für Schiffe und Wertpapiere.

bonded warehouse *offenes Zolllager, Zollfreilager, Zollniederlage* Lager unter Zollverschluss zur Lagerung von Waren, die erst kurz vor dem Verkauf oder der Weiterverarbeitung (**processing**) verzollt und dann entnommen werden.

branch *Zweigstelle, Filiale*

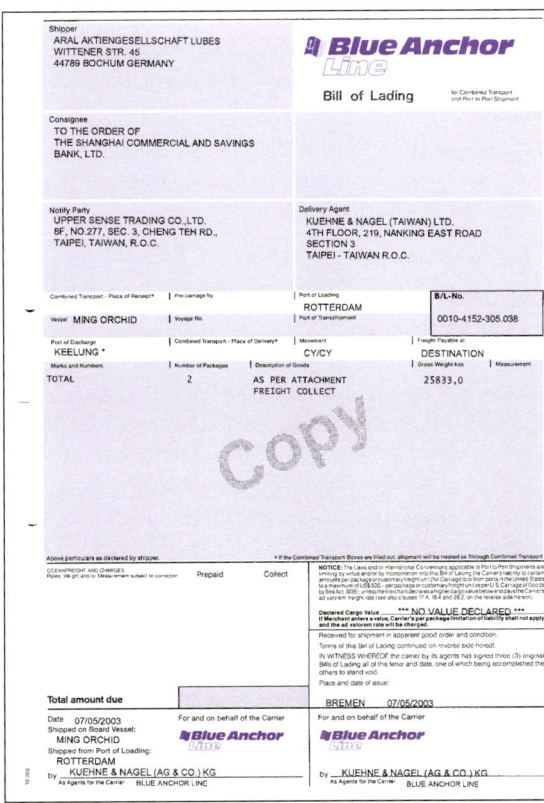

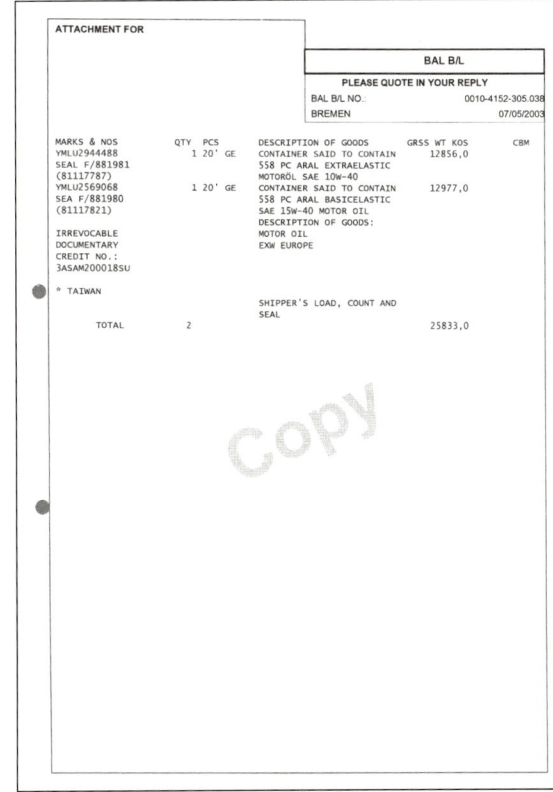

breach of contract *Vertragsbruch* Vertragswidriges Verhalten, das zu Schadenersatz (**damages**) oder Vertragsrücktritt (**revocation of contract**) berechtigen kann.

broker *Makler*

buyer's market *Käufermarkt* Marktsituation mit einem reichen Warenangebot und günstigen Einkaufsbedingungen (Preise, Rabatte), cf. **seller's market**.

C

cancellation *Stornierung* Vertragliche Verabredungen werden rückgängig gemacht.

carnet *Zollpassierscheinheft* Aufgrund internationaler Vereinbarungen wird die Einfuhr und zollmäßige Behandlung (**customs treatment**) bestimmter Warengruppen (Warenmuster (**samples**), Waren bei zeitlich beschränkter Einfuhr) im Carnet-Verfahren wesentlich vereinfacht.

Carriage and Insurance Paid to (CIP) ... *Fracht und Versicherung bezahlt bis ...* (Incoterm) Es gelten dieselben Bedingungen wie für **Carriage Paid To**, außer dass der Verkäufer bei dieser Lieferbedingung verpflichtet ist, Versicherungsdeckung zu den üblichen Mindestbedingungen bis zum Abschluss der Lieferung zu beschaffen und bezahlen. Gilt für jede Transportart.

carriage forward (carr. fwd.) *Fracht zu bezahlen* Frachtkosten (**freight charges**) sind vom Empfänger zu bezahlen. Bei **carriage paid (carr. paid)** werden die Frachtkosten vom Verkäufer übernommen.

Carriage Paid To (CPT) ... *Fracht bezahlt bis ...* (Incoterm) Der Verkäufer besorgt die Ausfuhrabfertigung (**customs clearance**) und trägt alle Kosten des Transports einschließlich der Entladung am Bestimmungsort. Hier geht das Risiko auf den Käufer über. Die Versicherungspflicht ist nicht geregelt. Gilt für jede Transportart.

carrier *Frachtführer, Spediteur* Der Frachtführer führt den Transport von Gütern durch. Der Spediteur (**forwarding/freight agent**) besorgt oder vermittelt den Transport und erbringt andere transportbezogene Dienstleistungen, insbesondere die Organisation von Transportleistungen, Lagerung (**warehousing**), Verpackung (**packing**), Verteilung (**distribution**) etc. Es wird unterschieden zwischen gewerblichen Frachtführern (**common carrier**), bahnamtlichen Rollfuhrunternehmern (**contract carrier**), Werksverkehr (**private carrier**).

carrier's risk (C.R.) *Gefahr beim Frachtführer* Transport von Gütern durch Eisenbahngesellschaften, bei denen der Frachtführer der Ware das Risiko durch Verlust oder Beschädigung während des Transports trägt.

cash against documents (CAD/c.a.d) *Kasse gegen Dokumente, Dokumente gegen Zahlung* Die Verschiffungsdokumente (**shipping documents**) werden nur Zug um Zug gegen Bezahlung der Ware ausgehändigt, so dass der Empfänger (**consignee**) erst nach Rechnungsbegleichung (**payment/settlement of the invoice**) über die Ware verfügen kann. Hierbei werden die Dokumente an eine Bank übergeben.

cash discount *Skonto, Barzahlungsrabatt* Nachlass (**reduction**) auf den Rechnungspreis für Zahlung innerhalb bestimmter Fristen.

cash on delivery (COD/c.o.d.) *Nachnahme* Einzugsverfahren (**method of collection**), z. B. bei Bahn und Post, bei dem das beförderte Gut nur gegen Bezahlung des Nachnahmebetrages ausgehändigt wird.

cash with order (CWO) *Bezahlung bei Auftragserteilung* Häufig im Versandgeschäft verwendete Zahlungsform (**method of payment**), z. B. Zahlung durch Scheck, Ermächtigung zur Belastung des Kreditkartenkontos (**debit mandate**).

certificate of damage *Schadensprotokoll* Aufstellung über Schäden bei Anlieferung von Ware im Hafen.

certificate of insurance *Versicherungsschein* Bestätigung der Versicherungsdeckung (**insurance cover**) durch die Versicherungsgesellschaft, in der Regel bei Akkreditivgeschäften (**letter of credit**) erforderlich.

certificate of origin *Ursprungszeugnis* Bestätigung über den Ursprung der Ware in einem bestimmten Land. Das Ursprungszeugnis findet z. B. im Handel zwischen EU-Staaten oder EFTA-Staaten zum Nachweis der Zollfreiheit (**customs exemption, zero-rating**) Verwendung. Die Beglaubigung erfolgt durch eine Industrie- und Handelskammer des Abgangslandes (**country of origin**).

chamber of commerce (and industry) *Industrie- und Handelskammer*

charter-party *Frachtvertrag* Schriftlicher Vertrag im See- und Lufttransport über die Vermietung des Fahrzeugs oder Teilen des Laderaums (**cargo hold**) für eine festgelegte Zeit oder Anzahl von Reisen (**voyage**).

cheque *Scheck* Bargeldloses Zahlungsmittel, mit dem der Aussteller (**drawer**) ein Geldinstitut, d.h. den Bezogenen (**drawee**), anweist, bei Vorlage aus seinem Guthaben einen bestimmten Geldbetrag zu bezahlen. Der Barscheck (**open cheque**) kann bar ausgezahlt oder gutgeschrieben werden. Der Betrag von einem Verrechnungsscheck (**crossed cheque**) kann nur einem Konto des Einreichers gutgeschrieben werden.

circular *Rundschreiben*

closed indent *Beschaffungsauftrag* Beschaffungsauftrag an Vertreter im Ausland mit Angabe der Beschaffungsquelle.

collateral *Sicherheit* Absicherung einer Schuld oder Zahlungsverpflichtung durch eine Wertsache.

collection agency *Inkassostelle, Inkassobüro* Kreditinstitut oder gewerbliches Unternehmen, das die Einziehung von Schecks, Wechseln, Lastschriften bzw. abgetretener Forderungen für das Gläubigerunternehmen (**collection order**) übernimmt.

commercial invoice *Handelsrechung* Dokument beim Kauf und Verkauf von Waren und Dienstleistungen, in dem Art und Umfang der erbrachten/verkauften Leistung detailliert beschrieben wird. Der Preis pro Einheit (**price per item**) und der Gesamtpreis (**total price**) sind angeführt. Die Rechnung weist darüber hinaus die gewährten Nachlässe (**reduction**), Rabatte (**discount**) und Skonti (**cash discount**) sowie die Zahlungsbedingungen (**terms of payment**) aus. Sie enthält Name und Anschrift des Leistungserbringers (**supplier, service provider**) und -empfängers sowie die Bankverbindung aus.

commission *Provision* Vergütung für die Tätigkeit des Vertreters (**commission agent**) bei der Vermittlung von Geschäften/Aufträgen, oft als Prozentsatz vom Auftragswert gewährt.

commodity 1 *Rohstoff* börsenmäßig gehandelter Rohstoff; 2 *Ware* jegliche Art von Ware.

Community Transit Procedure *gemeinschaftliches Versandverfahren* Vereinbarung zwischen den EU-Staaten zur Erleichterung der zollmäßigen Behandlung (**customs treatment**) bei der Durchfuhr (**transit**) bestimmter Waren.

company [GB] *Gesellschaft* Unternehmensform der Kapitalgesellschaft: Aktiengesellschaft (**public limited company**) oder Gesellschaft mit beschränkter Haftung (**private limited company**).

consignment note *Frachtbrief, Warenbegleitschein* Begleitpapier (**accompanying document**) und Beweisurkunde über das Transportgut, die in dreifacher Form ausgestellt wird. Ein Exemplar erhält der Absender (**shipper, sender**), eins der Frachtführer (**carrier, forwarder**), der nach Maßgabe des Frachtbriefs liefern muss. Das dritte begleitet das Gut und wird an den Empfänger (**recipient**) ausgehändigt.

consular invoice *Konsulatsfaktura* Das Konsulat (**consulate**) des Bestimmungslandes (**country of destination**) der Ware im Exportland bestätigt auf einem besonderen Vordruck, dass der Wert der Ware, wie er in der Rechnung angegeben ist, dem tatsächlichen Warenwert entspricht. Die Konsulatsfaktura dient zur Berechnung des Wertzolls (**ad valorem customs duty**) der Ware. Sie ist gegebenenfalls auch im Zusammenhang mit einem Akkreditivgeschäft (cf. **letter of credit**) bei der Wareneinfuhr vorzulegen.

contract of affreightment *Frachtvertrag, Befrachtungsvertrag* cf. **charter-party**.

corporation [USA] *Gesellschaft* cf. **company**.

Cost and Freight (CFR) ... *Kosten und Fracht ...* (Incoterm) Der Verkäufer schließt auf eigene Rechnung den Befrachtungsvertrag bis zum Bestimmungshafen (**port of destination**) ab und trägt alle Fracht- und Ausladekosten (**cost of carriage and unloading**) im Entladungshafen sowie das Risiko für die Ware, bis diese die Reling des Schiffes (**ship's rail**) im Verschiffungshafen (**port of shipment**) überschritten hat. Der Verkäufer besorgt die Ausfuhrabfertigung (**export clearance**) und beschafft die Ausfuhrbewilligung (**export licence**) und sonstige amtliche Bescheinigungen sowie ein reines (**clean**), begebbares (**negotiable**) „An Bord" (**on board**) oder Verschiffungs- (**shipped**) Konnossement (**bill of lading**). Der Käufer hingegen trägt alle Kosten für die Löschung (**discharge, unloading**) oder Leichterung (**lighterage**), die Verzollung (**customs clearance**) oder sonstige Einfuhrabgaben (**import levies**). Gilt für See- und Binnenwassertransport.

Cost, Insurance and Freight (CIF) ... *Kosten, Versicherung, und Fracht ...* (Incoterm) Der Verkäufer besorgt auf eigene Rechnung den Versand der Ware zum Bestimmungshafen (**port of destination**) und trägt alle Entladekosten (**costs of discharge/unloading**). Er versichert die Ware gegen alle üblichen Risiken für den Seetransport gegen Verlust und/oder Beschädigung zu F.P.A.-Bedingungen (**free from particular average**) und beschafft ein reines Konnossement (**bill of lading**). Der Verkäufer besorgt die Ausfuhrabfertigung (**export clearance**). Die Lieferung gilt als erfolgt, wenn die Ware die Reling des Schiffs im Verladehafen (**port of shipment**) überschritten hat. Zu diesem Zeitpunkt geht auch das Risiko auf den Käufer über (**transfer of risk**). Gilt für See- und Binnenwassertransport.

counterfoil *Kontrollabschnitt, Beleg* Abtrennbarer Teil einer Rechnung, eines Scheckformulars, einer Quittung, der als Nachweis für Betrag und Datum aufbewahrt wird.

cover note *Deckungszusage* Bestätigung der Versicherung über die Annahme des Versicherungsantrags (**insurance proposal**). Wird vor Ausgabe der Versicherungspolice (**insurance policy**) ausgestellt.

credit 1 *Guthaben* Frei verfügbarer Betrag auf dem Bankkonto. 2 *Gutschrift* Betrag, der dem Konto zugebucht wird. 3 *Kredit, Darlehen* Von einem Verleiher (Bank: **lender**) zur Verfügung gestellter Geldbetrag, der entsprechend der Vereinbarung zurückgezahlt werden muss. Der Verleiher erhält zum Ausgleich eine Vergütung (Zinsen: **interest**), die in Prozent zum ausgeliehenen Betrag berechnet (Zinssatz: **rate of interest**) und während der Vertragsdauer vom Entleiher (**borrower**) regelmäßig gezahlt wird.

credit inquiry *Kreditauskunft* Anfrage bei einer Bank oder Auskunftei (**credit agency**) über die Kreditwürdigkeit (**creditworthiness**) oder den finanziellen Status (**credit standing, credit rating**) eines Kunden.

current account *laufendes Konto, Girokonto* Bankkonto für die Abwicklung des gesamten Zahlungsverkehrs durch Daueraufträge (**standing order**), Lastschriftverfahren (**direct debiting**), Überweisungen (**bank transfer**), Scheckverkehr (**payment by cheque**). Die Gutschriften (**credit**) und Lastschriften (**debit**) sind dem Kontoauszug (**statement of account**) zu entnehmen, der auch den Saldo (**account balance**) ausweist.

customs duty *Zoll* Betrag, der von Staaten bei der Einfuhr, gelegentlich auch bei der Ausfuhr, von Waren aus einem anderen Staat erhoben wird.

customs invoice *Zollrechnung, Zollfaktura* Für Zollzwecke ausgestellte Rechnung, die den Warenwert ausweist und für die Wareneinfuhr erforderlich ist. Sie ist auch erforderlich für Waren, die nicht zum Verkauf bestimmt (**not intended for sale**) sind, z. B. Ausstellungsgüter (**exhibits**), Ansichtsware (**goods on approval**), Muster (**samples**).

D

damages *Schadenersatz* Ausgleich eines erlittenen Schadens (**damage**) oder Verlustes (**loss**).

daughter (company) [US] *Tochtergesellschaft* cf. **subsidiary**.

debit *Soll* 1 Betrag, der vom Konto abgebucht wird. 2 Geschuldeter Betrag.

debit note *Lastschriftanzeige* 1 Mitteilung über den offenen Betrag (**outstanding amount**) für die Lieferung von Waren oder Dienstleistungen. 2 Mitteilung über den verbuchten Sollbetrag.

del credere agent *Delkredereagent* Handelsvertreter, der für den Eingang der Zahlung für die durch ihn verkauften Güter haftet. Hierfür wird ihm eine Delkredereprovision (**del credere commission**) gewährt.

Delivered At Frontier (DAF) ... *Lieferung frei Grenze ...* (Incoterm) Die Pflicht des Verkäufers zur Übernahme der Kosten endet, sobald die Ware die Grenze des Ausfuhrlandes (**exporting country**) überschritten hat. Falls erforderlich oder üblich übernimmt der Verkäufer die Kosten des Löschvorgangs (**discharge, unloading**) am Lieferort an der Grenze (**place of destination**). Er besorgt die Ausfuhrabfertigung (**export clearance**) und beschafft dem Käufer bei Bedarf ein Durchfrachttransportpapier (**through transport document, transit document**). Gilt für jede Transportart.

Delivered Duty Paid (DDP) ... *geliefert und verzollt ...* (Incoterm) Die Ware wird dem Käufer an einem genannten Ort im Einfuhrland (**importing country**) verzollt und frei von allen Kosten zur Verfügung gestellt. Die Ware wird auf dem Transportfahrzeug (**means of transport**) zur Verfügung gestellt, d. h. nicht entladen. Der Käufer ist zur Übernahme der Ware (**taking delivery**) und aller Kosten von diesem Zeitpunkt an verpflichtet. Gilt für jede Transportart.

Delivered Duty Unpaid (DDU) ... *geliefert unverzollt ...* (Incoterm) Der Verkäufer liefert die Ware am benannten Bestimmungsort unverzollt an den Käufer. Die Ware wird auf dem Transportmittel (**means of transport**) zur Verfügung gestellt, d. h. nicht entladen. Gilt für jede Transportart.

Delivered Ex Quay (DEQ) ... *geliefert ab Kai ...* (Incoterm) Der Verkäufer trägt alle Kosten und Risiken bis zur Entladung im Bestimmungshafen. Er besorgt die Ausfuhrabfertigung (**export clearance**). Die Einfuhrabfertigung einschließlich der Entrichtung aller Gebühren, Zölle und Steuern wird vom Käufer durchgeführt. Gilt für See- und Binnenwassertransport.

Delivered Ex Ship (DES) ... *geliefert ab Schiff ...* (Incoterm) Der Verkäufer trägt alle Kosten und Risiken bis zum Zeitpunkt der Lieferung im Bestimmungshafen. Die Entladung ist darin nicht eingeschlossen. Er besorgt die Ausfuhrabfertigung (**export clearance**). Gilt für See- und Binnenwassertransport.

delivery note *Lieferschein* 1 Anweisung an den Lagerhalter (**stockist, storekeeper**) zur Auslieferung von Gütern. 2 Mitteilung des Versenders über eine Warenlieferung (**consignment**), wird vom Empfänger unterschrieben.

direct debit *Lastschrift* Vom Abnehmer einer Leistung autorisierte Abbuchung (**debit**) des fälligen Betrages (**amount due**) durch den Ersteller der Leistung. Hierzu ist ein Abbuchungsauftrag erforderlich (**direct debit mandate**).

discount 1 *Skonto, Rabatt* Abzug von einer Rechnung oder dem ausgezeichneten Warenpreis: bei Abnahme bestimmter Mengen (**quantity discount**), bei sofortiger Zahlung (**cash discount**), bei Verkauf an gewerbliche Kunden (**trade discount**). 2 *Disagio* Abzug vom Wechselbetrag bei Verkauf vor dem Fälligkeitstermin (**due date**).

discounting *Diskontierung* Ankauf der Bank von noch nicht fälligen Wechseln unter Abzug der Zinsen für die Restlaufzeit (**time to maturity**).

documentary bill/draft *Dokumentenwechsel, Dokumententratte* Der Wechsel wird in Verbindung mit Verschiffungsdokumenten (**shipping documents**) – Konnossement (**bill of lading**), Rechnung, Versicherungsschein etc. – weitergereicht; bei Außenhandelsgeschäften (**foreign trade**) zur Sicherung der Zahlung üblich.

documentary collection *Dokumenteninkasso* Bei den Zahlungsformen Dokumente gegen Annahme (cf. **documents against acceptance**) und Dokumente gegen Kasse/Zahlung (cf. **documents against payment, cash against documents**) werden die Warendokumente durch die ausländische Partnerbank nur gegen „Bezahlung" ausgehändigt.

documentary credit *Dokumentenakkreditiv, Dokumententratte.* Zahlungsform im überseeischen Warengeschäft unter Mitwirkung von Banken, häufig auf der Grundlage eines Kredits. Dabei dienen Fracht- und Versicherungspapiere (Dokumente) als Grundlage. Der Importeur lässt sich von seiner Bank den erforderlichen Kredit vor Abschluss des Geschäfts zusichern. Erfolgt die Zahlung durch Wechsel (cf. **bill of exchange**), wird die Tratte (**draft**) des überseeischen Verkäufers durch die Bank des Importeurs gegen Übergabe der Dokumente (cf. **documents against payment**) akzeptiert, cf. **letter of credit, documentary bill/draft**.

documents against acceptance (D/A) *Dokumente gegen Akzept* Eine Form der Zahlungsbedingung im Welthandel, cf. **documentary bill/draft**.

draft *Tratte* Gezogener Wechsel (Zahlungsaufforderung (**request for payment**), die noch nicht mit einem Akzept versehen ist).

drawback *Export-, Zollrückvergütung* Rückvergütung von Einfuhrzöllen (**refund of import duty**) bei Wiederausfuhr (**re-exportation**) der Waren.

drawee *Bezogener, Trassat* Beim Scheck oder Wechsel derjenige, an den die Zahlungsanweisung (**instruction to pay**) gerichtet ist.

drawer *Aussteller, Trassant* Der Aussteller (**issuer**) eines Wechsels gibt dem Bezogenen (cf. **drawee**) die Anweisung (**instruction**) zur Zahlung des Wechselpapiers. Der Aussteller eines Schecks gibt die Anweisung, dem Überbringer oder Einreicher (**bearer**) die in dem Scheck genannte Summe aus seinem Guthaben zu zahlen.

duty *Zoll* Steuer auf Waren, in der Regel bei der Einfuhr.

E

e-commerce *Internethandel* Warenbestellung und -bezahlung erfolgen auf elektronischem Wege.

EDI (electronic data interchange) *elektronischer Datenaustausch* Datenaustausch zwischen Unternehmen auf elektronischem Wege. Dies wird für Rechnungen, Warenbegleitpapiere, Mitteilungen über den Standort von Sendungen durch das GPS **(global positioning system)** oder über die Auslieferung von Waren genutzt. Teilweise werden die Daten über den Strichcode (cf. **bar code**) erfasst und weitergeleitet.

endorsement *Indossament* Vermerk auf der Rückseite eines Wechsels oder Schecks über die Übertragung **(transfer)** des Papiers und aller Rechte daraus auf einen Dritten (cf. **bill of exchange**). Auch für das Konnossement **(bill of lading)** im Akkreditivgeschäft üblich (cf. **letter of credit**).

entrepôt *Zwischenlager* Gebäude am Flughafen oder Hafen zur Zwischenlagerung **(temporary storage)** von Gütern.

entry of goods *Wareneinfuhr, Zollanmeldung* Vorführung von Waren bei der Einfuhr oder z. T. bei der Ausfuhr für die zollmäßige Abfertigung **(customs treatment)**. Hierzu ist in der Regel ein(e) Zollerklärung/Zollantrag **(bill of entry)** erforderlich.

errors and omissions excepted (E.&O.E.) *Irrtum vorbehalten* Klausel auf Rechnungen, die dem Aussteller eine spätere Berichtigung etwaiger Fehler gestattet.

escape clause *salvatorische Klausel* Vertragsklausel, die den Fortbestand des Vertrags sichert, sollte eine vertragliche Abmachung **(contractual agreement)** aus welchen Gründen auch immer ungültig werden. Sie ermöglicht den Ersatz der fehlerhaften Klausel durch eine andere, ohne die übrigen Teile des Vertrags zu berühren.

ex factory *ab Werk* cf. **ex warehouse**.

ex mill *ab Werk* cf. **ex warehouse**.

ex plantation *ab Plantage* cf. **ex warehouse**.

Export Credits Guarantee Department (ECGD) *Behörde für Exportkreditgarantien* Regierungsbehörde in Großbritannien zur Exportförderung **(promotion of exports)**, die Garantien für Exportgeschäfte gewährt. Diese Aufgabe wird in der Bundesrepublik Deutschland von der Hermeskreditversicherungs-AG im Auftrag des Bundes wahrgenommen.

ex quay duty paid / duty on buyer's account ... *ab Kai (un)verzollt ...* Der Verkäufer stellt die Ware am Kai des benannten Bestimmungshafens **(port of destination)** zur Verfügung und trägt alle Kosten und Abgaben einschließlich bzw. ausschließlich der Verzollungskosten **(costs of customs clearance)**, die sich bei der Einfuhr ergeben.

ex ship/steamer ... *ab Schiff ...* Der Verkäufer stellt die Ware an Bord des Schiffes im benannten Hafen zur Verfügung und trägt alle Kosten und Gefahren bis zu diesem Zeitpunkt. Er beschafft alle zur Übernahme der Ware erforderlichen Dokumente. Der Käufer trägt alle Gefahren und Kosten von dem Zeitpunkt, an dem die Ware zur Verfügung gestellt wurde.

ex stock *ab Lager* Lieferung der Ware ab Lager, keine Auftragsfertigung **(made-to-order production, contract manufacturing)**.

ex store cf. **ex warehouse**.

ex warehouse *ab Werk* Die Ware wird dem Käufer auf dem Werksgelände **(factory/plant premises)** des Verkäufers zur Abholung **(for collection)** zur Verfügung gestellt. Der Verkäufer trägt alle Kosten und Risiken bis zur Bereitstellung der Ware, erforderlichenfalls auch die Kosten der Qualitätsprüfung **(quality control, inspection)**, des Wiegens und Zählens. Der Käufer trägt die Kosten und Risiken vom Zeitpunkt der Bereitstellung und hat für die Verladung auf das von ihm zu beschaffende Beförderungsmittel **(means of transport)** zu sorgen und die Transportkosten **(transport costs)**, Zollgebühren **(customs duty)** und Kosten für die Beschaffung der erforderlichen Dokumente zu tragen.

ex wharf *ab Kai* cf. **ex quay**.

Ex Works (EXW) ... *ab Werk ...* (Incoterm) Lieferklausel mit den geringsten Verpflichtungen für den Verkäufer, der die Ware üblicherweise auf seinem Firmengelände für den Käufer zur Abholung bereitstellen muss, cf. **ex warehouse**.

F

factor 1 *Makler* Makler **(agent)**, der Ware im Auftrag eines Dritten auf eigene Rechnung und Gefahr **(on his own account and risk)** verkauft und anteilig am Erlös beteiligt wird. 2 *Absatzfinanzierungsinstitut* Ein Finanzierungsinstitut, das einem Verkäufer dessen Forderungen aus Warenlieferungen und Leistungen oft bei gleichzeitiger Übernahme des Ausfallrisikos **(factoring)** abkauft und bei Fälligkeit eintreibt **(collect)**. Der Verkäufer der Forderungen verfügt dadurch schneller über Geldmittel.

factoring *Factoring* Verkauf von Forderungen aus Warenlieferungen und Leistungen an eine Factoring-Bank, die das Inkasso **(collection)** auf eigene Rechnung, d. h. ohne Rückgriff **(without recourse)** betreibt.

fair average quality (faq) *gute Durchschnittsqualität* Die Qualität der Ware wird nicht nach einer bestimmten Warenprobe **(sample)**, sondern nach dem Durchschnitt einer Anzahl von Sendungen gemessen.

FOB airport ... *FOB airport ...* Der Verkäufer übergibt die Ware dem vom Käufer benannten Luftfrachtführer **(air carrier, airfreight forwarder)** an dem benannten Abgangsflughafen und schließt wenn vereinbart auf Kosten des Käufers einen Beförderungsvertrag **(contract of carriage)** ab. Der Käufer übernimmt alle Kosten und Risiken der Ware vom Zeitpunkt der Anlieferung am Flughafen und trägt insbesondere die Kosten der weiteren Beförderung.

force majeure cf. **Act of God**.

forfaiting *Forfaitierung* Ankauf von Handelswechseln **(commercial bills)** oder Forderungen im Außenwirtschaftsverkehr durch den Forfaitierer **(forfaiting house)**, der dann auf eigene Rechnung und eigenes Risiko, d. h. ohne Rückgriff **(without recourse)**, das Inkasso **(collection)** betreibt.

forwarder; forwarding agent *Spediteur* Dienstleistungsunternehmen (**service company**) im Transportgewerbe (**transport industry**), das die Abholung (**collection**), den Transport und die Auslieferung (**delivery**) der Ware organisiert bzw. selbst durchführt.

franchise *Lizenz, Konzession* Lizenz zur selbstständigen Führung eines Unternehmens unter dem Namen des Franchisegebers (**franchiser**), der dafür sein Produkt, sein Warenzeichen, sein Wissen und auch die Betriebseinrichtungen zur Verfügung stellt. Durch die Lizenzvergabe (**franchising**) sichert er sich längerfristig den Absatz seiner Produkte.

franco *frei* Die Lieferung der Ware erfolgt kostenfrei durch den Verkäufer an den vereinbarten Lieferort.

Free Alongside Ship (FAS) ... *frei Längsseite Schiff ...* (Incoterm) Der Verkäufer liefert die Ware an den Liegeplatz im benannten Verschiffungshafen (**place of shipment**) Längsseite Schiff an den vom Käufer benannten Ladeplatz. Er beschafft ein reines Konnossement (**clean bill of lading**), aus dem hervorgeht, dass er seinen Lieferverpflichtungen Längsseite Schiff nachgekommen ist, und trägt sämtliche bis zu diesem Zeitpunkt anfallenden Kosten einschließlich der Beschaffung des Konnossements. Der Käufer trägt alle Kosten und Risiken vom Zeitpunkt der Lieferung Längsseite Schiff und ist auch für die Ausfuhrabfertigung (**export clearance**) sowie die Beschaffung der üblichen Dokumente verantwortlich. Gilt für See- und Binnenwassertransport.

Free Carrier (FCR) ... *frei Frachtführer ...* (Incoterm) Der Verkäufer übergibt die Ware dem vom Käufer benannten Frachtführer (**carrier**) an dem benannten Ort und trägt alle Kosten und Risiken bis zu diesem Zeitpunkt. Der Verkäufer besorgt die Ausfuhrabfertigung (**export clearance**). Die Lieferung gilt als abgeschlossen, wenn die Ware auf das Fahrzeug des Käufers geladen ist. Der Käufer schließt den Beförderungsvertrag (**contract of carriage**) ab und informiert den Verkäufer entsprechend. Gilt für jede Transportart und ist für den multimodalen Verkehr (**multimodal transport**) geeignet.

free from particular average (fpa/FPA) *frei von besonderer Havarie* Klausel bei der Seeversicherung, durch die die Haftung des Versicherers für Teilschäden (**particular average**) ausgeschlossen wird. Sie sind vom Betroffenen zu tragen.

Free On Board (FOB) ... *frei an Bord ...* (Incoterm) Der Verkäufer liefert die Ware an Bord des vom Verkäufer angegebenen Seeschiffes und beschafft die erforderlichen amtlichen Bescheinigungen und die Ausfuhrbewilligung (**export licence**). Der Verkäufer besorgt die Ausfuhrabfertigung (**export clearance**). Er trägt alle Kosten und Risiken, Gebühren und Abgaben, bis die Ware die Reling des Schiffes überschritten hat (**cross the ship's rail**) und beschafft das übliche reine Konnossement. Der Käufer beschafft den erforderlichen Schiffsraum (**shipping space**) oder chartert ein geeignetes Schiff. Er übernimmt die Kosten und das Risiko von dem Zeitpunkt an, an dem die Ware die Reling des Schiffes überschreitet und trägt auch die Kosten und Gebühren für die Beschaffung der üblichen Dokumente einschließlich des Konnossements (**bill of lading**). Gilt für See- und Binnenwassertransport.

Free On Rail (FOR) ... *frei/franko Waggon ...* (Incoterm) Der Verkäufer hat bei einer vollen Waggonladung (**wagonload**) rechtzeitig auf seine Kosten einen geeigneten Waggon zu beschaffen und ihn zu beladen. Bei Teilladungen (**partial load**) ist die Ware rechtzeitig an der Bahnstation oder an ein von der Bahn gestelltes Fahrzeug zu übergeben. Er trägt Kosten und Risiko bis zur Übergabe der Ware oder des Waggons an die Bahn. Der Käufer übernimmt Kosten und Risiken vom Zeitpunkt der Übergabe der Ware an die Bahn, einschließlich der Kosten für die Beschaffung der erforderlichen Dokumente mit Ausnahme der Versanddokumente (**shipping/transport documents**).

free on truck (FOT) ... *frei/franko Lkw ...* (Incoterm) cf. **Free On Rail**.

freight carriage and insurance paid to ... *frachtfrei versichert ...* (cf. **freight or carriage paid to**) Der Verkäufer versichert zusätzlich die Ware auf seine Kosten gegen Untergang oder Schäden während des Transports.

freight or carriage paid to ... *frachtfrei ...* Der Verkäufer versendet die Ware auf eigene Kosten an den vereinbarten Ablieferungsplatz am Bestimmungsort und trägt das Risiko bis zur Übergabe der Ware an den ersten Frachtführer. Außerdem besorgt er die erforderlichen Ausfuhrbewilligungen (**export licence**). Der Käufer trägt das Risiko vom Zeitpunkt der Übergabe an den ersten Frachtführer sowie alle Einfuhrabgaben.

freight note *Frachtrechnung* Mitteilung des Frachtbesorgers (**forwarding/freight agent**) an den Versender (**shipper**) über die Höhe der zu zahlenden Frachtkosten.

G

general average *große/gemeinsame Havarie* Von allen Beteiligten gemeinsam zu tragender Schaden, wenn zur Abwendung eines noch größeren Schadens für das Schiff und/oder die Ladung Teile der Ladung über Bord geworfen werden müssen.

GPS (global positioning system) *weltweites satellitengestütztes Ortungssystem*

goods on approval *Ansichtsware* Bestellte oder unbestellte Ware zur Besichtigung, Auswahl und Abnahme.

goods on consignment *Kommissionsgut, Konsignationsware* Ware, die dem Handelsvertreter (**consignee**) zum Verkauf gegen Kommission überlassen wird. Der Unternehmer (**consignor/principal**) bleibt bis zum Verkauf Eigentümer der Ware.

group *Konzern, Gruppe* Zusammenschluss von mehreren Unternehmen, der von einer Obergesellschaft (cf. **parent company**) geführt wird.

H

haulage 1 *Transport* Warentransport per Straße, Schiene oder Binnenwasserstraße. 2 *Transportkosten* Gebühren für diese Art des Transports.

haulier; haulage contractor *Fuhrunternehmer* Der Fuhrunternehmer arbeitet häufig nur für bestimmte Kunden (cf. **carrier**).

I

import licence *Einfuhrgenehmigung* Staatliche Genehmigung der Wareneinfuhr zum Zwecke der Überwachung bei Devisenbewirtschaftungsmaßnahmen (**foreign exchange control measures**) oder der Einhaltung von staatlich verordneten Lieferkontingenten (**import quotas**).

Incorporation *Gründung einer Gesellschaft* Gründungsvorgang einer Kapitalgesellschaft durch Hinterlegung des Gesellschaftervertrags und der Satzung beim Amtsgericht (in GB **Registrar of Companies**) und Eintragung in das Handelsregister (**registration**).

Incoterms (International Commercial Terms) *Internationale Lieferklauseln* International gültige Lieferbedingungen, in denen die Verteilung der Kosten und Gefahren von Transport, Versicherung während des Transports und beim Be- und Entladen sowie der Kosten für das Be- und Entladen geregelt sind.

indent *Indentauftrag* Der Begriff wird heute oft allgemein für jede Art von Auslandsbestellung verwandt.

institute cargo clauses *Institut-Ladungsklauseln* Klauseln einer Gruppe von Londoner Versicherern im Seeversicherungszweig (**marine insurance**) für die Versicherung von außergewöhnlichen Risiken über die übliche Versicherungsdeckung (**coverage**) hinaus.

insurance certificate *Versicherungsbescheinigung* Bestätigung des Versicherers (**insurer/underwriter**), dass er das Versicherungsrisiko bei einem Transportgeschäft übernimmt. Es ist gegebenenfalls bei Akkreditivgeschäften (**letter of credit transaction**) vorzulegen.

insurance policy *Versicherungspolice, Versicherungsschein* Vom Versicherer ausgestellte Urkunde über den Abschluss eines Versicherungsvertrags, in dem sich der Versicherer verpflichtet, dem Versicherungsnehmer (**insured**) bei Eintritt eines Schadens (**in the event of a damage**) eine bestimmte Summe zu zahlen. Der Versicherungsnehmer verpflichtet sich zur Zahlung von Versicherungsprämien (**insurance premium**).

intermodal transport *multimodaler/kombinierter Verkehr* cf. **multimodal transport**.

International Chamber of Commerce (ICC) *Internationale Handelskammer* Verband der nationalen Handelskammerorganisationen mit Sitz in Paris.

inventory *Lagerbestand*

invoice *Rechnung* cf. **commercial invoice, consular invoice**.

L

LCL (less than carload/containerload) *Teilladung, Stückgut, Partiefracht* Güter, deren Menge nicht ausreicht, um einen Container oder Güterwaggon zu füllen.

Letter of Credit (L/C) *Akkreditiv* Zahlungsmodus bei Auslandsgeschäften, bei dem sich eine Bank verpflichtet, dem Verkäufer einer Ware bei termingerechter Vorlage der vom Käufer vorgeschriebenen Dokumente zum Nachweis des Versands (**proof of shipment**) der Ware einen bestimmten Betrag auszuzahlen. Das Akkreditiv wird auf Anweisung des Käufers (**applicant**) von seiner Bank (**issuing/opening bank**) zugunsten des Verkäufers (**beneficiary**) eröffnet. Nach Prüfung der Unterlagen und Kreditwürdigkeit schickt die eröffnende Bank (**opening/issuing bank**) eine Eröffnungsanzeige an die Bank im Verkäuferland (**correspondent bank**), die das Akkreditiv bei Vorliegen der Voraussetzungen lediglich weiterleitet oder aber ausdrücklich bestätigt (**advising/confirming bank**) und damit auch die Haftung für die Auszahlung übernimmt. Das Akkreditiv wird üblicherweise als Dokumentenakkreditiv (**documentary letter of credit**) ausgestellt. Zu den üblichen Dokumenten gehören Frachtbriefdoppel (**duplicate waybill**), Konnossement (**bill of lading**), Ladeschein (**carrier's receipt**), Spediteurübernahmebescheinigung (**forwarder's certificate of receipt / FCR**), quittierte Rechnung, Konsulatsfaktura (**consular invoice**), Versicherungbestätigung (**insurance certificate**). Das Akkreditiv ist in der Regel unwiderruflich und bestätigt (**irrevocable and confirmed**). In diesem Fall übernimmt die eröffnende Bank eine unwiderrufliche Verpflichtung zur Einlösung. Darüber hinaus wird zwischen bestätigten (**confirmed**) und unbestätigten (**unconfirmed**) Akkreditiven unterschieden. Das bestätigte Akkreditiv ist immer auch unwiderruflich. Durch die Bestätigung verpflichtet sich das avisierende Institut, die Dokumente einzulösen. Alle Akkreditive sind zeitlich befristet.

lien *Zurückbehaltungs-, Pfandrecht* Recht eines Schuldners, einen Gegenstand zurückzubehalten, bis der Gläubiger eine andere Leistung vollbracht hat, die ihm dem Schuldner gegenüber obliegt.

limited liability company *Kapitalgesellschaft* Gesellschaft, deren Haftung Dritten gegenüber beschränkt ist. Man unterscheidet zwischen der Gesellschaft mit beschränkter Haftung (GmbH, etwa: **private limited company / Ltd**) und der Aktiengesellschaft (AG, etwa: **public limited company / PLC**). Die GmbH ist eine selbstständige rechtliche Einheit (**legal entity**). Ihre Gesellschafter (**shareholders**) sind an dem Kapital der Gesellschaft beteiligt und haften beschränkt auf Ihren Kapitalanteil für die Verbindlichkeiten (**liabilities**) der Gesellschaft. Sie nehmen an dem Erfolg der Gesellschaft teil und haben ein Mitverwaltungsrecht. Die Organe der GmbH sind die Geschäftsführer (**general manager, managing director / MD**) und die Versammlung der Gesellschafter (**shareholders' meeting**). Die Gesellschafteranteile (**shares**) werden nicht öffentlich verkauft und können nur mit Zustimmung der übrigen Gesellschafter weiterveräußert

GLOSSAR

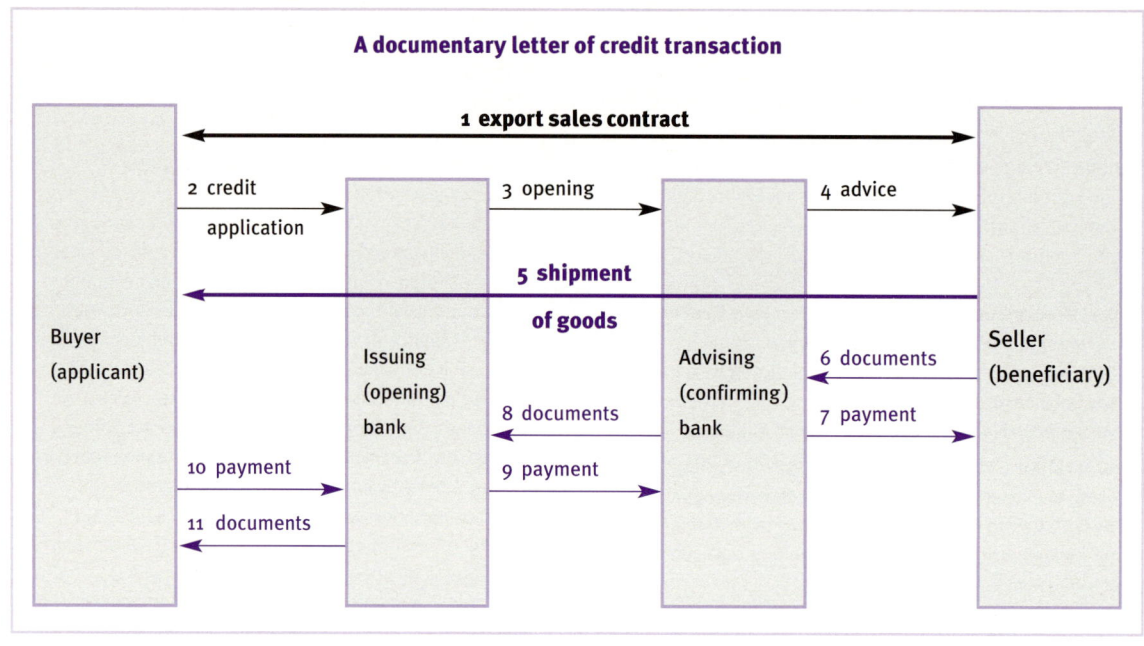

werden. Im Gegensatz dazu werden die Anteile an einer AG in der Regel einer größeren Öffentlichkeit zum Kauf angeboten. Ihre Organe sind die Hauptversammlung (**general meeting of shareholders**), der Aufsichtsrat (**supervisory board, board of supervisory/non-executive directors**) mit Kontrollfunktionen und der Vorstand (**executive board, board of executive/ managing directors**).

Lloyd's (of London) Internationaler Versicherungsmarkt, auf dem insbesondere Sachversicherungen abgeschlossen werden können. Die Haupttätigkeitsbereiche sind Seeversicherung (**marine insurance**), Luftverkehrsversicherung (**air transport insurance**), Kraftfahrzeugversicherung (**motor insurance**) und allgemeine Sachversicherung (**non-marine insurance**). Die Mitglieder von Lloyd's (**'Names'**) sind als Gruppen (**syndicates**) zusammengeschlossen und betreiben die Versicherung auf eigene Rechnung. Die im Markt tätigen Versicherer (**underwriters**) schließen Versicherungen nur mit ausdrücklich zugelassenen Mittelsmännern (**Lloyd's broker**) ab.

Lloyd's Register of Shipping *Lloyd's Schifffahrtsregister* Gesellschaft für die Klassifizierung von Schiffen, die Richtlinien für den Bau, Betrieb und die Reparatur von Schiffen aufgestellt hat. Sie ist eine Schwestergesellschaft von **Lloyd's of London** und veröffentlicht ein Schiffsverzeichnis mit detaillierten Angaben zur technischen Ausstattung von Schiffen, zu ihren Besitzern, Registrierungshafen (**port of registration**) und Flagge.

M

marine insurance *Seeversicherung*

mother company [US] *Muttergesellschaft* cf. **parent company**.

multimodal transport *multimodaler/kombinierter Verkehr* Transport, bei dem ein Verkehrsmittel auf ein anderes verladen wird, z. B. Transport von LKWs oder LKW-Anhängern (**trailer**) mit dem Zug (**piggyback service**) oder von LKWs und Eisenbahnwaggons mit dem Schiff (**roll-on/roll-off** bzw. **RoRo-service**).

N

negotiable *übertragbar* Wertpapier, Besitzurkunde, das/die problemlos an Dritte übertragen oder gegen Geld eingelöst werden kann (cf. **bill of lading**).

O

open indent *Beschaffungsauftrag* Beschaffungsauftrag an Vertreter im Ausland ohne Angabe der Beschaffungsquelle.

order *Kaufauftrag* Rechtsverbindlicher Auftrag zur Erstellung und/oder Lieferung von Waren oder Leistungen gegen Entgelt.

outstanding *offen, unbezahlt*

overdraft *Kontoüberziehung* Möglichkeit, ein Kontokorrentkonto (**current account**) ohne besondere Formalitäten für eine zuvor vereinbarte Zeit und bis einer vereinbarten Höhe (**agreed overdraft facility**) zu überziehen (**overdraw**).

owner's risk (O.R.) *Gefahr beim Eigentümer*

P

parent company [GB] *Muttergesellschaft* Unternehmen, das Mehrheitsanteile (bis zu 100 Prozent) (**majority ownership/ share**) an einem oder mehreren anderen Unternehmen (**subsidiary**) hält.

particular average *kleine Havarie, Teilhavarie* Beschädigungen an Schiff oder Ladung, die durch Sturm, Zusammenstoß (**collision**) oder zufällige Ereignisse eintreten und in der Regel von dem Geschädigten getragen werden.

payee *Zahlungsempfänger*

partnership *Personengesellschaft* Zusammenschluss von mindestens zwei Personen zum Betrieb eines Handelsgewerbes unter gemeinschaftlicher Firma. Es wird unterschieden zwischen der offenen Handelsgesellschaft (oHG: **general partnership**) und der Kommanditgesellschaft (KG: **limited partnership**). Bei der oHG haftet das gesamte Geschäftsvermögen und auch das Privatvermögen aller Gesellschafter (**partner**). Bei dieser Gesellschaftsform haftet jeder für die Folgen, die sich aus den Handlungen eines Mitgesellschafters ergeben. Bei der KG gibt es mindestens einen Gesellschafter (Komplementär: **general partner**), der voll haftet und einen Gesellschafter (Kommanditist: **limited partner**), der nur bis zur Höhe seiner Einlage (**contribution**) haftet. Der Komplementär ist zur alleinigen Geschäftsführung berechtigt.

premium *Prämie; Aufgeld, Agio* Geldbetrag, der vom Versicherungsnehmer (**insured**) an den Versicherungsgeber (**underwriter**) für den Versicherungsschutz (**coverage**) für ein Risiko zu bezahlen ist.

price ex warehouse *Preis ab Lager* Der genannte Preis gilt ab Lager und schließt die Lieferung nicht mit ein.

principal 1 *Unternehmer, Firmeninhaber* Leiter oder Inhaber eines Unternehmens. 2 *Kapitalsumme* Kapitalsumme, auf die Zinsen gezahlt werden. 3 *Kaufherr* Jemand, der eine Person zu seinem Vertreter benennt.

private limited company (Ltd, LTD) *Gesellschaft mit beschränkter Haftung (GmbH)* cf. **limited liability company**.

pro-forma invoice *Proforma-Rechnung* 1 Im Binnenhandel Rechnung an einen Kunden für Waren, die erst nach Begleichung der Rechnung ausgeliefert werden. 2 Im Außenhandel eine vorläufige Rechnung für ein Warengeschäft, die als Angebot gelten kann oder bei einer Geschäftsabwicklung auf Akkreditivbasis (**letter of credit- based transaction**) Bestandteil des Akkreditivs sein kann. 3 Musterrechnung für einen Auslandsvertreter (**foreign agent**) oder die Auslandsfiliale (**foreign branch**), auf deren Basis die Endpreise für Produkte festgesetzt werden können. 4 Vorläufige Rechnung an den Empfänger einer Warensendung zur Ansicht (**goods sent on approval**).

public limited company (plc, PLC) *Aktiengesellschaft (AG)* cf. **limited liability company**.

Q

quantity discount *Mengenrabatt* Abschlag (**reduction**) vom Verkaufspreis beim Bezug (**purchase**) größerer Mengen.

quota *Quote, Anteil* **1** Bei einem Kartell (**cartel**) der Anteil am Markt, der jedem Kartellmitglied zugestanden wird. **2** Bei Import- und Exportgeschäften von Waren, deren Mengen staatlichen Beschränkungen unterliegen, der Anteil an der Gesamtmenge, den ein Importeur oder Exporteur einführen bzw. ausführen darf.

R

rebate *Rückerstattung* Zahlung des Verkäufers an den Käufer nach Abschluss des Warengeschäfts (**completion of the purchasing transaction**).

receipt *Quittung, Empfangsbestätigung*

remittance *Überweisung* Bargeldlose Bezahlung (**cashless payment**) durch Überweisung des Geldbetrages auf das Bankkonto des Zahlungsempfängers (**payee**).

repeat order *Folgeauftrag* Auftrag für die Lieferung von Waren vom selben Lieferanten/Hersteller.

retail trade *Einzelhandel* Letzte Station in der Vertriebskette (**chain of distribution**). Hier werden Waren in kleinen Mengen an den Endverbraucher (**end user**) abgegeben.

returns *Retouren, Rückläufe* Waren, die vom Käufer zurückgegeben werden, weil sie fehlerhaft (**faulty**) oder unverkäuflich (**unsal(e)able**) sind.

roll-on/roll-off (ro-ro) *Fahrzeug für den Huckepackverkehr* (**piggyback service**) Schiff oder Eisenbahnwaggon mit Auffahrrampe, die für den Transport von Fahrzeugen geeignet sind.

S

sale on description *Verkauf nach Warenbeschreibung* Waren werden auf der Grundlage einer genauen Beschreibung ihrer Qualität und Beschaffenheit (**condition**) verkauft.

sale by sample *Verkauf gemäß Muster* Der Verkauf erfolgt auf der Grundlage, dass die gelieferte Ware dem vorgelegten Muster (**sample**) oder Musterstück (**specimen**) entspricht.

sale or return *Verkauf mit Rückgaberecht* Der Lieferant erklärt sich bereit, unverkaufte Ware zurückzunehmen und nur die verkaufte Ware in Rechnung zu stellen (**charge for**).

sample *Muster, Probe* Teil eines Produkts zu Prüfzwecken (**for test(ing) purposes**).

seller's market *Verkäufermarkt* Marktsituation mit einem knappen Warenangebot und wenig günstigen Einkaufsbedingungen (Preise, Rabatte), cf. **buyer's market**.

shipper *Versender* Hersteller oder Kaufmann, der Waren zum Versand bringt.

shipping agent *Spediteur* cf. **forwarder; forwarding agent**.

shipping documents *Versandpapiere* Die gebräuchlichsten Dokumente im internationalen Warenverkehr sind:
1. Verladedokumente: im Seeverkehr Konnossement (**bill of lading**) und Seefrachtbrief (**seaway bill**) (nicht begebbar: **not negotiable**), im Landverkehr Bahnfrachtbrief (**railway/railroad bill of lading, CIM-waybill**), Duplikatfrachtbrief (**duplicate of railway/railroad consignment note**), CMR-Frachtbrief (**international truck waybill**) und Flussladeschein (**inland waterways bill of lading**), Spediteurübernahmebescheinigung (**forwarding agent's certificate of receipt**), im Luftverkehr Luftfrachtbrief (**air waybill**) und im Postverkehr Posteinlieferungsschein (**parcel post receipt**);
2. Begleitdokumente verschiedenster Art: Handelsrechnung (**commercial invoice**), Konsulatsfaktura (**consular invoice**), Zollfaktura (**customs invoice**), Versicherungspolice oder -zertifikat (**insurance policy, oder certificate of insurance**), Ursprungszeugnis (**certificate of origin**) sowie Gesundheitszeugnis (**sanitary certificate**), Gewichtsbescheinigungen (**weight note/certificate**) und Packliste (**packing list**).

short delivery *unvollständige Lieferung*

shrinkage *Schwund* Verlust von Warenbeständen (**loss of stock**) durch Diebstahl (**pilferage**), Beschädigung bei der Herstellung oder beim Transport oder Buchungsfehler (**bookkeeping error**).

sole proprietor(ship), sole trader *Einzelkaufmann, Einzelunternehmung*

specimen *Muster* Produkt in Originalgröße zu Prüfzwecken, cf. **sample**.

standards *Normen*

statement of account *Kontoauszug* **1** *Bank* Periodische Aufstellung der Bewegungen auf einem Konto. **2** *Handel* Periodische Aufstellung des Kundenkontos mit Angaben über die Lieferungen von Waren und Dienstleistungen und die eingegangenen Zahlungen (**payments received**).

status inquiry *Kreditanfrage* Anfrage über die finanzielle Leistungsfähigkeit (**solvency**) und Kreditwürdigkeit (**creditworthiness**) eines Geschäftspartners.

(joint) stock corporation [US] *Kapitalgesellschaft* cf. **limited liability company**.

stock-in-trade *Warenbestand*

storage 1 *Lagerung* **2** *Lagerraum*

subsidiary *Tochtergesellschaft* Unternehmen, das mehrheitlich oder zu 100 Prozent einem anderen Unternehmen gehört (cf. **parent company, group**).

survey *Übersicht, Untersuchung* Im Bereich der Marktforschung (**market research**) Erhebung von Daten von einer Auswahl von Menschen (**sample**).

surveyor *Sachverständiger, Gutachter*

SWIFT (Society for Worldwide Interbank Financial Telecommunications) Internationaler Zusammenschluss von Banken zur Abwicklung von Überweisungsaufträgen (**transfers**) auf elektronischem Wege.

T

tare *Tara* Bezeichnung für das Gewicht der Warenverpackung.

terms of delivery *Lieferbedingungen* Vereinbarungen über die Pflichten von Käufer und Verkäufer im Zusammenhang mit dem Transport der Ware, die sich auf die An- und Abfuhr, Frachtkosten **(freight costs, carriage)**, Wiegegebühren **(weighing charges)**, Verladekosten **(loading charges)**, aber auch auf die Versicherung der Ware während des Transports beziehen. Bei Auslandsaufträgen werden in der Regel die **Incoterms** zugrunde gelegt.

terms of payment *Zahlungsbedingungen* Zwischen Verkäufer und Käufer zu vereinbarende Bedingungen über die Art und Weise und die Fristen für die Begleichung der Rechnung **(settlement of the invoice)**. Folgende Zahlungsbedingungen sind üblich: 1. Vorauszahlung **(cash in advance)**, z. B. Barzahlung bei Auftragserteilung **(cash with order / CWO)**; 2. Übergabe gegen Zahlung **(payment on receipt of goods)**, z. B. gegen Nachnahme **(cash on delivery / c.o.d.)**; 3. Zahlung nach Übergabe **(payment after delivery)**, z. B. Sofortkasse **(spot cash)**, gegen bar **(cash payment)**; 4. Vereinbarung eines Zahlungsziels, z. B. zahlbar in 30 Tagen ohne Abzug **(30 days net)**, zahlbar innerhalb von 10 Tagen abzüglich 2 % Skonto **(10 days 2%; less 2% cash discount for payment within 10 days)**. Bei Außenhandelsgeschäften kann auch Zahlung mittels Akkreditiv **(letter of credit)**, Dokumente gegen Kasse / Akzept **(documents against payment / acceptance)** vereinbart werden.

terms of trade *Austauschrelationen* Maßstab für die Außenhandelssituation eines Landes. Dabei wird das durchschnittliche Verhältnis der Preise für Exportgüter zu den Preisen für Importgüter gemessen, d.h. wie viele Einheiten von Importgütern mit einer Einheit von Exportgütern gekauft werden können.

time charter *Zeitchartervertrag* Vertrag für die Nutzung eines Schiffs oder Flugzeugs zu Transportzwecken für einen befristeten Zeitraum, cf. **voyage charter**.

trade bill *Handelswechsel* Wechsel für die Bezahlung von Gütern.

trade discount *Handelsrabatt, Wiederverkäuferrabatt* Nachlass vom Bruttopreis der Ware für gewerbliche Verbraucher oder Händler.

trade terms **1** *Lieferklauseln* Wenn keine Incoterms (cf. **Incoterms**) vereinbart sind, gelten die nationalen Vertragsklauseln. Diese sind wie die Incoterms von der Internationalen Handelskammer in Paris zusammengestellt worden. Die **trade terms** der USA sind in der Bezeichnung oft identisch mit den **Incoterms**, unterscheiden sich aber vielfach hinsichtlich des Zeitpunkts des Gefahrenübergangs **(transfer of risk)** und der Frage der Versicherung. **2** *Konditionen für den Handel* Besondere Preisgestaltung (z. B. durch Rabatte) für Wiederverkäufer.

transit *Transit* Beförderung der Ware, oft durch ein drittes Land.

U

underwriter *Versicherer*

V

value added tax (VAT) *Mehrwertsteuer* Umsatzsteuer **(output tax)**, die bei jeder Weitergabe von Waren an einen Dritten **(third party)** in der Phase der Erzeugung **(production)** und des Vertriebs **(distribution)** erhoben wird. Hierbei wird jeweils nur der zusätzlich geschaffene Wert besteuert. Die Vorsteuer **(input tax)** wird erstattet. Der Endverbraucher **(end user)** zahlt allerdings die volle Mehrwertsteuer.

voyage charter *Reisecharter* Chartervertrag **(charterparty)** für ein Schiff für eine festgelegte Reise, cf. **time charter**.

W

warehouse-to-warehouse *von Haus zu Haus* Versicherungsklausel, mit der ein Versicherungsschutz **(insurance cover)** während des Transports der Ware vom Lager des Verkäufers bis zum Lager des Käufers vereinbart wird.

warrant **1** *Garantieschein* Zusicherung einer verabredeten Leistung bzw. Produktqualität. **2** *Empfangsbestätigung* Bestätigung über den Empfang einer Ware.

warranty *Garantie*

waybill *Frachtbrief, Warenbegleitschein* cf. **consignment note**.

wholesale trade *Großhandel*

without engagement *freibleibend* Diese Klausel ermöglicht es dem Verkäufer, den Preis nach Angebotsabgabe **(making an offer)** entsprechend den Marktverhältnissen **(market situation)** noch zu ändern.

Wörterverzeichnis A–Z

Diese Liste enthält alle Wörter in alphabetischer Reihenfolge. Hier sind jedoch die Wörter, die zum Grundwortschatz gehören, sowie internationale Wörter wie *fax*, *hotel* oder *job* nicht aufgeführt. Die Zahl nach dem Stichwort bezieht sich auf die Seite, auf der das Wort zum ersten Mal erscheint.

T = das Wort befindet sich in den *Transcripts* zu der *Listening*-Übung auf der betreffenden Seite.

30 days net 54 *30 Tage netto*

A

ability to meet financial obligations 125 *Zahlungsfähigkeit*
accessories 36 *Zubehör(teile)*
accommodate so. 96 *jdm. entgegen kommen*
account, clear/settle an ~ 92, 98 *Rechnung begleichen, Konto ausgleichen*
account, collect an ~ 98 *Rechnungsbetrag eintreiben*
account, credit an ~ with 98 *dem Konto gutschreiben*
account, debit an ~ with 98 *Konto belasten mit*
account facility, open ~ 98 *Konto mit periodischer Abrechnung*
account, overdue ~ 87 *offen stehende/überfällige Rechnung*
account terms, open ~ 81 *offenes Zahlungsziel, Kontokorrentbedingungen*
accounting department 110 *Rechnungsabteilung*
acknowledgement of order 67 *Auftragsbestätigung*
action, legal ~ 67 *rechtliche Schritte*
addressee 9 *Adressat/in, Empfänger/in*
adequate 35 *angemessen, geeignet*
advantage, take ~ of 11 *nutzen*
advice 115 *Rat(schlag)*
advice note 79 *Versandanzeige*
advice of dispatch 67 *Versandmitteilung, Versandanzeige*
advise 41, 64 *(an)raten; benachrichtigen, informieren*
aforesaid 121 *vorgenannt, oben genannt*
agent 26 *(Handels)Vertreter/in, Vermittler/in*
aggravate 101 *verschlimmern*
agreement, confirm the ~ 51 *eine Vereinbarung bestätigen*
air, by ~ 77 *mit dem Flugzeug, auf dem Luftweg*
air freight, as/by ~ 80 *als/per Luftfracht*
Air Mail, By ~ 7 *(Mit) Luftpost*
air waybill, airway bill (AWB) 79 *Luftfrachtbrief*
A-level (exam(inations)) 129 *etwa: Abiturprüfung*
A-levels, pass one's ~ 140 *etwa: Abitur machen/bestehen*
allocate 51 *hier: zuordnen*
allowance of credit 116 *Fristgewährung, Kreditgewährung*
alternative 40 *Alternative*
amount, outstanding ~ 81 *fälliger/offener Betrag*
amount, credit so. with an ~ 84 *jdm. einen Betrag gutschreiben*

answering machine 23 *Anrufbeantworter*
anticipated 70 *erwartet*
apologies, please accept our ~ (for) 113 *wir entschuldigen uns (für), wir bitten um Entschuldigung*
apologies, offer one's ~ 113 *sich entschuldigen*
apologise 70 *sich entschuldigen*
applicant 139 *(Stellen)Bewerber/in*
application form 5 *Antragsformular, Bewerbungsformular*
application, approve an ~ 5 *Antrag genehmigen/annehmen*
application, unsolicited ~ 126 *Initiativbewerbung*
apply 64 *Gültigkeit haben, gelten*
appointment, new ~ 14 *Neubesetzung*
appointments diary 131 *Terminkalender*
appreciate 17 *dankbar sein für, zu schätzen wissen*
apprentice 141 *Lehrling, Auszubildende/r*
apprenticeship, serve an ~ 141 *eine Lehre/Ausbildung machen*
apprenticeship 141 *Ausbildung(splatz)*
approach 114 *sich wenden an*
approval, on ~ 39 *zur Ansicht, zur Probe*
approximate 100 *ungefähr*
arise from 108 *sich ergeben aus*
arrange for sth. to be done 66 *veranlassen/dafür sorgen, dass ...*
arrangement of appointments 14 *Vereinbarung von Terminen*
arrival, late ~ 113 *verspätete Ankunft, verspätetes Eintreffen*
article, customised/tailor-made ~ 50 *Sonderfertigung, Einzelstück, nach Kundenangaben hergestellter Artikel*
articulate 138 *klar im Ausdruck*
as per 77 *gemäß*
assembly 49 *Montage, Zusammenbau*
assignment, long-term ~ 127 *langfristige Anstellung/Beschäftigung*
assistance, be of ~ 116 *helfen (können)*
assortment 100 *Auswahl, Partie*
assurance 100 *Zusicherung, Sicherheit*
assure 40 *zusichern*
at 90 d/s (days sight) 98 *auf 90 Tage Sicht*
attention line 8 *Zeile für den persönlichen Empfänger*
attention to detail 130 *Genauigkeit*
attention, escape ~ 92 *der Aufmerksamkeit entgehen*

attention, receive immediate ~ 68 *umgehend bearbeitet/ erledigt werden*
augmented by 130 *hier: ergänzt durch*
authorities 108 *Behörden*
availability 42 *Verfügbarkeit*
average, above ~ 132 *überdurchschnittlich*

B

B&B accommodation 24 *Übernachtung mit Frühstück*
B.A. (Bachelor of Arts) 141 *erster akad. Grad in angelsächsischen Ländern (in Geisteswissenschaften)*
B.Sc. (Bachelor of Science) 141 *erster akad. Grad in angelsächsischen Ländern (in Natur- oder Ingenieurwissenschaften)*
back office support 138 *administrative Unterstützung*
background, educational ~ 140 *Bildungsgang; (Hoch)Schulbildung*
bag 80 *Beutel*
balance 5 *Restbetrag, Restsumme, Saldo*
balance, outstanding ~ 97 *offener Betrag*
balance sheet 121 T *Bilanz*
bale 80 *Ballen*
bank/banker's transfer 52, 98 *Banküberweisung*
banking industry 127 *Bankwesen, die Banken*
bankrupt 125 *konkurs, pleite*
bankruptcy (file for ~) 125 *Konkurs (anmelden)*
bargain, tempting ~ 5 *verführerisches Angebot, "Schnäppchen"*
barrel 80 *Fass*
based in (London), (London)-based 36 *mit Sitz in (London), in (London) ansässig*
basis, on the ~ of 51 *auf der Grundlage von*
batch 108 *Partie, Sendung*
benefits 11, 127 *Leistungen; Zulagen, freiwillige Sozialleistungen*
bent 111 *verbogen*
bilingual 127 *zweisprachig*
bill, a three-month ~ 115 *3-Monats-Wechsel*
bill of exchange (B/E) 66 *Wechsel*
bill of lading (B/L) 79 *Seefrachtbrief, Konnossement*
blame, be to ~ 99 *verantwortlich/schuld sein*
blame 99 *Schuld*
blot 108 *Flecken, Klecks*
board marker 108 *Schreibstift*
body of the letter 9 *Brieftext*
booking of accommodation 14 *Buchung einer Unterkunft*
booklet 39 *Heft, Faltblatt*
born 129 *geboren am*
borrowing activities 116 *Kreditaufnahme*

bottling machine 64 *Abfüllmaschine*
bottom 80 *unten*
breach of contract 113 *Vertragsbruch*
brisk 35 *lebhaft*
broaden 34 *verbreitern, ausweiten*
brochure 29 *Prospekt, Broschüre*
Bros (Brothers) 6 *Gebrüder*
browse 86 *durchblättern, durchstöbern*
bulk purchase 50 *Großeinkauf*
bulk 48 *größter Anteil*
bundle 80 *Bündel*
business 83 *hier: das Geschäft*
business administration 128 *Betriebswirtschaft*
business conduct 125 *Geschäftsgebaren*
business contacts 128 *Firmenkontakte, Kundenkontakte*
business dealings 125 *Geschäftsverkehr*
business relationship 116 *Geschäftsbeziehung*
buyer, prospective ~ 50 *Kaufinteressent/in, potenzielle/r Kunde/Kundin*
buying 39 *Beschaffung, Einkauf*

C

cabinet, roll-fronted ~ 111 *Rollschrank*
Cadeaux (F) 19 *Geschenke*
call on 40 *besuchen, aufsuchen*
cannot but 99 *nur noch tun können*
capacity, be working to ~ 50 *voll ausgelastet sein, die Kapazität voll ausschöpfen*
capital base 116 *Kapitalausstattung*
capital, tied-up ~ 114 *gebundenes Kapital*
car fleet 49 *Fahrzeugflotte*
car polish 48 *Autopolitur*
carbon copy 10 *Durchschlag*
carboy 80 *Korbflasche*
card balance 5 *Kreditkartensaldo*
care, handle with ~ 75 *Vorsicht, nicht werfen*
career centre 126 *Berufsinformationszentrum*
career, professional ~ 141 *beruflicher Werdegang, Berufslaufbahn*
careers office 137 *Berufsberatung*
carpet salesroom 102 *Teppich-Verkaufsraum*
carriage forward (C/F) 79 *unfrei, per Frachtnachnahme*
carriage paid (C/P) 79 *frachtfrei, Fracht bezahlt*
carrier 75 *Spedition, Frachtführer, Transportunternehmer*
carry 79 *transportieren*
case 51 *Kasten*
cash against documents (C/D; CAD) 114 *Kasse gegen Dokumente*
cash discount 40 *Skonto, Barzahlungsrabatt*

cash on delivery (COD) 114 *gegen Nachnahme*
cash payment 46 *Barzahlung*
cash settlement 66 *sofortige Rechnungsbegleichung*
cash situation, strain the ~ 88 *die Kassenlage anspannen*
cash with order (CWO) 114 *Bezahlung bei Auftragserteilung*
cashflow 88 *Cashflow, Liquidität*
catalogue *(GB)*, catalog *(US)* 10 *Katalog*
Caution! 80 *Vorsicht!*
certificat pratique de la langue française *(F)* 131 *Französisch-Zertifikat*
certificate 140 *Bescheinigung, Zeugnis, Zertifikat*
certificate of origin 79 *Ursprungszeugnis*
Chamber of Commerce 26 *(Industrie- und) Handelskammer*
charge, at no extra ~ 97 *ohne zusätzliche Kosten, kostenlos*
charges 40 *Gebühren*
charges, postal ~ 13 *Postgebühren*
charges, rental ~ 36 *hier: Standgebühren/-miete*
chart 138 *Schaubild, Grafik*
check, end-of-line ~ 69 *Endkontrolle*
chief officer 6 *Geschäftsführer/in, Vorstandsvorsitzende/r*
china 28 *Porzellan*
circumstance 86 *Umstand*
circumstances beyond our control 75 *Umstände, auf die wir keinen Einfluss hatten*
claim for compensation 113 *Schadensersatzanspruch*
claim, reject the ~ 99 *Forderung zurückweisen*
clerkship 141 *Praktikum*
clientele 41 *Kundschaft, Kunden*
Co (company) 6 *Firma (Fa)*
code, postal ~ 8 *Postleitzahl (PLZ)*
coincide 108 *zusammenfallen mit*
collection agency 82 *Inkassobüro*
collection letter 82 *Mahnschreiben, Mahnung*
college 131 *Fachschule; Kolleg, Akademie*
college, secretarial ~ 141 *Sekretärinnenschule*
colour code 48 *Farbstruktur, Farbkodierung*
colouring 28 *Farbe, Farbgebung*
come back to 36 *sich wieder melden*
come up to 36 *hier: entsprechen*
commitments, meet the ~ 88 *(Zahlungs)Verpflichtungen erfüllen/nachkommen*
committed 138 *engagiert*
commonly 51 *allgemein, üblicherweise*
communicate 14 *kommunizieren, sich austauschen*
communication, inter-company ~ 4 *Kommunikation zwischen Unternehmen*
communication, intra-company ~ 4 *unternehmensinterne Kommunikation*

communication skills 127 *Kommunikationskompetenz*
company report 114 *Geschäftsbericht*
company stationery 6 *Firmenbriefpapier*
compatible with 130 *vereinbar mit*
compensation 101 *Ausgleich, Erstattung*
compensation, ask for ~ 113 *um Entschädigung bitten*
compensation, insist on ~ 113 *auf Entschädigung bestehen*
compensation, claim ~ 112 *Ersatz/Ausgleich beanspruchen*
competitive 35 *günstig, wettbewerbsfähig*
complain about 100 *sich beschweren über*
complaint 67 *Mängelrüge, Beschwerde*
complimentary close 4 *höfliche Schlussformel*
comply with 114 *einhalten, (den Vorschriften) entsprechen*
comprehensive 35 *umfassend*
compromise solution 99 *Kompromiss*
computer literacy 137 *Computerkenntnisse*
computer-literate 127 *mit Computerkenntnissen*
concessions, offer/grant ~ 39 *Vergünstigungen einräumen/gewähren*
condition, in good ~ 68 *in gutem Zustand*
condition, be in a marketable ~ 99 *noch verkauft werden können*
conference facilities 14 *Tagungsmöglichkeiten*
conference room 5 *Tagungsraum, Sitzungszimmer*
confident 52 *zuversichtlich*
confidential, strictly ~ 115 *streng vertraulich*
confidential, be treated as ~ 114 *vertraulich behandeln*
conformity, in ~ with 51 *gemäß*
consequently 100 *folglich, daher*
considered, be ~ 126 *in die engere Wahl ziehen*
consignee 77 *(Sendungs)Empfänger/in*
consignment 53 *Sendung, Lieferung, Ladung, Partie*
consignment, grouped ~ 79 *Sammelladung*
consignment note 79 *Frachtbrief*
consignor 79 *Versender, Verfrachter*
consistent 130 *beständig*
consolidate 110 *zusammenführen*
constitute 51 *darstellen, bedeuten*
consular invoice 81 *Konsulatsrechnung, Konsulatsfaktura*
contact, initiate ~ 132 *Verbindung/Kontakt aufnehmen*
container 80 *Container; Behälter*
Continent 132 *Europa (ohne britische Inseln)*
contract of sale 67 *Verkaufsvertrag*
contract, award a ~ 64 *Auftrag erteilen*
contract, hold so. to a ~ 113 *auf die Einhaltung des Vertrags drängen*
contract, negotiate a ~ 121 T *Vertrag aushandeln*
contract, place a ~ 48 *Auftrag erteilen/vergeben*

contributor 131 hier: *Autor/in*
convenience, at your ~ 36 *bei Gelegenheit*
convenience, at your earliest ~ 17 *möglichst umgehend*
convenience, for your ~ 64 *zu Ihrer Verwendung*
convention 4 *Gewohnheit, Konvention*
conveyor belt system 49 *Transportbandanlage*
copy, rough ~ 13 *Briefentwurf, Konzept*
copy typing 127 *Übertragen von Texten*
copywriting 131 *Texterfassung*
core of the business 122 *Hauptgeschäft/-geschäftsaktivitäten*
Corp (Corporation) *(US)* 6 *Gesellschaft mit beschränkter Haftung (GmbH)*
correctness, political ~ 7 *korrektes Verhalten*
correspondence, follow-up ~ 10 *nachfolgene/weitere Korrespondenz*
cost and risk, at so.'s ~ 99 *auf jds. Kosten und Gefahr*
cost, overall/total ~ 50 *Gesamtkosten*
cost-saving 114 *Kosten sparend*
cotton shirt 112 *Baumwollhemd*
couched, be ~ 99 hier: *formuliert*
count on 36 *damit rechnen, darauf zählen*
counteroffer 51 *Gegenangebot*
course, in due ~ 52 *bei Gelegenheit; zu gegebener Zeit*
course, attend a ~ 137 *einen Kurs besuchen*
cover letter 84 *Kurzbrief, Begleitzettel*
cover, under separate ~ 40 *mit getrennter Post*
crate, wooden ~ 69 *Holzkiste*
credit agency, commercial ~ 114 *Kreditauskunftei*
credit enquiries 114 *Kreditauskunft*
credit entry 98 *Gutschrift*
credit facilities, long-term ~ 66 *langfristige Zahlungsziele*
credit line 125 *Kreditrahmen, Kreditlinie*
credit note/memo 81, 98 *Gutschriftanzeige*
credit record 86 hier: *Ruf als pünktlicher Zahler, Kreditwürdigkeit*
credit reference/status agency 125 *Auskunftei*
credit standing/status 115 *Kreditstatus, -würdigkeit, Bonität*
credit, allow/grant ~ 115 *Kredit gewähren/einräumen*
credit, extend a ~ 98 *Kreditverlängerung gewähren*
credit transfer 81 *Überweisung*
creditworthiness 125 *Kreditwürdigkeit*
current 34 *aktuell, derzeit gültig*
curriculum vitae (CV) 126 *Lebenslauf*
customer database 127 *Kundendatenbank*
customer, discerning ~ 42 *anspruchsvoller Kunde*
customer enquiries, process ~ 131 *Kundenanfragen bearbeiten*
customer, long-standing ~ 35 *langjähriger Kunde*
customer, prospective ~ 40 *potenzieller Kunde, Kaufinteressent*

customer relationship manager 128 *Kundenbetreuer/in*
customer, accommodate the ~ 99 *dem Kunden entgegen kommen*
customer's specifications, produce to the ~ 67 *nach Kundenangaben herstellen*
customised 46 *nach Kundenangaben gefertigt/hergestellt*
customs clearance 77 *Verzollung, zollamtliche Abfertigung*
customs duty 75 *Zoll(gebühr)*
customs invoice 81 *Zollrechnung, Zollfaktura*
cutlery 46 *Besteck*

D

damage (of goods) in transit 69 *Transportschaden*
damaged, badly/slightly ~ 113 *schwer/leicht beschädigt*
damaged en route/in transit 113 *während des Transports beschädigt*
data analysis 138 *Datenanalyse*
data gathering 138 *Datenerhebung*
data protection legislation 114 *Datenschutzgesetze*
data sheet, personal ~ (PDS) 140 *(tabellarischer) Lebenslauf*
date 127 *datieren, mit einem Datum versehen*
date, expiry/use-by/best before ~ 113 *Haltbarkeitsdatum*
date of birth 140 *Geburtsdatum*
date of invoice 47 *Rechnungsdatum*
date of maturity 98 *Verfalltag, Fälligkeitsdatum/-termin*
date, stipulated ~ 75 *gewünschtes Datum*
date, to ~ 128 *bisherig*
dates, on the due ~ 121 *bei Fälligkeit*
days of receipt, within (14) ~ of 54 *innerhalb von (14) Tagen nach Erhalt von*
deadline, fail to meet the ~ 66 *Frist versäumen, Frist nicht einhalten*
deadline, meet the ~ 66 *Termin einhalten, Frist wahren*
dealings 108 *Geschäftsabschlüsse*
dealings, in their ~ 122 *in ihrer Geschäftstätigkeit*
debit entry 98 *Lastschrift*
debit note/memo 81, 98 *Belastungsanzeige*
debt(s), bad ~ 114 *Außenstände*
deck, do not stow on ~ 80 *nicht an Deck verstauen*
default 98 *in Verzug sein/kommen*
defective 99 *fehlerhaft, mangelhaft*
delay in delivery 67 *Lieferverzug, Lieferverzögerung*
delay in payment 82 *Zahlungsverzug*
delayed, be ~ 75 *verzögert werden*
delete 41 *tilgen, löschen;* hier: *aus dem Programm nehmen*
delivery 26 *Lieferung*
delivery date 40 *Lieferdatum, Liefertermin*
delivery date, meet a ~ 50 *Liefertermin/Lieferfrist einhalten*
delivery date, quote a ~ 50 *Liefertermin nennen*

delivery, early/prompt ~ 66 *baldige/sofortige Lieferung*
delivery note 79 *Lieferschein, Lieferzettel*
delivery period 34 *Lieferfrist, Lieferzeitraum*
delivery, special ~ *(US)* 13 *durch Eilboten*
delivery, make ~ 70 *liefern*
demand (for) 34 *Nachfrage (nach), Bedarf (an)*
dented 111 *mit Dellen, eingedellt*
depending on 26 *je nach*
deposit 84 *Anzahlung*
design 28 *Design, Gestaltung, Ausführung*
design, interior ~ 127 *Innenarchitektur*
desk, international ~ 131 *Abteilung für internationale Angelegenheiten*
despatch 79 *versenden, zum Versand bringen, liefern*
despatch note 79 *Versandanzeige, Lieferschein*
detail, in sufficient ~ 40 *hinreichend detailliert*
detailed below 66 *nachstehend aufgeführt*
deterioration 113 *Verderb*
diagnosis equipment 34 *Diagnosegeräte*
diligence 130 *Sorgfalt, Fleiß*
Director level 127 *Geschäftsführungsebene*
discount 26 *Rabatt, Preisnachlass*
discount, grant/allow a ~ 48 *Rabatt gewähren*
discrepancy 63 T *Unterschied, Unstimmigkeit, Differenz*
discretion, treat with ~ 122 *vertraulich behandeln*
discretion, with the strictest ~ 125 *streng vertraulich*
discrimination 127 *Diskriminierung*
dispatch 40 *versenden, zum Versand bringen, liefern*
dispatch department 99 *Versandabteilung*
dispatch note 79 *Versandanzeige, Lieferschein*
dispatch, ready for ~ 67 *versandfertig*
display 61 *ausstellen, zeigen*
display 36 *Anzeige, Ausstellung, Ansicht*
disposal, at so.'s ~ 51 *zu jds. Verfügung*
disposal, place at the ~ of 62 *zur Verfügung stellen*
disregard 92 *nicht beachten, ignorieren*
distribution 129 *Vertrieb*
distributor 34 *Vertrieb(sgesellschaft)*
diverse 138 *verschieden(artig)*
divorced 140 *geschieden*
document 128 *belegen, dokumentieren*
documentation 69 *Papiere*
documents against acceptance (D/A) 77 *Dokumente gegen Annahme (der Tratte) (Wechsel)*
documents against payment (D/P) 61 *Dokumente gegen Kasse*
draft, first ~ 13 *Briefentwurf, Konzept*
draft for acceptance 98 *Tratte zur Annahme*
draft, accept our ~ 69 *unsere Tratte akzeptieren*
drive 136 *Dynamik*

driving licence, clean ~ 129 hier: *ohne Eintragung in die Flensburger Kartei*
drop, do not ~ 80 *nicht fallen lassen*
drum 75 *Tonne, Trommel*
due date 98 *Verfalls-/Fälligkeitsdatum*
duplicate 92 *Kopie, Zweitschrift*
duplicate, in ~ 79 *in zweifacher Ausfertigung*
duration 22 *Dauer*
duty forward 79 *unverzollt*
duty paid 79 *verzollt*

E

earthenware 28 *Steingut*
e-commerce 122 *Internet-Handel*
economics 129 *Volkswirtschaftslehre, Wirtschaftswissenschaften*
economics, graduate in ~ 140 *im Fach Wirtschaftswissenschaften sein Examen machen*
education 127 *Erziehung, schulischer Werdegang*
education, higher/tertiary ~ 140 *Hochschulbildung*
education, primary ~ 140 *Primarstufe*
education, secondary ~ 140 *Sekundarstufe*
effective, become ~ 50 *wirksam werden, in Kraft treten*
employment agency 126 *Stellenvermittlung*
employment contract 141 *Arbeitsvertrag*
enclosure 10 *Anlage*
encourage 40 *ermutigen, ermuntern*
engineer 64 *Techniker*
engineering company 131 *Maschinenbauunternehmen*
English-speaking environment 128 *englischsprachiges Umfeld*
enhanced 131 hier: *erweitert, ergänzt*
enquiry 26 *Anfrage*
en-suite facilities, with ~ 15 *mit Bad und WC*
entail 51 *nach sich ziehen, zur Folge haben*
enterprises, medium-sized ~ 123 *mittelständische Unternehmen*
entitled, be ~ to 11 *Anspruch haben auf, berechtigt sein zu*
envelope, reply-paid ~ 5 *portofreier/frei gemachter Briefumschlag*
envelope, self-/stamp-addressed ~ (SAE) 13 *adressierter Freiumschlag*
environment, economic ~ 122 *wirtschaftliche Rahmenbedingungen, wirtschaftliches Umfeld*
erection 65 hier: *Montage*
error 63 T *Irrtum*
error, redress an ~ 113 *Irrtum wiedergutmachen*
errors and omissions excepted (E&OE) 98 *Irrtümer und Auslassungen vorbehalten*
evidence, credible ~ 99 *glaubwürdiger Nachweis/Beweis*

exceeding 48 *über, von mehr als*
excess, in ~ of 41 *über, von mehr als, höher als*
execute 67 *ausführen*
execution 40 *Ausführung, Erledigung*
execution of order 78 *Auftragsausführung*
exhibit 39 *Ausstellungsstück*
exhibition 37 *Ausstellung*
exhibitor 19 *Aussteller/in*
expansion 116 *Wachstum, Geschäftsausweitung*
expectations 35 *Erwartungen*
expense, be at so.'s ~ 66 *zu jds. Lasten gehen*
experience, industry-related ~ 130 *Erfahrung in der Industrie*
expertise 138 *Kompetenz, Können*
explanation, ask for an ~ 86 *um eine Erklärung bitten*
export price 36 *Exportpreis, Ausfuhrpreis*
exposure, extensive ~ 131 *hier: langjährige Erfahrung*
exposure to 128 *hier: Kontakte zu, Tätigkeit in*
Express, (By) ~ 13 *durch Eilboten*
extension of credit 93 *Fristverlängerung*
extension, ask for an ~ 82 *um Verlängerung des Zahlungsziels bitten*
extension, grant an ~ 93 *einen Zahlungsaufschub gewähren*

F

fabrics 48 *Stoffe, Gewebe*
fabrics, woven ~ 70 *Webstoffe*
facilities, technical ~ 15 *technische Ausstattung*
fail in doing sth. 96 *etw. nicht tun*
failure in the performance 67 *Nichterfüllung*
failure to pay 97 *Nichtzahlung*
fair 19 *(Fach)Ausstellung, (Fach)Messe*
fair display 138 *Messeauslagen*
fair stand 19 *Messestand*
faith, in the utmost good ~ 116 *in gutem Glauben*
family name 140 *Familienname*
family status 127 *Familienstand*
fashion house 36 *Modehaus*
fashion show 36 *Modeschau*
fault 67 *Fehler, Mangel, Defekt*
fault, be at ~ 102 *schuld sein*
favourable 62 *günstig*
feedback 19 *Rückmeldung*
field sales team 138 *Vertriebsmitarbeiter, Vertriebsmannschaft*
field work 131 *praktische Tätigkeit*
file number 6 *Aktennummer, Aktenzeichen*
files 13 *Akten(ablage), Aktenvorgänge, Registratur*
filing 13 *Ablage*
filing cabinet 111 *Aktenschrank*
filling material 75 *Füllmaterial*
finalize 16 *endgültig festlegen*
finalized, be ~ 15 *hier: endgültig bestätigen/entscheiden*
finish 53 *Endbearbeitung, hier: Verarbeitung*
finishing 110 *Verarbeitung*
fire, damaged by ~ 113 *durch Feuer beschädigt*
fitting 69 *Einbau*
flammable 80 *feuergefährlich*
flexi part time 127 *Teilzeitarbeit mit Gleitzeit*
fluency (in) 127 *Flüssigkeit, flüssiger Gebrauch (von)*
fluent 136 *fließend*
follow-up order 51 *Folgeauftrag*
font 126 *Schrifttyp*
force majeure (F) 64 *(Vers.) höhere Gewalt*
form, available in printed ~ 40 *gedruckt/in gedruckter Form verfügbar*
form, blank/filled-out ~ 13 *leeres/ausgefülltes Formular*
form, in tabular ~ 127 *tabellarisch*
form letter 13 *Musterbrief, Formbrief*
fortnight 41 *14 Tage*
forward 115 *versenden, liefern, nachsenden*
forward, please ~, to be ~ed 13 *bitte nachsenden*
forwarder, forwarding agent 62, 75 *Spediteur, Spedition, Versender*
forwarding instructions 67 *Versandanweisungen*
fragile 75 *zerbrechlich*
franco domicile 54 *frei Haus*
freelancer 141 *Freiberufler/in*
freight, exclusive of ~ 79 *ausschließlich Fracht*
freight, inclusive of ~ 79 *einschließlich Fracht*
freight charges 75 *Frachtgebühren, Frachtkosten*
freight collect 79 *unfrei, per Frachtnachnahme, Fracht bezahlt Empfänger*
freight forwarder 99 *Spediteur, Spedition*
freight note 79 *Frachtbrief*
freight paid 79 *Fracht bezahlt*
freight prepaid 79 *frachtfrei, Fracht bezahlt*
fringe benefits 141 *freiwillige Sozialleistungen (des Arbeitgebers)*
full-block form 9 *Blockform*
fundamentals 130 *Grundlagen*
furious 109 T *wütend*
furniture, occasional ~ 36 *Kleinmöbel*

G

garments 36 *Bekleidung, Bekleidungsstücke*
gazette 121 T *Blatt, Anzeiger*
GCSE examination (general certificate of secondary education) (GB) 140 *zentrale staatliche Prüfung zum Abschluss der Sekundarstufe I*

genuine 126 *echt, ehrlich*
Glass with care 80 *Vorsicht Glas*
glassware, ornamental ~ 42 *Einzelstücke aus Glas*
glassware 42 *Glasprodukte, Glasartikel*
gloves 36 *Handschuhe*
goal-focused 138 *zielorientiert*
goods await collection 75 *die Ware ist zur Abholung bereit*
goods in stock 50 *vorrätige Ware*
goods in transit 69 *Transitwaren*
goods out of stock 50 *nicht mehr vorrätige Ware*
goods, second-rate ~ 113 *Waren minderer Qualität*
goods, substandard ~ 99 *minderwertige Ware*
goods, accept the ~ 67 *Ware(n) annehmen*
goods, deliver ~ 66 *Ware anliefern/ausliefern*
goods, deliver ~ by (date) 66 *Ware bis zum ... liefern*
goods, lay/take ~ in stock 50 *Ware auf Lager nehmen*
goods, supply ~ 66 *Ware liefern*
goodwill 93 hier: *guter Wille*
goodwill, preserve the ~ 99 *das Wohlwollen erhalten*
government-run office 126 *staatliche Behörde/Stelle*
grade 129 *Note*
graduate 132 *Hochschulabsolvent/in*
graduate calibre 136 *mit Hochschulabschluss*
grant 36 *gewähren*
guarantee, carry our full ~ 69 *der vollen Garantie unterliegen*
guesthouse 24 *(Ferien)Pension*

H

handbag 36 *Handtasche*
handle 131 hier: *bearbeiten*
handling (rough ~) 108 *(unsachgemäße) Behandlung, Handhabung*
hand-woven 102 *handgewebt*
haulage company 79 *Straßenspediteur, (Güter)Spedition*
headquarters 127 *Hauptverwaltung, Hauptsitz*
heat, damaged by ~ 113 *durch Hitze beschädigt*
heat, stow away from ~ 80 *vor Hitze schützen*
high school, graduate from ~ (US) 137 *Schulabschluss erreichen, Schule beenden*
highlight 42 *besonders herausstellen*
highly inflammable 80 *leicht entzündlich, Vorsicht Feuergefahr*
high-quality 35 *hochwertig, von guter Qualität*
high-tech product 23 *technisch hochwertiges Produkt*
hinge 121 T *Angel, Scharnier*
hold 112 hier: *zurückhalten*
hold so. responsible (for) 108 *jdn. verantwortlich machen (für)*
holiday entitlement 141 *Urlaubsanspruch*
holiday, paid ~ 141 *bezahlter Urlaub*

holiday season 94 T *Urlaubszeit*
honours degree (GB) 137 *qualifizierter Hochschulabschluss*
hooks, use no ~ 80 *keine Haken*
hospitality 19 *Gastfreundschaft*
hotel lounge 36 *Eingangsfoyer, Empfangshalle*
human resources 127 *Personal, Mitarbeiter/innen*
human resources management 127 *Personalwesen, Personalverwaltung*

I

ignore 97 *ignorieren, nicht beachten*
illustrated 35 *bebildert*
imitation leather armchair 36 *mit Kunstleder bezogener Sessel*
implement 132 *umsetzen*
implications, legal ~ 51 *rechtliche Folgen*
important, all the more ~ 101 *umso wichtiger*
impracticable 110 *unpraktisch*
impressive 28 *eindrucksvoll*
Inc (Incorporated) 6 *eingetragene Gesellschaft (AG, GmbH)*
incident 99 *Vorfall*
inconvenience 70 *Unannehmlichkeit, Schwierigkeiten*
inconvenience incurred 101 *Unannehmlichkeiten*
indentation 14 *Einrückung*
indented 9 *eingerückte Briefform*
indicate 36 *angeben*
indication 51 *Hinweis*
infant school 140 *Vorschule*
inferior 70 *von geringerer Qualität, minderwertig*
inflammable 75 *entzündlich, entflammbar*
information, confidential ~ 125 *vertrauliche Auskunft*
information on the credit status and reliability 125 *Auskunft über die Kreditwürdigkeit und Zuverlässigkeit*
information pack 36 *Info-Mappe*
information, reliable ~ 125 *zuverlässige Auskunft*
initials 10 *Initialen*
inland postage 13 *Inlandsporto*
innovative 132 *innovativ*
insist on 100 *bestehen auf*
insolvency 125 *Insolvenz, Zahlungsunfähigkeit*
insolvent 125 *zahlungsunfähig, illiquide*
inspection, customary ~ 67 *übliche Prüfung*
inspection, for ~ 112 *zur Ansicht/Prüfung*
instalments, in equal ~ 88 *in gleichen/gleich hohen Raten*
instructions, as per our written ~ 66 *gemäß unseren schriftlichen Anweisungen*
instructions for dispatch 79 *Versandanweisungen*
insurance certificate 79 *Versicherungsschein*
insurance policy 79 *Versicherungspolice*

interest rate offer 5 *günstiges Zinsangebot*
interest, arouse ~ 126 *Interesse wecken*
internship 141 *Praktikum*
interpreting work 131 *Dolmetschtätigkeit*
intervals, at very short ~ 110 *kurz hintereinander*
intranet 126 *firmeneigenes Netz*
investigations 99 *Nachforschungen*
invoice 41 *Rechnung*
invoice 112 *in Rechnung stellen, berechnen*
invoice amount 69 *Rechnungsbetrag*
invoice-based 121 *gegen Rechnung*
invoice, commercial ~ 79 *Handelsrechnung, Handelsfaktura*
invoice, pro-forma ~ 79 *Proformarechnung*
invoice, make out an ~ 85 *Rechnung ausstellen*
involve 26 *bedeuten, mit sich bringen*
irregularity 101 *Unregelmäßigkeit*
irrespective of 99 *ungeachtet der Tatsache*
item, each ~, per ~ 66 *pro Stück*
item number 51 *Artikelnummer*
itinerary 17 *(Reise)Route*

J

jar 80 *Glas*
job advertisement 126 *Stellenanzeige, Stellenausschreibung*
job application 126 *Stellenbewerbung*
job centre 141 *etwa: Arbeitsamt*
job exchange 126 *Stellenbörse*
job experience 141 *praktische Erfahrung, Berufserfahrung*
job listing 128 *Stellennachweis*
job profile 136 *Stellenbeschreibung, Stellenprofil*
job seeker 126 *Arbeitsplatzsuchende/r, Stellensuchende/r*
job title 10 *Berufsbezeichnung, Stellenbezeichnung*
job vacancy 126 *freie Stelle*
justified, be ~ 99 *gerechtfertigt sein*

K

keen 36 *hier: äußerst preisgünstig*
keep cool 80 *Kühl aufbewahren*
keep dry 75 *Trocken lagern, vor Nässe schützen*
key account manager 128 *(Groß)Kundenbetreuer/in*
keyboard(ing) skills 136 *EDV-Fähigkeiten*
keying error 92 *Eingabefehler*
kitchen, fitted ~ 110 *Einbauküche*
knowledge 128 *Kenntnis(se)*

L

lampshade 37 *Lampenschirm*
layout 126 *äußere Form und Gestaltung*

leaflet 39 *Informationsblatt, Prospekt*
leak 108 *lecken*
leakage 113 *(Flüssigkeit) Auslaufen, Leck, Leckage; Schwund*
legally binding 40 *rechtsverbindlich*
letter form, printed ~ 13 *Briefvordruck*
letter of application 126 *Bewerbungsschreiben*
letter of credit (L/C) 64 *Akkreditiv, Kreditbrief*
letter of credit, irrevocable and confirmed documentary ~ 64 *unwiderrufliches und bestätigtes Dokumentenakkreditiv*
letterhead 6 *Briefkopf*
letters, incoming ~ 13 *Briefeingang, Posteingang*
liability, accept ~ 64 *Haftung übernehmen*
liability, without ~ 125 *ohne Gewähr*
lift here 80 *hier anheben*
linguistic skills 137 *Sprachkompetenz*
list of charges 15 *hier: Preisliste*
listed below 66 *nachstehend aufgeführt*
literature 28 *Informationsmaterial, Prospekte*
load-carrying capacity 65 *Tragkraft*
logistics 129 *Logistik*
long-standing 35 *langjährig*
look forward (to) 28 *sich freuen (auf)*
lorry, by ~ 80 *mit Lastkraftwagen/Lkw*
loss incurred 108 *erlittener/entstandener Verlust*
loss, cover a ~ 113 *Verlust decken/ausgleichen*
lot 50 *Partie, Gebinde*
low-cost 5 *kostengünstig, zu geringen Kosten*
LTD/Ltd (Limited = Private Limited Comp.) 6 *Gesellschaft mit beschränkter Haftung (GmbH)*

M

M.A. (Master of Arts) 138 *Magister (in Geisteswissenschaften)*
M.Sc. (Master of Science) 141 *Magister (in Natur- oder Ingenieurwissenschaften)*
machine, customised ~ 69 *nach Kundenangaben gebaute Maschine*
machine operators 64 *Bedienungspersonal*
magazine advertisement 27 *Zeitschriftenanzeige*
maiden name 140 *Mädchenname*
mail, inward ~ *(US)* 13 *Briefeingang, Posteingang*
mail order 122 *Versandhandel*
mail, outgoing/outward ~ *(US)* 4 *Ausgangspost, Briefausgang*
mail, with/by same ~ 13 *mit gleicher Post*
maintenance 69 *Wartung*
major 28 *groß*
Major *(US)* 138 *Hauptfach, Leistungskurs*
major in *(US)* 140 *Abschluss mit ... als Hauptfach machen*
managing director 139 *Geschäftsführer/in*

manufacturing company 128 *Hersteller*
margin, left ~ 9 *linker Rand*
margin of profit 92 *Gewinnspanne*
marine engineering 129 *Schiffbautechnik*
mark 140 *Note*
market 28 *vermarkten, verkaufen, vertreiben*
market, fast-moving ~ 41 *schnellen Veränderungen unterliegender Markt*
market leader 127 *Marktführer/in*
market, local ~ 52 *hiesiger/heimischer Markt*
marketing company 34 *hier: Vertriebsgesellschaft*
marketing graduate 132 *Hochschulabsolvent/in in Marketing*
marketing initiative 92 *Absatzinitiative*
married 140 *verheiratet*
matter, printed ~ 7 *Drucksache*
matter, registered ~ 7 *Einschreiben*
matter, investigate the ~ 113 *Angelegenheit untersuchen*
matter, look into the ~ 102 *Angelegenheit untersuchen lassen*
matter, take the ~ up with 108 *Angelegenheit mit ... besprechen*
means 115 *Finanzmittel*
means, by legal ~ 98 *auf dem Rechtsweg/Klageweg*
meantime, in the ~ 53 *zwischenzeitlich*
measurements 51 *Maße*
media studies 138 *Medienwissenschaft(en)*
medium-sized 121 *mittlere/r/s*
memo pad 13 *Notizblock*
mention: bien *(F)* 131 *Note: gut*
merchandise 101 *Ware*
message, urgent ~ 4 *dringende Nachricht*
Minor *(US)* 138 *Nebenfach, Grundkurs*
minor in *(US)* 141 *Abschluss mit ... als Nebenfach machen*
mistake 12 *Fehler*
misunderstanding 51 *Missverständnis*
model letter 4 *Musterbrief, Formbrief*
model number 51 *Modellnummer*
moist 111 *feucht, nass*
money order 81 *Postüberweisung, Zahlungsanweisung*
moved, address unknown 13 *Empfänger unbekannt verzogen*
multiple 131 *vielfältig*

N

name, first/given/Christian ~ 140 *Vorname*
necessitate 70 *erfordern, notwendig machen*
negotiating skills 136 *Verhandlungssicherheit*
non-availability 70 *Nichtverfügbarkeit*
non-delivery 113 *Nichtlieferung*
non-payment 114 *Nichtzahlung*

notice-board 126 *Schwarzes Brett, Anschlagtafel*
notice, escape so.'s ~ 108 *jds. Aufmerksamkeit entgehen*
numerate 136 *kompetent im Rechnen*

O

obligation(s), financial ~ 120 *finanzielle Verpflichtung, Zahlungsverpflichtung*
obligation to accept the goods 51 *Verpflichtung zur Annahme der Ware*
obligation to supply 51 *Lieferverpflichtung*
obligation, without (any) ~ 50 *(Angebot) unverbindlich, ohne Kaufverpflichtung, freibleibend*
obligations, contractual ~ 108 *vertragliche Verpflichtungen*
obligations, meet one's (financial) ~ 93 *seinen (Zahlungs) Verpflichtungen nachkommen*
oblige 99 *verpflichten*
occupational 141 *Berufs-, beruflich*
occurred 108 *vorgekommen*
occurrence, become an infrequent ~ 99 *selten werden/ vorkommen*
OEM product 116 *Originalprodukt*
offer 40 *Angebot*
offer discount, introductory ~ 66 *Einführungsrabatt*
offer, firm ~ 51 *verbindliches Angebot*
offer, submit an ~ 39 *Angebot machen/unterbreiten*
office communication 14 *Bürokommunikation*
office equipment 35 *Büroausstattung, Bürogeräte*
office, registered ~ 6 *eingetragener Sitz*
O-levels, pass one's ~ *(GB)* 138 *Abschlussprüfung (etwa: Abschluss der Sekundarstufe I) machen*
ominous 109 T *unheilvoll*
omit 127 *auslassen*
omitted 29 *ausgelassen*
open here 80 *hier öffnen*
opening of the credit 64 *Akkreditiveröffnung*
operation, put sth. into ~ 64 *etw. in Betrieb setzen*
operations 116 *Aktivitäten, Geschäftstätigkeit*
order 35 *Auftrag, Bestellung*
order 66 *Auftrag erteilen*
order discount, initial ~ 66 *Nachlass für Erstaufträge*
order, firm ~ 50 *feste Bestellung, Festauftrag*
order, follow-up ~ 50 *Ersatzbestellung, Nachfolgebestellung*
order form 51 *Auftragsformular, Auftragszettel*
order, in reverse chronological ~ 127 *in umgekehrter chronologischer Reihenfolge*
order, initial ~ 50 *Erstauftrag, Neuauftrag*
order number 51 *Auftragsnummer*
order on call 51 *Auftrag auf Abruf*

order, regular/standing ~ 51 *Dauerauftrag*
order, repeat ~ 50 *Ersatzbestellung, Nachfolgebestellung*
order, acknowledge an ~ 79 *Auftrag bestätigen*
order, cancel an ~ 79 *Auftrag stornieren*
order, complete an ~ 66 *Auftrag ausführen/fertig stellen*
order, confirm the ~ 67 *Auftrag bestätigen*
order, deliver an ~ 79 *Auftrag ausliefern*
order, execute/fill/fulfil an ~ 41 *Auftrag ausführen/erledigen*
order, handle/meet/process an ~ 46 *Auftrag bearbeiten/ausführen*
order, make up an ~ 101 *Auftrag zusammenstellen/fertig stellen*
order, place an ~ 37 *Auftrag erteilen*
order, refuse/reject/turn down an ~ 75 *Auftrag ablehnen/zurückweisen*
order, suspend an ~ 93 *Auftrag nicht (weiter) bearbeiten*
order volume, minimum ~ 48 *Mindestauftragsvolumen*
organisation, professional ~ 127 *Berufsorganisation, Standesorganisation, Fachverband*
outlet 28 *Geschäft, Laden*
out-of-stock 41 *nicht mehr vorrätig*
outright 99 *rundweg*
overcharge 113 *zuviel berechneter Betrag, Überforderung*
overdue 86 *überfällig*
overseas order 41 *Auslandsauftrag*
overseas postage 13 *Auslandsporto*
oversight, through an ~ 78 *aufgrund eines Versehens*
over-the-counter trade 122 *Geschäft im stationären Handel*
overworked 86 *überarbeitet*

P

P.O. Box 13 *Postfach*
packaging 41 *Verpackung*
packing, improper ~ 108 *unsachgemäße Verpackung*
packing instructions 67 *Verpackungsanweisungen*
packing list 79 *Packliste*
packing, seaworthy ~ 64 *seemäßige Verpackung*
pallet 75 *Palette*
parentage 131 *Eltern*
partner 7 *Teilhaber/in*
partnership 7 *Personengesellschaft*
parts, spare ~ 69 *Ersatzteile*
pattern 26 *(Stoff etc.) Muster*
pattern book 48 *Musterbuch*
pattern, match the ~ 66 *dem Muster entsprechen*
pay off 92 *sich auszahlen*
pay package 136 *Vergütung*
payee 98 *Zahlungsempfänger*

payment by crossed cheque 66 *Zahlung durch Verrechnungsscheck*
payment discount, early ~ 66 *Skonto, Barzahlungsrabatt*
payment habits 116 *Zahlungsverhalten, Zahlungsgewohnheiten*
payment in advance 66 *Vorauszahlung*
payment on invoice 125 *Zahlung bei Rechnungserhalt*
payment performance 125 *Zahlungsgewohnheiten*
payment terms, deferred ~ 125 *langfristiges Zahlungsziel*
payment within a fortnight of receipt of invoice 41 *Zahlung innerhalb von 14 Tagen nach Rechnungserhalt*
PC-literate 129 *mit Computerkenntnissen*
PDS (personal data sheet) 140 *tabellarischer Lebenslauf*
peers 138 *Gleichgestellte, Kollegen*
per annum 126 *jährlich*
performance 108 *Leistung*
performance of the contract 67 *Vertragserfüllung*
period of delivery 67 *Lieferzeit, Lieferfrist*
period, probationary ~ 141 *Probezeit*
period, within the ~ stated 66 *innerhalb der angegebenen Zeit/Frist*
perishable 80 *verderblich*
perks 136 *freiwillige Sozialleistungen*
personal 13 *persönlich*
petrol station 49 *Tankstelle*
pick up 75, 88 *abholen; hier: sich (wieder) beleben*
pile 101 *(Teppich) Flor*
pilferage 113 *(geringfügiger) Diebstahl*
place of birth 140 *Geburtsort*
plant 64 *Fabrik, Werk*
PLC/plc (Public Limited Company) 6 *Aktiengesellschaft (AG)*
plug 63 *Stecker*
poisonous 75 *giftig*
policy of caution 116 *hier: Vorsicht*
polytechnic *(GB)* 140 *Fachhochschule*
portable 37 *tragbar*
post, with/by same ~ 13 *mit gleicher Post*
postage 13 *Porto*
post-graduate 141 *Student/in in einem weiterführenden Studiengang (4./5. Studienjahr)*
pp, per pro 10 *in Vertretung für (i.V.)*
practical 129 *Praktikum*
practice, common ~ 40 *allgemein üblich*
preceded, be ~ by 51 *etw. vorausgehen*
preferably 127 *vorzugsweise*
preferred 10 *bevorzugt; hier: am häufigsten gebraucht*
premises 102 *Geschäftsräume*
prerequisite 136 *Voraussetzung*

press, come off the ~ 42 *gerade erschienen sein*
prevent from 86 *hindern an*
price, agreed ~ 51 *vereinbarter Preis*
price, at a ~ of 66 *zum Preis von*
price, competitive/keen ~ 36 *wettbewerbsfähiger/günstiger Preis*
price, gross ~ 47 *Bruttopreis*
price-list 10 *Preisliste*
price-list, current ~ 35 *gültige/aktuelle Preisliste*
price, moderate ~ 24 *günstiger Preis*
price, net ~ 40 *Nettopreis*
price, special introductory ~ 49 *Einführungssonderpreis*
priced at 66 *zum Preis von*
prices, off net ~ 36 hier: *von den Nettopreisen abgezogen*
prices, quote firm ~ 40 *ein Festpreisangebot machen*
principal 39 *Auftraggeber/in, Unternehmer/in*
private and confidential 8 *persönlich und vertraulich*
proactive 132 *mit Eigeninitiative*
procedures, improve ~ 78 *Verfahren verbessern/optimieren*
processing 7 *Bearbeitung*
procurement 39 *(Staat) Beschaffung*
product line 29 *Produktgruppe, -reihe*
product, pharmaceutical ~ 77 *Pharma-Produkt*
product, promote a ~ 50 *Produkt herausstellen/fördern*
production schedule 76 *Produktionsplan*
profession 141 *Beruf (mit akad. Ausbildung)*
proficiency 127 *Können, Kompetenz*
profile, personal ~ 137 *Lebenslauf, Werdegang, Bewerbungsmappe, -unterlagen*
profile, professional ~ 131 *berufliches Profil*
project development 131 *Projektentwicklung*
promise, make good one's ~ 100 *sein Versprechen halten*
proofreading 131 *Korrekturlesen*
propose 115 *vorschlagen, bitten um*
prospects, ruin our ~ 100 *Chance/Aussicht zunichte machen*
prospectus 35 *(Schule/Universität) Werbeprospekt; Börsenzulassungsprospekt*
provide so. with 39 *jdm. etw. zukommen lassen*
provided 51 *vorausgesetzt*
Pty (proprietary company) 6 *etwa: GmbH*
public relations department 138 *Abteilung für Öffentlichkeitsarbeit*
purchase 51 *kaufen, erwerben*
purchase price 99 *Kaufpreis*
purchasing 39 *Beschaffung, Einkauf*
purchasing department 7 *Einkauf(sabteilung)*
purchasing manager 38 *Einkaufsleiter/in*
putting into operation 49 *Inbetriebnahme*

Q

quadruplicate, in ~ 79 *in vierfacher Ausfertigung*
qualification, vocational ~ 141 *Berufsbildungsabschluss*
qualify for 110 *berechtigen zu*
qualities, self-starting ~ 131 *Eigeninitiative*
quality, inferior ~ 102 *minderwertige/schlechte Qualität*
quantity discount 34 *Mengenrabatt*
queries 36 T *Rückfragen*
query, further ~ 16 *Rückfrage, weitere Frage*
question, in ~ 40 *fraglich*
quintuplicate, in ~ 79 *in fünffacher Ausfertigung*
quotation 26 *(Preis)Angebot*
quotation, offer/make a favourable ~ 39 *ein günstiges Angebot vorlegen/machen*

R

rail, by ~ 80 *per Bahn*
range (of products) 19 *Sortiment, Produktpalette*
range, full ~ 34 *komplettes/gesamtes Sortiment*
rates, postal ~ 13 *Postgebühren*
rebate 34 *Nachlass*
receipt, (up)on ~ of 52 *nach Erhalt von*
receipt of order, after ~ 39 *nach Auftragseingang, nach Eingang der Bestellung*
receipt of your invoice, within ... upon ~ 52 *innerhalb von ... nach Eingang Ihrer Rechnung*
recent 28 *neueste/r/s*
recipient 5 *Empfänger/in*
reciprocate 23 *Gegendienste leisten, Gefälligkeit erwidern*
recognize 116 *erkennen, sich bewusst sein*
recommend 116 *empfehlen*
records 13 *Akten(ablage), Aktenvorgänge*
recruitment agency 126 *Stellenvermittlung*
recruitment officer 130 *Sachbearbeiter/in für Personaleinstellungen*
reduction 46 *Preisnachlass*
refer to 27 *sich beziehen auf, Bezug nehmen auf*
reference 29 *Empfehlungsschreiben, Referenz; Verweis*
reference, first-class ~ 36 *erstklassige/vorzügliche Referenz*
reference, furnish/submit/supply a ~ 39 *eine Referenz vorlegen*
reference, give a favourable ~ 114 *eine positive Auskunft geben*
reference, make ~ to 6 *verweisen auf*
reference number 6 *Geschäftszeichen*
reference, provide a ~ 29 *eine Referenz angeben*
refined 130 hier: *ergänzt, vervollkommnet*
refreshments, light ~ 16 *kleine (Pausen)Erfrischung*
refund 99 *(Rück)Erstattung, Rückzahlung*

refund 108 *zurückerstatten*
refurbish 36 *modernisieren, umbauen*
Registered (Mail) 13 *Einschreiben*
registration number 6 *Registernummer*
reimbursement 113 *Rückerstattung*
rejection 99 *Zurückweisung, Ablehnung*
related 34 hier: *dazugehörig*
relevant 28 *einschlägig*
reliability 122 *Zuverlässigkeit*
reliable 36 *zuverlässig*
remainder 92 *Restbetrag, Restsumme*
reminder 81 *Zahlungserinnerung, Erinnerungsschreiben*
remittance to so.'s account with/at … (bank) 66 *Überweisung auf jds. Konto bei der …*
remittance 61 *Überweisung*
remittee 98 *Zahlungs-/Überweisungsempfänger*
remitter 98 *Überweisender, Geldsender*
remuneration package 139 *Vergütungspaket*
replacement 75 *Ersatz(stück), Ersatzlieferung*
replacement offer 67 *Ersatzangebot*
reply coupon 26 *Antwortabschnitt*
reply coupon, international postal ~ 13 *Internationaler Postantwortschein*
report 140 *(Schule, Hochschule) Zeugnis*
representative 26 *Vertreter/in, Repräsentant/in*
repro furniture 36 *Stilmöbel*
reputation 67 *Ruf*
reputation, enjoy a good ~ 116 *einen guten Ruf genießen*
request for credit 125 *Bitte um Kreditgewährung*
request for information 26 *Bitte um Auskunft/Information(en)*
request, comply with a ~ 125 *einer Bitte entsprechen*
requested, if ~ 64 *falls gewünscht*
require 26 *brauchen; erfordern, erforderlich machen*
requirement 86 *Bedarf, Bestellung*
requirements, meet the ~ 126 *den Anforderungen entsprechen*
resources, financial ~ 120 *Finanzmittel*
resources, sufficient ~ 93 hier: *ausreichende (Geld)Mittel*
respective 10 hier: *betreffend, jeweilig*
responsibility, assume ~ 116 *Verantwortung übernehmen*
responsible, be ~ (for) 102 *Verantwortung tragen für*
restock 50 *das Lager (wieder) auffüllen*
résumé, resumé *(US)* 130 *Lebenslauf*
return if undelivered 13 *zurück, falls unzustellbar*
return (of mail/post), by ~ 13 *postwendend, umgehend*
returnable, be ~ 75 *umtauschbar sein*
reveal 127 *offen legen*
reverse (of letter) 13 *Briefrückseite*
review 130 hier: *lesen*

reward 127 *belohnen*
road, by ~ 80 *per Straße*
road haulier 79 *Straßenspediteur, (Güter)Spedition*
roller guide 111 *Rollenführung*
room, twin ~ 15 *Doppelzimmer mit getrennten Betten*
rota 136 *Dienstplan, Einsatzplan*
rotation, in strict ~ 46 *streng der Reihe nach, in der Reihenfolge des Eingangs*
run-up, in the ~ to 19 *vor, im Vorfeld von*
rush of orders 70 *hoher Auftragseingang, Flut von Aufträgen*

S

sack 80 *Sack*
salary 126 *Gehalt*
sale or return, on ~ 39 *mit Rückgaberecht, in Kommission*
sale, attract a ~ 41 *zum Auftrag führen*
sales 129 *Verkauf*
sales drive 61 *Absatzkampagne*
sales letter 5 *Werbebrief*
sales letter, draft a ~ 131 *Angebotsschreiben entwerfen*
sales literature 26 *Prospektmaterial, (Verkaufs)Prospekte*
sales manager 7 *Verkaufsleiter/in*
sales material 39 *Prospektmaterial, Prospekte*
sales outlet 61 *Vertriebsstätte, Laden*
salutation 9 *Grußformel*
sample 26 *Muster, Probe(stück)*
sample, be up to/correspond to the ~ 63, 66 *dem Muster entsprechen*
satisfaction, give ~ 108 *zufrieden stellend funktionieren*
satisfactory 99 *zufrieden stellend*
scanner pen 62 *Scannergriffel*
schedule 130 hier: *Termin festlegen für*
scheduled, be ~ 15 *geplant/angesetzt sein*
school, comprehensive ~ 138 *Gesamtschule*
school, junior/primary ~ 140 *Grundschule*
school leaving certificate 140 *Abschlusszeugnis*
school, secondary/high ~ *(US)* 137 *weiterführende Schule, Oberschule*
school, attend ~ 140 *Schule besuchen*
school, leave ~ 140 *von der Schule abgehen*
school, vocational ~ 141 *Berufsschule, Berufskolleg*
scope 4 *(Spiel)Raum*
scratch 111 *Kratzer*
scratched 111 *verkratzt, zerkratzt*
sealed 112 *verschweißt*
seaport 64 *Seehafen*
season, festive ~ 19 hier: *Weihnachtszeit*
seating capacity 15 hier: *Sitzplätze*

seconds 101 *minderwertige Ware, zweite Wahl*
security, without ~ 125 *ohne Stellung von Sicherheiten*
seepage 113 *(Flüssigkeit) Durchsickern*
selection 52 *Auswahl*
selection procedure/process 126 *Auswahlverfahren*
selector 126 *Personalsachbearbeiter/in*
self-driven 132 *dynamisch*
self-employed, be ~ 141 *selbstständig sein (beruflich)*
selling, door-to-door ~ 137 *Türverkauf*
selling point 40 *Verkaufsargument*
semi-block form 9 *Flattersatz*
send 5 *versenden*
senior secretary/PA 127 *Chefsekretärin/Assistentin*
sensitive 114 *heikel, problematisch*
service, after-sales ~ 69 *Kundendienst*
service (and maintenance) department/division 37 *Kundendienst(abteilung)*
service, fast ~ 42 *hier: schnelle Erledigung*
settee 36 *(Sitz)Couch*
settle amicably 113 *gütlich regeln/beilegen*
settlement 50 *(Rechnung) Begleichung*
settlement in full 98 *zum vollen Ausgleich*
settlement, in ~ of your statement 98 *zum Ausgleich Ihres Kontoauszuges*
settlement of our invoice 97 *Begleichung unserer Rechnung*
shape 28 *Form*
shifting of contents 113 *Verrutschen der Ware*
ship 42 *versenden, absenden*
ship, by ~ 80 *mit dem Schiff, auf dem Seewege*
shipload 115 *Schiffsladung*
shipment 68 *Sendung, Lieferung*
shipment, ready for ~ 75 *versandbereit*
shipment, arrange ~ 66 *den Versand veranlassen, für den Versand sorgen*
shipments, consolidate ~ 79 *Sammelladung zusammenstellen*
shipper 75 *Versender, Befrachter*
shipping advice 79 *Versandanzeige, Verschiffungsanzeige*
shipping agent 79 *Spediteur, Spedition*
shipping company 79 *Schifffahrtsgesellschaft, Reederei*
shipping documents 69 *Versandpapiere, Verschiffungspapiere*
short-delivered, short-shipped 111, 113 *(Minderlieferung) zu wenig geliefert*
shorthand 127 *Kurzschrift, Steno(grafie)*
shortlist 126 *Auswahl treffen*
showroom 39 *Ausstellungsraum, Musterlager*
sight draft 98 *Sichttratte, Sichtwechsel*
sincere 99 *aufrichtig*
single 129 *ledig*

skills 127 *Fähigkeiten, Fertigkeiten*
skills, organisational ~ 127 *Organisationsfähigkeit, Organisationstalent*
skills, social ~ 127 *Sozialkompetenz*
skills, sophisticated secretarial ~ 131 *umfassende Kompetenz in Sekretariatsangelegenheiten*
slack 92 *flau*
snag 19 *Problem*
soap, herbal ~ 61 *Kräuterseife*
soiled 113 *angeschmutzt*
solicit 130 *auffordern (zu)*
solicitor 96 *(Rechts)Anwalt*
solution, mutually acceptable ~ 87 *beiderseitig zufrieden stellende Lösung*
solvency 125 *Zahlungsfähigkeit*
solvent 125 *zahlungsfähig, liquide*
Son(s) 6 *Sohn (Söhne)*
sophisticated 99 *hier: gut, ausgereift*
source 29 *Herkunft, Ursprung*
specialist magazine 126 *Fachzeitschrift*
specialist retail trade 34 *Facheinzelhandel*
specialist retailer 28 *Fachhändler*
specimen 28 *Muster(stück) (in Originalgröße)*
specimen letter 13 *Musterbrief, Formbrief*
speed up 75 *beschleunigen*
staff 14 *Personal, Mitarbeiter/innen*
staff, (highly) skilled ~ 34 *(hoch)kompetente Mitarbeiter/innen*
stand 34 *(Messe)Stand, Firmenstand*
standard practice 67 *übliche Praxis*
standard, be up to ~ 39 *den Anforderungen entsprechen*
standing contract 100 *Dauerauftrag*
standing, financial ~ 122 *finanzielle Lage, Vermögenslage*
state of affairs 101 *Lage, Stand der Dinge, Situation*
state, unsatisfactory ~ 112 *unbefriedigender Zustand*
statement, duplicate ~ 97 *Rechnungsdoppel, Rechnungskopie*
statement, monthly ~ 98 *Monatauszug, Monatsabrechnung*
statement of account 92 *Kontoauszug*
statement, quarterly ~ 66 *(Konto) Quartalsauszug, vierteljährlicher Auszug*
state-of-the-art 136 *hochmodern, allerneueste/r/s*
stationery 4 *Schreibpapier, Schreibwaren*
statistics, compile ~ 138 *Statistiken erstellen*
status, financial ~ 125 *finanzielle Lage, Vermögenslage*
steel frame 111 *Stahlrahmen*
steps, legal ~ 98 *gerichtliche Schritte*
stipulated 75 *festgelegt*
stock clearance 50 *Lagerräumung*

stock, ex/from ~ 46 *ab Lager*
stock, from ~ 67 hier: *mit Lagerprodukten*
stock, in ~ 67 *vorrätig, auf Lager*
stock, out of ~ 46 *nicht (mehr) vorrätig*
stock, be made for ~ 67 *auf Lager fertigen/produzieren*
stock, supply from ~ 79 *ab Lager liefern*
stockist 40 *Großhändler, Fachhändler*
stock-keeping 69 *Lagerhaltung*
stocks, clear/reduce ~ 50 *die Läger/Lagerbestände räumen*
stocks, replenish ~ 50 *das Lager (wieder) auffüllen*
storage costs 75 *Lagerkosten*
store 75 *lagern*
strictly private 116 *streng vertraulich*
subject line 5 *Betreffzeile*
subject, main ~ 140 *Hauptfach, Leistungskurs*
subject, subsidiary ~ 129 *Nebenfach, Grundkurs*
subject to 61 *auf der Grundlage von, vorbehaltlich*
subject to confirmation 40 *unverbindlich, ohne Kaufverpflichtung, freibleibend*
subject to these conditions 70 *gemäß diesen Bedingungen*
substandard 99 *unzureichend; (von) minderer Qualität*
substantial 35 *beträchtlich, erheblich*
substitute 70 *Ersatzprodukt*
suede and leather goods 36 *Lederwaren*
suggestion 40 *Vorschlag*
suitability 126 *Eignung*
suitable 17 *geeignet, passend*
sum total 98 *Gesamtbetrag*
superb 127 *großartig*
supplier 34 *Lieferant*
supplier, potential ~ 26 *möglicher Lieferant*
supply 50 *Vorrat, (Lager)Bestand, Lieferung; Angebot*
supply guarantee 42 *Liefergarantie*
supply period 35 *Lieferzeit, Lieferfrist*
supply so. with 40 *jdm. schicken, jdn. beliefern mit*
support services 36 T *Service-Unternehmen*
surname 140 *Familienname*

T

tally 108 *übereinstimmen*
tamper with 112 *sich zu schaffen machen an*
team leader 131 *Gruppenführer/in*
team player, be a ~ 132 hier: *teamorientiert sein/arbeiten*
telephone manners 136 *Telefonkompetenz*
telesales marketing 127 *Telefonverkauf*
temp 141 *Zeitarbeiter/in*
temp 141 *Zeitarbeit machen*
temping 141 *Zeitarbeit*

temporary 127 *zeitlich befristet, temporär*
terms and conditions 34 *(allgemeine) Geschäftsbedingungen*
terms, in legal ~ 51 *rechtlich gesehen*
terms of delivery 40 *Lieferbedingungen*
terms of payment and delivery 26 *Liefer- und Zahlungsbedingungen*
terms of the contract 113 *Vertragsbedingungen*
terms stated in the offer 63 *Angebotsbedingungen*
test programme, put through a ~ 69 *genau testen*
test, rigorous ~ 48 *strenger Test*
testimonial 126 *(Arbeitgeber) Zeugnis, Nachweis*
texture 39 *Beschaffenheit, Struktur*
thank you letter 14 *Dankesschreiben*
ticket, complimentary ~ 19 *Freikarte*
timber 115 *(Nutz)Holz*
time, full ~ 127 *Vollzeit*
time, in the ~ 66 *innerhalb der angegebenen Zeit/Frist*
time management 131 *Zeitplanung, Terminplanung*
time schedule 36 T *Zeitplan*
title 7 *Titel, Anrede*
tool box 61 *Werkzeugkasten*
top 80 *oben*
total 83 *Gesamtbetrag*
track record 128 *Erfolg (in der Vergangenheit), Werdegang*
track record, proven ~ 127 *nachweislicher Erfolg*
trade association 26 *Handelsverband*
trade customers 42 *gewerbliche Kundschaft, Wiederverkäufer*
trade directory 26 *Branchenbuch, Branchenverzeichnis*
trade discount 36 *Wiederverkäuferrabatt, Handelsrabatt*
trade fair 39 *(Fach/Handels)Messe, Ausstellung*
trade journal/magazine 28 *Fachzeitschrift*
trade reference 114 *Handelsauskunft*
trading partner, prospective ~ 124 *potenzieller Geschäftspartner*
trainee 137 *Auszubildende/r, Volontär/in*
traineeship 132 *Volontariat, Praktikum, Ausbildungsplatz*
training 64 *Ausbildung; Fortbildung*
training, further ~ 141 *Weiterbildung, Fortbildung*
training, in-house/in-company ~ 141 *betriebliche Weiterbildung*
training, in-service ~ 141 *berufliche Fortbildung/Weiterbildung*
training, practical/vocational ~ 141 *Berufsausbildung*
transfer to so.'s account with/at ... (bank) 66 *Überweisung auf jds. Konto bei der ...*
transferee 98 *Zahlungs-/Überweisungsempfänger*
transferor 98 *Überweisender, Geldsender*
transit, in ~ 99 *während des Transports*
transmission, speedy ~ 4 *schnelle Übermittlung*

trial order 35 *Probeauftrag*
trial shipment/supply 39 *Probesendung, Probelieferung*
triplicate, in ~ 79 *in dreifacher Ausfertigung*
truck, by ~ 80 *mit Lastkraftwagen/Lkw*
trucking operations 19 *Lkw-Betrieb*
trust, be based on ~ 114 *auf Vertrauen beruhen*
turnover 35 *Umsatz*

U

ullage 113 *Flüssigkeitsverlust, Auslaufen*
ultimately 67 *letztendlich*
undelivered 113 *(Minderlieferung, Fehlmenge) nicht/zu wenig geliefert*
undercharge 113 *zu wenig berechneter Betrag, Unterforderung*
undergraduate 141 *Student/in in den ersten 3/4 Studienjahren*
understand, we ~ 61 *wir nehmen zu Kenntnis*
understanding, on the definite ~ 100 *unter der eindeutigen Voraussetzung*
understood, it is ~ 52 *es gilt als vereinbart*
undertaking, definite ~ 100 *festes Versprechen, feste Zusage*
unfounded 102 *unbegründet*
unit, per ~ 54 *pro Verpackungseinheit/Gebinde*
update 41 *aktualisieren, auf den neuesten Stand bringen*
update 16 *hier: Aktualisierung; neuester Stand*
urgent 4, 13 *dringend; Eilt*

V

vacation, annual ~ (US) 141 *Jahresurlaub*
valid 40 *gültig*
value added tax (VAT) 24 *Mehrwertsteuer (MwSt)*
variety 28 *Vielfalt, breite Palette*
VAT number 6 *Mehrwertsteuer-Nummer (MwSt-Nr.)*
venue 16 *Tagungsort*
vice-president 15 *Direktor, Abteilungsleiter*
visitor (to the fair) 39 *Messebesucher*

W

wage 141 *Lohn*
warehouse 49 *hier: Lagerhalle, Lager*
warehousing 129 *Lagerhaltung, Lagerei*
warrant 116 *rechtfertigen*
warranty 35 *Gewährleistung, Garantie*
water, damaged by ~ 113 *durch Wasser beschädigt*
way, this ~ up 75 *hier oben*
wear and tear 113 *(natürlicher) Verschleiß*
website 26 *Webseite, Internetseite*
weight, dead ~ 80 *Eigengewicht, Leergewicht*
weight, gross ~ 75 *Bruttogewicht*
weight, net ~ 75 *Nettogewicht*
well-established 28 *alteingesessen, gut eingeführt*
well-founded 99 *gut begründet*
wholesaler 35 *Großhändler*
widowed 140 *verwitwet*
work experience 127 *praktische Erfahrung, Berufserfahrung*
work freelance 141 *freiberuflich tätig sein*
work full-time 141 *voll/ganztags arbeiten*
work part-time 139 *Teilzeit/halbtags arbeiten*
work, part-time ~ 141 *Teilzeitarbeit*
work placement 138 *Praktikum, Praktikumsplatz*
working day 48 *Arbeitstag*
working hours 141 *Arbeitszeit*
working week, 37 hour ~ 41 *Wochenarbeitszeit von 37 Stunden*
workmanship 47 T *Verarbeitung*
workmanship, faulty/poor ~ 99 *schlechte Verarbeitung, fehlerhafte Arbeit*
wrapping instructions 69 *Verpackungsanweisungen*
wrapping material 75 *Umschlagmaterial*
wrapping paper 80 *Packpapier*

XYZ

Yellow Pages 26 *Gelbe Seiten*

Transcript

 Unit 2 Exercise C5

... Bitte hinterlassen Sie eine Nachricht nach dem Signalton.

Boulder: This is Peter Boulder. I'm phoning from the train, but I'm afraid we have only just left Hanover. The train from Berlin had engine failure, so we had to get on another train at Wolfsburg and then change again in Hanover. I don't think I can be in Düsseldorf for the meeting later this morning. Will you please tell everyone that I'll arrive at Düsseldorf station at about 2 o'clock and hope to be at your office approximately half an hour later. I'm very sorry to upset everybody's plans. But I hope it's OK if we have the meeting at three. See you then and thank you.

3 Unit 2 Exercise C6

Jennings: Keele Park Hotel. Events management. Can I help you?
Bauer: This is Bianca Bauer from MTV in Germany. Good afternoon. My company is organising a meeting of our British sales staff and I would like to make a booking.
Jennings: Yes, certainly. Could I just make a note of your name?
Bauer: Bianca Bauer from MTV in Germany.
Jennings: Yes, I've got that. And when is the conference?
Bauer: The conference begins on 16 April in the morning and ends on 18 April after lunch.
Jennings: Let me just have a look at our bookings list. ... That wouldn't be a problem. And how many people would be attending the conference?
Bauer: Well, I would think about eight people, our five British sales staff and three people from our head office here in Germany. They would be accompanied by their partners. So, we need five single rooms and three double rooms for three nights, that is from 15 to 18 April.
Jennings: Let me just check with reception. ... Right, I'm back again. So, the five single rooms are OK. But I'm afraid we can only offer you one double room and two twin rooms. Would that be all right? All the other double rooms are already booked.
Bauer: Yes, fine, but the rooms must have en-suite facilities.
Jennings: That's no problem. All our rooms are en-suite.
Bauer: And how about charges?
Jennings: Well, the price per room is £85.00 for bed and breakfast for a single room and £100.00 for the twin rooms. And in this case we'll charge the same for the double room. And for conferences we can also offer half-board or full-board arrangements.
Bauer: And what are your prices for half board and full board, please?
Jennings: Our rate for half board is £107.50. And for full board we charge £125.00.
Bauer: That sounds fine. And how about the conference room?
Jennings: Well, you said eight people will be attending the conference. So, one of our smaller conference rooms would do. Actually, I can offer you our Stafford room which seats about 12 people. That would be suitable, wouldn't it?
Bauer: Yes, that would be fine. And what about the price?
Jennings: The charge is £175.00 per day. And that also covers all the usual conference facilities plus refreshments in the mornings and in the afternoons.
Bauer: That sounds OK. So, would you please book that for us? And could you please also let me have some brochures, so that I can show my boss?
Jennings: No problem. I'll send you the literature straight away. And I'll also make the booking. But I need your written confirmation. So, who do I send the brochure to?
Bauer: OK. So, the address is ...

 Unit 3 Exercise C9

This is Wagner GmbH in Reutlingen/Germany. Today our International Sales Department is closed because of a public holiday. But you can leave a message after the tone and we will deal with it as soon as possible. Thank you for calling.

Howard: This is Michael Howard from Vickers Imports Pty in Durban, South Africa. We visited your stand at the recent Made in Germany Fair here in Johannesburg where we picked up some leaflets about your products. We are especially interested in your range of electrical gardening tools. Please send your full catalogue and current price-list to the following address:
    Vickers Imports Pty
I'll spell that: V-I-C-K-E-R-S Imports Pty
Attention: Michael Howard, that's H-O-W-A-R-D
    15 Bridge Road
    Durban (D-U-R-B-A-N)
    South Africa
Or you can call us on 0027 for South Africa, 31 for the area code and then the number is 250 84 180. I repeat 0027 31 250 84 180. Thank you.

Unit 3 Exercise C10

Janet: Birmingham Exhibition Centre, Janet speaking. How can I help you?

Petra: This is Petra Schnitzler from Stellmacher Plastik in Erfurt, Germany. From a trade magazine published here in Germany we see that you are organising the INTERPLAS in October next year, and our company is interested in taking part as an exhibitor and we would like some details.

Janet: That's no problem. It's still early days yet. Will this be the first time you'll be coming to Birmingham?

Petra: Yes. We've never been to the INTERPLAS before.

Janet: Well, in that case it would be best for me to send you our full information pack.

Petra: That sounds fine. And what information does your pack contain?

Janet: Well, obviously, information about the Birmingham Exhibition Centre, our facilities generally, and then more detailed information that you as an exhibitor will require, for example, about our services, hall plans, the stands, their sizes and rental charges, time schedule, hotels, useful addresses for support services, etc. I suggest you study this material and then come back to us. Let's say in two or three weeks' time. And then we can discuss details. Does that sound OK for you?

Petra: Yes, that's fine.

Janet: Good. And who shall I send the information pack to?

Petra: Oh, just send it to me. I'll give you the details. My company is Stellmacher GmbH. I'll spell that: S-T-E-L-L-M-A-C-H-E-R, new word G-M-B-H, Metallstraße (like metal with a double l) number 17 in 99086 Erfurt (E-R-F-U-R-T) Germany.

Janet: I think I've got that. Let me just repeat. So the company is Stellmacher GmbH, Metallstr. 15 in 99086 Erfurt, Germany.

Petra: Yes, that's it exactly. And my name is Petra (P-E-T-R-A) Schnitzler (S-C-H-N-I-T-Z-L-E-R).

Janet: OK. I've got that. So I'll send you the information pack today. And get back to me when you've made up your mind or if there are any queries, of course.

Petra: Fine. Thank you very much. Bye.

Janet: Thank you. Bye.

Unit 4 Exercise C6

Julia: Schumann Import GmbH. Was kann ich für Sie tun?

Helen: This is Helen Palmer from Royston Crystal in Glasgow. Could I speak to someone in your purchasing department, please?

Julia: Just a moment please, I'll put you through.

…

Sandra: Sandra Peters from Purchasing. Hello, Ms Palmer. How can I help you?

Helen: Well, you see, we got an e-mail enquiry from your company this morning and I'm not quite sure I understand exactly what you want.

Sandra: I'm sorry about that; one of our trainees wrote the e-mail. What would you like to know?

Helen: Basically, what product lines you're interested in, because we sell all sorts of different products and don't have a full catalogue. But there are leaflets for all the different ranges. Do you want us to send you a selection or do you need them all?

Sandra: Yes, we would like to have everything you've got on your cut glass ranges. Not just the sets, but also the individual pieces that you sell.

Helen: OK. And a price-list, I presume?

Sandra: And that too, of course.

Helen: Right. And your trainee mentioned specimens. Is there anything particular you are interested in?

Sandra: Any item will do. We would just like to check the workmanship and test the quality.

Helen: Would two or three pieces be enough?

Sandra: That would be fine.

Helen: That's no problem at all. And who shall I send the literature and specimens to? The address wasn't quite clear.

Sandra: I'm sorry about that. Our trainee really must have made a mess of things. OK. So, our company is: Schumann Import GmbH. I'll spell that for you: S-C-H-U-M-A-N-N I-M-P-O-R-T G-M-B-H. And our address is: Hafenstrasse 128, that's H-A-F-E-N-S-T-R-A-S-S-E in – and now the postal code – 55118 and the town is Mainz, M-A-I-N-Z. And please send it to my name. I am S-A-N-D-R-A P-E-T-E-R-S.

Helen: Fine. I think I've got that. So I'll send off all our cut glass leaflets to you today plus our current price-list and some specimens.

Sandra: Yes, that would be lovely. Thank you very much. And I'm sorry you had to go to so much trouble. Bye then.

Helen: Bye.

Unit 5 Exercise C7

Carsten: Schneider, Einkauf. Guten Tag. Kann ich Ihnen helfen?

Peter: This is Peter Ashcroft from Thomson Incorporated in Philadelphia. Hello, is that you Carsten?

Carsten: Yes. It's me. Hello, Peter. How are you? Haven't heard from you for a long time.

Peter: Oh, I'm fine. Thank you. Everything OK at your end?

Carsten: Yes, everything is OK. No problem. I'm just on my way home. Anyway, what can I do for you today?

Peter: Yes, of course, lucky you. That's the time difference:

I've still got more than half a day to go. Well, the reason why I'm ringing you is that I've just got this order from you, and there are a couple of points I would like to clear up.

Carsten: Is that the order we sent off last Friday? Order No. 5825?

Peter: Yes, that's it. Order No. 5825. The written confirmation of your telephone order. There are one or two discrepancies, I'm afraid.

Carsten: That sounds bad.

Peter: Well, you see, under item number 3 you say you need 17 pieces. I've got 70 down on my telephone memo.

Carsten: Let me just check that on my computer. – Yes, it should be 17, odd number, but that's what we need.

Peter: OK. So it's 17. And then item 7. You put down 55 pieces for catalogue number HB 4635, whereas I've got 55 for catalogue number HV 4635.

Carsten: Sorry Peter. That must be a keying error on our part. It's definitely HB 4635. What a silly thing to do.

Peter: And finally, in your order you say that the colour for item 9 should be light grey. But my notes say light green. Which is it to be? Light grey or light green?

Carsten: Well, we wanted light green really, if you've got that in stock. If not, light grey will do, as long as the price is the same, which I think it is.

Peter: Yes, the price is the same and stocks are no problem.

Carsten: Well, make it light green then. That would certainly be a better fit. We really seem to have got things badly wrong this time round.

Peter: No problem. We've got things sorted out now, and that's the main thing. I suggest we both make notes of what's been decided so that when the goods arrive there won't be any problems. So, that's 17 pieces for item 3, 55 pieces for item 5, catalogue number HV 4635.

Carsten: Sorry Peter, now you've got it wrong. It's catalogue number HB 4635 like Bravo.

Peter: You're right. So, I repeat: 55 pieces for catalogue number HB like Bravo 4635 and light green for item 9 of your order.

Carsten: Now, we've got it. Thanks for being so attentive Peter.

Peter: No problem. We want satisfied customers, don't we?

Carsten: Yes, you're right there. Anyway, thanks again.
((SFX: fade out))

8 Unit 6 Exercise C6

Hier ist der automatische Anrufbeantworter der Firma Feldmann & Söhne. Unser Büro ist nach 17 Uhr nicht mehr besetzt. Wir freuen uns jedoch, wenn Sie uns eine Nachricht hinterlassen. Sprechen Sie nach dem Signalton.

This is Stewart Hauliers from Perth, Scotland, Michael Douglas speaking. One of our drivers just phoned me to say that the lorry carrying your consignment has broken down with engine trouble just south of Newcastle. The lorry has to be taken to a garage for repairs. I'm sorry to say that it will miss the Hull ferry to Rotterdam tonight. And the consignment won't reach you tomorrow afternoon as agreed. We'll do everything we can to have the fault put right, but a lot will depend on whether the garage has all the necessary spare parts to carry out the repairs. You will realise that loading the goods onto another vehicle is not really possible. At the moment we are also exploring the possibility of rerouting the lorry via Dover to take advantage of the shorter crossing time. But at this stage, I can't say anything definite. I'll get in touch again first thing tomorrow morning to keep you posted. I'm very sorry about this. Thank you.

9 Unit 7 Exercise C7

Andreas: Winter. ABC Reisen. Guten Morgen. Was kann ich für Sie tun?

Roger: This is Roger Baines from the Norfolk Hotel Group.

Andreas: Oh. Hello Roger. How are you?

Roger: Hello, Andreas. Fine, thank you. And yourself? Did you have a good start to the holiday season?

Andreas: I'm fine, thank you. Business could be a bit more cheerful, I must say. But then again we mustn't grumble, I suppose.

Roger: No, I suppose not. ... Look, I'm sorry to have to bring this up, Andreas, but we seem to have a slight problem.

Andreas: Oh dear. What's that then?

Roger: Well, two of our invoices still seem to be outstanding.

Andreas: Oh. That does surprise me. Could you perhaps give me the details?

Roger: Yes, of course. The first is invoice KT 2846F for Foxtrot, dated 24 April and amounting to £2485.50, and ...

Andreas: Sorry, could you repeat that so that I can take down the details?

Roger: Yes, of course. So the first is invoice KT 2846F for Foxtrot, dated 24 April. And the amount is £2485.50.

Andreas: OK. I've got that. And the other one?

Roger: The other one is KT 3003 and again F for Foxtrot dated 25 May this time. And the amount is £3056.75.

Andreas: Right. So KT 3003, and the amount is £3065.75.

Roger: No, sorry. The amount is £3056.75.

Andreas: So sorry, Roger.

Roger: You see, Andreas, these invoices are six and ten weeks overdue. And in both cases there were queries regarding the amounts the guests in your party had to pay for their drinks at the hotel bar. But I thought we had sorted that out.

Andreas: Yes, of course. So did I. I mean, I did put your invoices on hold for a while until this issue was settled. But as things have been sorted out between us, I can't quite understand why the amounts haven't been transferred yet. The accounts should have been cleared long ago. I'll look into it and call you back as soon as I can.
Roger: Thank you, Andreas. That's what I wanted to hear. And you'll keep me informed?
Andreas: Of course, I will. Sorry about this.
Roger: That's OK. Bye for now, then.
Andreas: Bye.

10 Unit 8 Exercise C7

Patrick: Compusoft Ltd. Patrick Wilmots speaking.
Bianca: Hello, good morning. This is Bianca Ritter from Mediapark.
Patrick: Sorry. I didn't quite get your name. It's rather noisy in the background. Would you mind …
Bianca: No, of course not. I'm Bianca Ritter from the purchasing department of Mediapark in Vienna.
Patrick: Yes, of course. So sorry. I didn't get your name the first time round. And what can I do for you, today? – A new order perhaps?
Bianca: Not this time, I'm afraid. Quite the opposite, in fact.
Patrick: Oh dear. That sounds ominous. Is there anything wrong?
Bianca: Well, yes, I'm afraid there is. Something went badly wrong with our last order and my boss is furious and asked me to get in touch with you straight away. So I thought I'd better phone rather than send you an email.
Patrick: I'm very sorry to hear that. So what's the problem then?
Bianca: Well, you see, your last consignment contained the wrong goods, and the quantities don't tally with our order, and we didn't get the usual discount.
Patrick: That really does sound very bad indeed. Could you just give me the order number and the date and then I can check things on the computer.
Bianca: Well, the order number is FD4837X of 13 February and the invoice number is 43075G.
Patrick: OK. I've got that. Just a sec … Here we are. Mediapark Vienna, sent off on the 16th. So we have 50 items of catalogue number B10003 and 100 items of catalogue number B10501 and …
Bianca: No, no, no! 150 items of catalogue number B10008 (Jim: we did this because she says they got the wrong items) and 150 items of catalogue number B10501 and 200 items of catalogue number B10858 …
Patrick: I haven't got that one here. Mmh. … You know, if you say there are so many things wrong with this consignment I think there must have been a mix-up with another order.

Bianca: That may well be the case.
Patrick: But I really can't understand why. Tell you what. You fax me a copy of your order straightaway and I'll try and chase up your order form here to see where the problem is. In the meantime, I'll have your order made up and dispatched today. – And if I send it by express you should have the stuff the day after tomorrow at the very latest. How does that sound?
Bianca: That sounds absolutely fine. And what do I do about the faulty consignment?
Patrick: Well, if you could just hang on to that till I've got an idea whose consignment it might be, that would be very kind of you.
Bianca: That should be no problem.
Patrick: That's great. And I'll get back to you as soon as I can. Perhaps today even.
Bianca: That would be super because we've got customers waiting …

11 Unit 9 Exercise C6

Peter: Hello, Peter Wood speaking.
Ann: Ann Gilbertson from Whittaker and Partners. Hello Peter.
Peter: Good morning Ann. Good to hear you. How are things?
Ann: All Right, Peter. Everything's fine. And yourself?
Peter: Same here, everything's OK. Can't grumble. And how's business?
Ann: Busy as usual. You know us. Now, the reason why I'm calling you is this. We're just in the process of negotiating a pretty big contract with a new customer in Germany. And we're wondering, you know, with all your contacts over there …
Peter: Yes …
Ann: Well, whether you could perhaps help us with some information.
Peter: Yes. And what is it exactly that you need?
Ann: Well, you see, the firm we are dealing with at the moment is TN Automotive in Schwelm.
Peter: Say that again, Ann.
Ann: TN Automotive in Schwelm. They produce parts for almost all the German car manufacturers.
Peter: Yes, I think the name rings a bell. Well, let me think. – Yes, that's it. Don't they produce door hinges and stuff like that?
Ann: That's it exactly. And they want us to supply them with input material on a more regular basis because they can't produce everything themselves.
Peter: Sounds promising. Interesting for you, I bet. Just your line, eh?
Ann: You can say that again. Just the thing we've been looking for. But somehow it's too good to be true. And we don't want this to go wrong.

Peter: *I can understand that. And now you want me to tell you something about them?*

Ann: *Yes, Peter. If you could. That would be very helpful indeed. I think you realise that.*

Peter: *Of course, I do. Well, you see. We haven't really done much business with them recently simply because we have moved in a different direction as you know. But, as far as I can recall, there have never been any problems. Personal contacts were good, they all speak excellent English over there. The order volume was quite reasonable, a few hundred thousand pounds every year, with orders coming in regularly. And we never had any problems with payments either. So, everything went quite smoothly really.*

Ann: *I'm pleased to hear that, Peter. And thank you. You see, as I said, we're talking about something really substantial, for us anyway. You wouldn't have anything more concrete, by any chance?*

Peter: *No, I'm afraid I haven't, Ann. But if you're really that interested I would get on to the Anglo-German Chamber of Commerce or maybe look things up in the Bundesanzeiger, you know, this federal German gazette. You might get something about their balance sheet there.*

Ann: *Thanks, Peter. That sounds like a good suggestion. I think we should follow that up. – Well, thank you very much again for your help. That's great.*

Peter: *Don't mention it. And I wish you the best of luck. Bye, Ann.*

Ann: *Bye, Peter. And thanks again.*

INCO-Terms 2000 im Überblick

Gruppe	\multicolumn{2}{c}{Gültig für jede Transportart}	\multicolumn{2}{c}{Gültig für den Transport zur See oder auf Binnenwasserstraßen}
	Abkürzung	Erklärung	Abkürzung	Erklärung
E	EXW	Ex Works (... named place) *Ab Werk (...benannter Ort)*		
F	FCA	Free Carrier (named place) *Frei Frachtführer (... benannter Ort)*	FAS	Free Alongside Ship (... named Port of Shipment) *Frei Längsseite Schiff (... benannter Ort)*
			FOB	Free On Board (... named Port of Shipment) *Frei an Bord (... benannter Verschiffungshafen)*
C	CPT	Carriage Paid To (... named place of destination) *Frachtfrei (... benannter Bestimmungsort)*	CFR	Cost and Freight (... named Port of Destination) *Kosten und Fracht (... benannter Bestimmungshafen)*
	CIP	Carriage and Insurance Paid To (... named place of destination) *Frachtfrei versichert (... benannter Bestimmungsort)*	CIF	Cost, Insurance and Freight (... named Port of Destination) *Kosten, Versicherung, Fracht (... benannter Bestimmungshafen)*
D	DAF	Delivered At Frontier (... named place) *Geliefert Grenze (... benannter Ort)*	DES	Delivered Ex ship (... named Port of Destination) *Geliefert ab Schiff (... benannter Bestimmungshafen)*
	DDU	Delivered Duty Unpaid (... named place of destination) *Geliefert unverzollt (...benannter Bestimmungsort)*	DEQ	Delivered Ex Quay (... named Port of Destination) *Geliefert ab Kai (... benannter Bestimmungshafen)*
	DDP	Delivered Duty Paid (... named place of destination) *Geliefert verzollt (...benannter Bestimmungsort)*		

Cornelsen

In Übung bleiben ...

... ist das Erfolgsrezept gewiefter Könner – sei es beim Rudern oder Gehirnjogging. Hier empfehlen wir Ihnen Materialien für Ihr persönliches Englisch-Fitness-Training, abgestimmt auf *Advanced Commercial Correspondence*.

Adv. Commercial Correspondence – Audio-CD und Key
Lauschen Sie den *native speakers*: Aufgenommen sind alle Hörverständnisübungen. –
Im *Key* finden Sie die Lösungen zu den Übungen des Kursbuches und eine Musterprüfung für Fremdsprachenkorrespondenten.

Audio-CD ca. 45 Min.
ISBN 3-464-02802-X   ◇ 19,95 €
Key 48 Seiten
ISBN 3-464-02791-0   4,95 €

Cornelsen English Grammar Große Ausgabe
Sie umfasst alle wesentlichen Strukturen der englischen Grammatik. Die Regeln sind einfach formuliert und mit Beispielen verdeutlicht. Viele Vergleiche mit dem Deutschen helfen Fehler zu vermeiden. Spezielle Einträge widmen sich nicht nur dem „korrekten" Sprachgebrauch, sondern auch sprachlicher Variation, wie britisch/amerikanisch oder formell/informell.
Die *Practice Books* liefern die passenden Übungen.

Cornelsen English Grammar:
Große Ausgabe (auf Deutsch)
248 Seiten
ISBN 3-464-053342   16,95 €
English Edition
248 Seiten
ISBN 3-464-06310-0   16,95 €
Practice Book 1
ISBN 3-464-06311-9   11,50 €
Practice Book 2
ISBN 3-464-063127   11,50 €

Das große Oxford Wörterbuch für Schule und Beruf
Englisch–Dt./Dt.–Englisch.
100.000 Stichwörter mit etwa 230.000 Übersetzungen:
Das Wörterbuch unterstützt fortgeschrittene Lerner u. a. mit farbigen Hervorhebungen wichtiger Konstruktionen. Viele Beispielsätze helfen, Fehler zu vermeiden.

1372 Seiten, Festeinband
ISBN 3-464-10441-9   24,90 €

Words for Business – New Edition
Das thematisch geordnete Lernwörterbuch vermittelt die wichtigsten 3000 Vokabeln, damit man im internationalen Business mitreden kann. Themen sind zum Beispiel *Commercial Correspondence*, *Insurance* oder *Travel*.

320 Seiten
ISBN 3-464-02550-0   15,95 €

Oxford Business English – Business Grammar & Practice
Dieses einsprachige Übungsbuch greift bereits vorhandene Grammatikkenntnisse auf und bindet sie in berufsbezogene Kontexte ein. Vielfältige *exercises* (mit Lösungen) sichern den Lernerfolg.

232 Seiten
ISBN 3-464-11001-X   ◇ 25,50 €

Im Buchhandel erhältlich.
◇ = Unverbindliche Preisempfehlung.
Stand der Preise 1.1.2004.

Cornelsen Verlag
14328 Berlin
www.cornelsen.de